Classic Rock

CLASSI

GREAT BRITISH ROCK-CLIMB

C ROCK

COMPILED BY KEN WILSON

Other books in this series:

Hard Rock
The Big Walks
Extreme Rock
Classic Walks
Cold Climbs
Wild Walks

Front cover: The second pitch of Pegasus (Hard Severe) one of the many fine classic climbs on Chair Ladder, Cornwall. *Climber: Dave Bradney. Photo: Ken Wilson*

Back cover: The crux pitch of Moss Ghyll (Gill) Grooves (Mild Very Severe) on Scafell Crag. *Climbers: Unknown. Photo: Al Phizacklea*

Frontispiece: The popular southern end of Stanage Edge from Martello Buttress to the Black Hawk Area. This is, arguably, the busiest and the finest edge in Britain being richly endowed with hundreds of fine outcrop climbs in all grades with three star Diffs hob-nobbing with some of the hardest gritstone testpieces. Though high and exposed it is curiously sheltered, dries quickly and can be climbed in all seasons. With something for everyone, this is the ultimate democratic crag. *Photo: Ken Wilson*

ACKNOWLEDGEMENTS *(for the first edition)*: The choice of routes involved a number of advisers, each of whom has an intimate knowledge of his area. In this respect I would particularly like to thank Allen Fyffe, Ron James, Robin Campbell and Paul Nunn.

The photographs were collected from many sources but a number of climbers made special efforts for the book. Chris Hall in particular has been a tireless seeker after the ultimate photograph of many cliffs, and Donald Bennet has also made a great effort to secure rare views, besides placing his comprehensive collection of Scottish photographs at the disposal of the book. Other photographers whose contributions have added significantly to the interest of the book include John Cleare, Tom Weir, Bill Brooker, W. A. Poucher, C. Douglas Milner, John Woodhouse and Ken Crocket; and mention must be made of their patient subjects, who have frequently loitered in precarious places, all in the name of art. Other important contributions have been made to the book by Brian Evans, who drew the diagrams, and Mike Pearson and Heather Ann Jones, who worked on the manuscript.

Finally, a debt of gratitude is owed to the essayists, who have produced such interesting articles within the rather rigid formula dictated by this type of book.

In many ways it is unfair to single out people for special mention, as all the contributions act in combination to increase the final quality of the book. The following is a full list of all who have helped with the book, either as writers or photographers, or in some advisory or assisting role: Bob Allen, Jancis Allison, Chris Astil, Allan Austin, David Avens, F. G. Balcombe, Mike Banks, Bob Barton, Liza Beasant, Patricia Bell, Donald Bennet, Chris Bonington, Paul Brian, Tony Brooder, Bill Brooker, Nigel Bruce, Martin Burrows Smith, Robin Campbell, Charles Clark, Dave Cook, David Cox, Ken Crocket, Harold Drasdo, Dave Dunn, Al Evans, Sir Charles Evans, John Evans, Angela Faller, John Fitzgerald, Ian Fulton, L. W. P. Garland, Colin Grant, Dennis Gray, Tony Greenbank, Joann Greenhow, Harry Griffin, Roger Grimshaw, Fred Harper, Michael Hawkins, Dave Hillebrand, Lord Hunt, Barbara James, Ron James, John Jones, Alan Kimber, John Kingston, Doug Lang, Brian Lawrie, Kenneth Leech, Adrian Liddell, Graham Little, John MacKenzie, Ted Maden, Bill Marshall, C. Douglas Milner, Nea Morin, Tony Moulam, W. H. Murray, Jim Neville, Paul Nunn, Roger O'Donovan, Mike Papworth, John Peck, Jim Perrin, Martin Plant, Walter Poucher, Tom Price, Ian Roper, Chris Ryder, Klaus Schwartz, Brian Shuttleworth, Bill Skidmore, Malcolm Slesser, Roger Stokes, Greg Strange, Showell Styles, John Sumner, Mike Thompson, Robin Thompson, Tony Toole, Tom Weir, Anne Wheatcroft, John Woodhouse, Jim Worthington, Ian Wright, Walt Unsworth and Charlie Vigano. My apologies are due to anyone whose name I may inadvertently have omitted.

I would also like to thank Roger Schlesinger and his colleagues at Granada Publishing for their enthusiasm for the project.

In closing, I would like to acknowledge my debt to the journals of the Scottish Mountaineering Club, the Climbers' Club, the Rucksack Club and the Fell and Rock Climbing Club, as ever valuable sources of reference. The history of British climbing would indeed be poorly documented if these clubs had not maintained such a comprehensive record of affairs for so long.

(regarding the 1989 revisions): In order to shadow the definitive guidebooks a variety of grading comments were added at this stage.

(regarding the 1997 revisions): A Historical Commentary has been added. Other revisions involve further grading updates and layout reorganisations to introduce new colour photographs and some portraits of the great pioneers. I am indebted to those who have given assistance in this 'face-lift', namely Chris Bonington, Paul Bradbury, Gordon Gadsby, Alan Hankinson, John Hartley, Frank Loftus, Simon Massey, Rob Phillips, Al Phizacklea, Stephen Reid, Graham Rowe, Don Sargeant, Chris Schiller, Stuart Scott, Gordon Stainforth, John Stockdale and Walt Unsworth. The original photo credits pages have been removed but a list of each contributing photographer's contribution follows: Ashley Abraham ix, Bob Allen 117; Donald Bennet 14, 15, 17, 22, 24, 25(2), 29, 32, 40, 46, 61, 86, 87; Chris Bonington 96, 102, 123; Bill Brooker 52, 57, 60, 75, 76, 77(2); W. D. Brunskill 126; John Cleare 18, 21, 160, 161, 166, 174, 175, 182, 183, 230/1; Alan Craig 43; Ken Crocket 33, 50, 52, 53(3), 71; John Fitzgerald 154; Ian Fulton 14; Allen Fyffe 64; Gordon Gadsby 89, 92, 146; L. W. P. Garland 191; Alan Grey 80; Chris Hall 12, 16, 17, 41, 94, 98(2), 103, 104, 110, 112(2), 113, 114, 116, 117, 124, 126, 127, 131, 133, 135, 138, 139, 141, 144, 205; John Hartley 134; John Higham 60; Brian Lawrie 67; Christine Little 91, 93, 94; Graham Little 90; Bill Marshall 72, 77; J. E. McEwan 28; C. Douglas Milner 20, 142, 171, 191, 197; John Moore 76; Tony Moulam 148(2); Bob Moulton 232; Jim Neville 224; Al Phizacklea *back cover*; W. A. Poucher 20, 33, 42; Stephen Reid 140, 145(2); Ian Roper 130; Graham Rowe 92; Stuart Scott 233; Klaus Schwartz 25, 36, 62, 63, 90; Rebecca Schwartz 36; Gordon Stainforth vi; John Stockdale 217; Greg Strange 55, 56, 58; John Sumner 204(2); Tom Weir 48, 49; J. D. B. Wilson 28; John Woodhouse 154/5, 214, 215, 221, 224; Ian Wright 128. All other pictures are taken by the compiler or are from his archive.

British Library Cataloguing in Publication Data (available)

ISBN 1 898573 11 5

First published in 1978 by Granada Publishing

Reprinted in 1979, 1981 and 1985 (Grafton)

Revised and reprinted in 1989 (Diadem)

Revised and reprinted in 1997 by Bâton Wicks Publications, London

All trade enquiries to:
Cordee, 3a De Montfort Street, Leicester LE1 7HD

Printed and bound in Singapore by the Kyodo Printing Company

Contents

Gordon Stainforth

Preface

Classic Rock is the second in a series of books dealing with the great rock climbs of the British Isles. The excellent reception given to *Hard Rock* indicated that a similar book dealing with easier climbs might find favour. But then there arose the question of grade. Eventually, it became clear that such a book would have to be limited to climbs of up to Hard Severe grade, as these can generally be tackled by any climber, regardless of age, experience or fitness. The many fine Very Severe climbs clearly belong to a class of their own, as they involve a greater degree of commitment.

It should not be concluded that classic climbs lack the challenge and interest of the harder climbs. Such qualities come as much from the theatricality of a route as from its difficulty – the architecture of its crag setting, and the intricacy, variability and positioning of its pitches. To illustrate this I have only to refer to an experience I had while preparing the book. I had dragged a friend up to Scotland for a photography session. We spent two days dodging showers to do some good climbs on the Cobbler and the Buachaille, but, on the third day, my companion vetoed further classic climbing and demanded an expedition of a more demanding nature. Accordingly, we turned our attention to one of Britain's finest routes – the stunning Yo-Yo on Aonach Dubh. Elated after a memorable ascent, we returned to the valley to plan our next day on the classics. I could see that my companion did not relish the prospect believing that it would be a terrible anticlimax after Yo-Yo. But how wrong he was. On a brilliant autumn day we climbed the superlative Ardverikie Wall which gave us an ascent just as stimulating as our Yo-Yo climb.

Such is the power of the classics to impress. Britain is lucky indeed to possess a wealth of such climbing, accumulated during more than a century of discovery. One could easily spend a lifetime exploring them – possibly working them into challenging mountain-walking days. Many are little-frequented and situated on remote mountains. They are ripe for rediscovery and renewed patronage – some will lack quality but others will be forgotten gems awaiting the attention of the connoisseur.

In this book we have concentrated on a range of the better known climbs. Eighty have been selected, each possessing one or more of the attributes that are generally agreed to make a climb notable. The magnificent mountain scenery surrounding Tower Ridge and many of the other big Scottish routes contrasts with the warm yet dramatic coastal atmosphere of the Cornish climbs. The seemingly endless complexities of Ardverikie Wall balance the demanding scrambling and sharp pitches of the Cuillin Ridge. There are challenging gully climbs, choice outcrop test-pieces, convenient small-crag favourites, long mountain climbs on high cliffs – all are encompassed in this book. Moreover, many are truly classic being encrusted in history, their first ascents often having been pivotal events in the development of British climbing. A few are quite recent discoveries that have been rapidly acclaimed for their quality, and all are honest and straightforward, in that

Left: Climbers on Arrow Route, Sron na Ciche. This climb forms an elegant and logical link between Cioch Direct and Integrity (which follows the obvious slanting crack on the upper wall). *Climbers: Unknown*

they can reasonably be undertaken in boots and with no more than a handful of slings.

The outcrops receive less emphasis than in *Hard Rock*. There are of course hundreds of superb classic Gritstone and Sandstone climbs but few are long enough or demanding enough to leave a really profound impression – their character tending to come across when one does a group of them in one session. Limestone is less well-endowed with suitable climbs and only one example is included in this book, perhaps no bad thing in view of the tendency for limestone to polish up with over use.

Unlike those in *Hard Rock*, the essays in this volume have an air of restraint and maturity that perhaps reflects the more relaxed nature of the climbing. There are a number of contributions by older climbers who made their ascent while the routes in question still enjoyed an aura of reputation. Indeed, with loose rock and very basic equipment, some of the bigger climbs must have been formidable undertakings, and one should remember that years of consolidation and improvements in protection techniques have greatly reduced the problems originally encountered by the pioneers. To appreciate fully the fearsome reputations once held by these routes, one has only to consider how daunting Main Wall must have been, on a completely unexplored buttress, replete with creaking flakes and loose turf, or think of the commitment involved in the runnerless first ascents of greasy and delicate routes like Moss Ghyll Grooves or Avalanche.

It has been said of *Hard Rock* that it made the featured climbs unduly popular. In order to reduce the possibility of overcrowding, therefore, a detailed appendix lists other fine climbs close to the routes described – each a fine alternative to the described route.

The counter argument is that *Classic Rock* should encourage climbers to travel and develop interest in new areas, thus broadening the general appreciation of climbing in Britain and bringing us into contact with our opposite numbers elsewhere. Popularisation refreshes our awareness of the diversity of mountain treasures we have to enjoy. Having always gleaned inspiration from a new guide, an account of an interesting ascent, or even a good photograph, I offer no apologies for continuing the tradition.

Whether you are a novice moving hesitantly up your first climbs, an expert soloing, a veteran seeing if the body will still perform what the mind decrees, or an instructor introducing pupils to their first experience of climbing, or just an ordinary climber enjoying a day on the hill – these classic routes have a hoard of marvellous secrets and situations awaiting discovery.

A note for the 1997 edition: Recent guidebooks have upgraded a number of the climbs. With the exception of four Scottish climbs and one in Wales, this is a questionable trend that threatens to disrupt the overall balance of the grading system. Another change that is noted is the decline in booted climbing, a much prized skill for those with alpine aspirations and strongly reflected in the photographs. These days the fashion is to use lightweight footwear and, where necessary, carry their boots in a sac. Surely this too is a retrograde trend as boot skills are always valuable?

KEN WILSON 1978 & 1997

Some Thoughts on the Early Days of Classic Climbing

The inspiring period when rock climbing in Britain developed into an identifiable sport, took place during the three decades that spanned the turn of the century. Prior to this explorers of the British mountains had tackled the most obviously craggy summits and precipices by the easiest possible routes, but in 1886, W. P. Haskett-Smith's solo ascent of Napes Needle signalled the start of a more intense period. At a stroke exploration on rock was charged with a more sporting character – the pursuit of challenging and gymnastic recreation for its own sake.

Napes Needle, despite its diminutive size, provided a symbol that inspired climbers in much the same way that the ascent of the Matterhorn fired the imagination of alpinists. It was, for example, the books of Whymper, Stephen and Tyndall and then a photograph of Napes Needle in a shop window in the Strand that motivated a youthful Owen Glynne Jones in the early 1890s. Yet when one considers the remarkable growth of alpinism that had begun in the 1850s and which, by the 1880s, had reached a point where three of the Matterhorn ridges had been climbed as well as hard rock peaks like the Dru and the Meije, the most surprising aspect of British rock climbing was that it took so long to get going. Once started, the sport advanced quickly, fuelled by the confidence engendered by those years of alpine activity. Even before Haskett-Smith's seminal climb this confidence had been evident in the rapid exploration in the 1870s of the Cuillin of Skye. The 1883 ascent of the West Buttress of Lliwedd by Stocker and Wall, and the exploration of the two main buttresses of Ben Nevis by the Hopkinson family during two days in September, 1892, were further indicators of alpine confidence. Cecil Slingsby brought his Norwegian rock experience to underpin his forays on Scafell and Ben Nevis. Other alpinists to the fore in early explorations included Norman Collie and Geoffrey Hastings, though their contemporaries Alfred Mummery and Clinton Dent were notable by their absence from new route activities on the home front.

But after the Napes Needle ascent, the achievements of established alpinists were matched, if not exceeded, by climbers whose main focus was the home mountains, the combination of the two groups adding a new dynamism in each of the main mountain areas. Ambitious teams were soon at work – Haskett-Smith, Owen Glynne Jones and the Abraham brothers operating mainly in the Lakes; J. M. Archer Thomson, Oscar Eckenstein, W. R. Reade and their friends in Wales; and Naismith, Raeburn, Collie, Bell, Brown, King and Collier in Scotland.

Yet we should be careful to avoid giving regional tags to these climbers, as a remarkable aspect of early British rock climbing in those days of the railway and the horse-drawn carriage is the degree to which the active climbers made their mark in all the areas. Thus we see Archer Thomson, in the company of H. O. Jones and Leslie Shadbolt, tackling the formidable North-

West Face of Sgurr a'Mhadaidh on Skye. The Abraham brothers, famed for their Lakeland and Welsh climbs, teamed up with the gritstone experts Puttrell and Baker to snatch the prestigious first direct ascent of Crowberry Ridge in 1900. While the Scottish pioneer Norman Collie, made his mark in the Lakes with the first ascent of Moss Ghyll (1892). In Scotland Collie often climbed with the ubiquitous Godfrey Solly and the equally widely travelled Dr Collier both of whom led early Lakeland VS climbs (Eagle's Nest Ridge, 1892, and Collier's Climb, 1893). Jones alternated his activities between the Lakes and Wales. Nor let us forget the achievements in many regions of Scotland of Harold Raeburn whose early Cairngorm climbs and Raeburn's Arête (1902) on the Ben's North-East Buttress and his solo ascent of Observatory Ridge (1901) are particularly notable.

At this time ropework, belaying and equipment were at a very primitive stage of development. Climbers wore heavily nailed boots and, for the most part, climbed in a brutish, inelegant style. Early climbs therefore followed buttresses with frequent ledges, where progress could be made by short pitches, or gullies and narrow slots that offered some degree of security. Nevertheless, some open climbs of a higher order of difficulty were done. Napes Needle and Eagle's Nest Ridge must surely have been climbed with a more precise style? Archer Thomson perfected a balance climbing technique for tackling the jugless ribs and slabs of Lliwedd, a skill that he presumably employed to overcome Tryfan's Yellow Slab (1894). W. W. Naismith's climb on the Bhasteir Tooth (1898) was very exposed, demonstrating what climbers were happy to tackle, providing the holds were large and the situation secure.

Gullies and chimneys favoured more forceful techniques and in this sphere Owen Glynne Jones, with his renowned strength, reigned supreme. But, in 1895, it was two little-known climbers, J. Kelsall and A. W. Hallet, who made the most impressive ascent of the gully era – the imposing Waterpipe Gully in Skye, a climb that still merits a Very Severe grade. This might be compared to Great Gully on Craig yr Ysfa, (Archer Thomson, Simey and Clay, 1900) which, though shorter and easier, with its crux being reserved to the final (apparently) inescapable pitch, might well have been equally taxing in the usual wet conditions.

The gully-climbing phase reached its zenith by the turn of the century but by then new challenges were beginning to beckon from the steeper cliffs and buttresses. Jones led his exposed climb up Scafell Pinnacle from Lord's Rake in 1898 and the Abrahams constructed their New West Climb on Pillar in 1901. Archer Thomson initiated a decade of intense activity on Lliwedd. But belaying techniques were still too rudimentary for such exposed and serious climbs and the harsh penalties that lurked were to be tragically demonstrated. In the early days some climbers had regarded ropes with distaste. Haskett-Smith had, after all, climbed the Needle "with no rope or other illegitimate means" a comment that betrays an attitude in British climbing that persists to this day: the feeling that the mountain or cliff should be given a chance by being "tackled on equal terms". Such attitudes may have discouraged climbers from developing the proper belaying techniques that their new sport manifestly required. This oversight was forcefully exposed by Jones's fatal accident (with three guides) on Dent Blanche in 1899 and four years later by the death of four more climbers on Scafell Pinnacle – both parties being torn from the cliff because of the absence of proper belays. The photographs

Right: A. H. Binns and H. Harland on the 'Great Pitch' of Waterpipe Gully – Ashley Abraham's fine photograph specially set up during his Skye trip of 1907. Amongst the new climbs made on this visit Abraham and Harland captured Cioch Direct.

W. P. Haskett-Smith 1859-1946

Cecil Slingsby 1849-1929

Norman Collie 1859-1942

W. W. Naismith 1856-1935

Dr Joseph Collier 1855-1905

Ashley Abraham 1876-1956

George Abraham 1872-1965

Godfrey Solly 1858-1942

SOME PIONEERS OF CLIMBING IN BRITAIN 1880-1910

Harold Raeburn 1865-1926

Owen Glynne Jones 1867-1899

J. M. Archer Thomson 1863-1912

of the Abraham brothers reveal the pitifully inadequate belaying of the pioneers, but after these accidents there was a slow improvement and the rope antics of Herford, Sansom and Holland on their historic ascent of Scafell's Central Buttress (1914) demonstrated that at least some of the lessons had been learned.

Siegfried Herford and his mentors John Laycock and A. R. Thomson made their first appearance in the mountains in the years before the First World War. Along with Puttrell, Baker, Jeffcoat and Botterill, they were outcrop-trained climbers, and it was this group that was to push climbing forward to more demanding levels of difficulty. Their founding father was Cecil Slingsby who, in the 1870s, had brought gritstone techniques to his Norwegian climbs and later to the British mountains. In 1903 Puttrell and Baker's ascent (with Oppenheimer) of Beinn Nuis Chimney on Arran, and Fred Botterill's eponymous slab climb on Scafell, both graded VS, were harbingers of a new order that was to be established by the Central Buttress climb and consolidated in the interwar years. Gritstone's rounded and weathered character tends to encourage friction and balance climbing, exactly the style that was required for this advance. In Europe similar skills perfected on the Saxony sandstone towers were being applied to the great limestone peaks of the Eastern Alps at the same time.

These advances are beyond the scope of a book concentrating on *classic* climbing, a style that usually offers unsustained difficulties, short pitches and large stances and where the best climbs are often based on lines of weakness up otherwise formidable cliffs. Many of the chapters that follow give vivid reflection of this early stage of the sport's development.

It all came to an end with the trauma of World War I. Thereafter climbing matured into its next phase. This was more regionalised and perhaps more parochial, pursuing climbs of greater difficulty, mindful of the greater risks and thus more cautious – somehow lacking the innocent bravura quality of the discoveries of those confident Victorian and Edwardian years. Yet fine climbs of that early classic character have continued to be found in every decade since, each one adding to the repertoire of the pioneers.

A. S. Bullough

Above: H. M. Kelly 1884-1980 (*left*) and J. H. B. Bell c1896-1976 (*right*) – two later pioneers who added climbs of great distinction (Tophet Wall and Moss Ghyll Grooves; Eagle Ridge Direct and The Long Climb) to the classic repertoire.

It is possible to trace the detailed story of this inspiring saga of sporting development by careful study of the definitive guidebooks and in a clutch of scholarly histories.* Knowledge of our sport's history enriches the enjoyment of our classic-climbing days. It reminds us of the background that underpins our own climbing and puts us all on our mettle to cherish an enviable legacy and build on a great tradition.

* *Mountaineering in Britain* by R. W. Clark and E. C. Pyatt (Dent/Phoenix House, 1957); *The First Tigers* by Alan Hankinson (Heinemann, 1972); *The Mountain Men* by Alan Hankinson (Heinemann, 1977); *High Peak* by Eric Byne and Geoffrey Sutton (Secker and Warburg, 1966); *A Century of Scottish Mountaineering* Edited by W. D. Brooker (SMC/T, 1988); *The Mountains of Snowdonia* by H. R. C. Carr and G. A. Lister (Bodley Head, 1925); *Snowdon Biography* by G. W. Young, G. Sutton and C. W. F. Noyce (Dent, 1957).

First-ascent chronology of climbs in the book

with original and *current* grades (the latter in italics)
(*note:* the grades in text were those at the time of first publication)

- 1884 **Needle Ridge** W.P.Haskett-Smith M/*D*
- 1886 **Napes Needle** W.P.Haskett-Smith D/*HS*
- 1892 **Tower Ridge** Descended by four members of the Hopkinson family D/*D*
- 1894 **Tower Ridge** Ascended in winter by J.N.Collie, G.A.Solly and J.Collier; summer: W.W.Naismith and G.Thomson
- 1894 **Pinnacle Rib** (Yellow Slab) J.M.Archer Thomson and H.Hughes D/*D*
- 1896 **Naismith's Route** W.W.Naismith and party D/*VD*
- 1898 **Jones's Route Direct** O.G.Jones and G.T.Walker S/*HS*
- 1900 **Great Gully** (Craig yr Ysfa) J.M.Archer Thomson, R.I.Simey, and W.G.Clay VD/*VD*
- 1900 **Parsons' Chimney** W.Parsons and (?) F.Botterill S/*HS*
- 1901 **New West Climb** G.D. and A.P.Abraham, C.W.Barton and J.H.Wigner
- 1902 **Gashed Crag** H.B.Buckle and G.Barlow D/*VD*
- 1902 **Bowfell Buttress** T.Shaw, G.H.Craig, G.R.West, C.Hargreaves and L.J.Oppenheimer D/*VD*
- 1904 **Recess Route** H.Raeburn (and party?) D/*VD*
- 1907 **Avalanche** and **Red Wall** J.M.Archer Thomson and E.S.Reynolds VD/*VD*
- 1907 **Direct Route** (Glyder Fach) K.M.Ward and H.B.Gibson S/*HS*
- 1907 **Amen Corner** ('B' Route) H.B.Lyon, J.Stables and A.S.Thompson S/*S*
- 1907 **Cioch Direct** H.Harland and A.P.Abraham S/*S*
- 1909 **Central Climb** (Hen Cloud) J.Laycock S/*S*
- 1910 **Milestone Direct** G.Barlow and H.Priestley Smith D/*VD*
- 1911 **Grooved Arête** E.W.Steeple, A.G.Woodhead, G.Barlow, H.E.Bowren and A.H.Doughty. VD/*VD*
- 1911 **The Cuillin Ridge** L.G.Shadbolt and A.C.McLaren VD/*VD*
- 1912 **Gillercombe Butt.** H.B.Lyon and W.A.Woodhead S/*S*
- 1914 **Troutdale Pinnacle** F.Mallinson and R.Mayson MS/*MS*
- 1915 **Hope** Mrs E.H. Daniell, I.A.Richards, T.J.Roxburgh and R.B.Henderson D/*VD*
- 1918 **'C' Route** A.P.Wilson, G.H.Jackson and A Brundritt S/*S*
- 1918 **Murray's Route** D.G.Murray, W.J.Borrowman and B.L.Martin S/*S*
- 1919 **Rib and Slab** H.M.Kelly and C.G.Crawford
- 1920 **Black and Tans/Tech Slab/Via Dolorosa** A.S.Piggott and R.Morley Wood S/*HS*
- 1920 **Crypt Route** R.Morley Wood, J.Wilding and A.Piggott VD/*VD*
- 1920 **The Chasm** Mr and Mrs N.Odell and R.F.Stobart S/*VS*
- 1920 **Ash Tree Slabs** G.S.Bower and A.W.Wakefield VD/*VD*
- 1922 **Flying Buttress** (Stanage) F.Graham HD/*VD*
- 1922 **Lazarus** I.A.Richards and D.Pilley (crux climbed as a finish to Piton Route) HVD/*S*
- 1923 **Tophet Wall** H.M.Kelly and R.E.W.Pritchard S/*HS*
- 1923 **Bracket and Slab** H.B.Lyon and J.Herbert S/*S*
- 1926 **Moss Ghyll Grooves** H.M.Kelly, Blanche Eden Smith and J.B.Kilshaw S/*MVS*
- 1928 **Black Slab** A.T.Hargeaves HS/*VS*
- 1928 **April Crack** H.Hartley HS/*HS*
- 1929 **The Arête** F.E.Hicks, C.B.Warren and A.L.Spence VD//*VD*
- 1929 **North Face Route** J.H.B.Bell and A.Harrison VD/*VD*
- 1930 **The Cracks** B.L. a nd H.C.H.Bathurst (with aid) *FFA*. C.F.Kirkus later in the same year. S/*HS*
- 1930s **Pendulum Chimney** (upper section) J.E.Littlewood and party VD/*S*
- 1931 **Spiral Stairs** J.M.Edwards and S.B.Darbyshire HD/*VD*
- 1931 **Flying Buttress** (Wales) J.M.Edwards, who originally called the climb Sodom! HD/*VD*
- 1932 **Grey Slab (Lost Boot Climb)** A.S.Bullough, J.Cooper and J.Marchington S/*VS*
- 1933 **Sail Buttress** B.Smith and B.Connelly HVD/*VS*
- 1933 **The Cumming/Crofton Route (Mitre Ridge)** M.S.Cumming and J.W.Crofton S/*S*
- 1935 **Crackstone Rib** J.M.Edwards and J.B.Joyce VD/*S*
- 1935 **Main Wall** P.L.Roberts and J.K.Cooke HS/*HS*
- 1935 **Climbers' Club Ordinary** A.D.M.Cox and R.Bere MVS/*MVS*
- 1936 **Piton Route** F.G.Balcombe and J.C.Shepherd S/*VS*
- 1936 **Agag's Groove** J.F.Hamilton, A.Anderson, A.C.Small VD/*VD*
- 1938 **Clachaig Gully** W.H.Murray, A.M.MacAlpine, J.K.W.Dunn and W.G.Marskell VD/*S*
- 1940 **Terrier's Tooth** J.Mallory, A.Roster, A.M.Greenwood and B.Donkin HVD/*HVD*
- 1940 **The Long Climb** J.H.B.Bell and J.D.B.Wilson S/*VS*
- 1941 **Eagle Ridge Direct** J.H.B.Bell and Nancy Forsyth S/*S*
- 1941 **Nea** Nea Morin and J.M.Edwards S/*VS*
- 1943 **Labryinth** G.C.Curtis and H.Moneypenny VD/*VD*
- 1943 **Demo Route** J.F.Barry S/*HS*
- 1944 **Sou'Wester Slabs** G.H.Townend, G.C.Curtis, H.Hore and M.J.H.Hawkins VD/*VD*
- 1945 **Savage Slit** R.B.Frere and J.D.Walker VD/*VD*
- 1946 **Little Chamonix** B.Beetham VD/*VD*
- 1947 **Wrinkle** M.P.Ward, J.E.Q.Barford and B.Pierre S/*VD*
- 1947 **Archer Ridge** W.H.Murray and D.B.MacIntrye VD/*VD*
- 1947 **Pendulum Chimney** (complete) J.Cortland Simpson and E.Stones S/*S*
- 1948 **Ardgarten Arête** J.Cunningham S/*VS*
- 1949 **Punster's Crack** J.Cunningham and W.Smith S/*S*
- 1949 **Integrity** D.A.Haworth and I.E.Hughes S/*MVS*
- 1951 **Creagh Ddu Wall** J.Cunningham, W.Smith and P.Vaughan HS/*HS*
- 1951 **Topsail** D.Penlington and E.Marshall S/*VS*
- 1951 **Powder Monkey Parade** D.Penlington and E.Byne HVD/*S*
- 1953 **Squareface** T.W.Patey and J.M.Taylor VD/*VD*
- 1953 **Long Crack** L.S.Lovat and J.M.Johnson S/*S*
- 1955 **Doorpost** B.M.Biven, H.T.H.Peck and P.Biven HS/*HS*
- 1956 **The Talisman** W.D.Brooker and K.A.Grassick S/*HS*
- 1956 **Red Pencil Direct** A.Greenbank and party S/*S*
- 1961 **Clean Sweep** R.Smith and G.Tiso S/*VS*
- 1961 **Devil's Slide** K.Lawder and J.Logan S/*HS*
- 1967 **Ardverikie Wall** D.F.Lang and G.F.Hunter S/*S*
- 1968 **The Cioch Nose** T.W.Patey and C.J.S.Bonington VD/*VD*
- 1972 **Will-o'-the-Wisp** J.Sumner, Miss J. Henderson HVD/*HVD*

1 The Cuillin Ridge

by Ted Maden

Route Traverse of the main Cuillin Ridge. Very Difficult. 6 miles. 10,000ft. of ascent.
Location The Black Cuillin Mountains. Isle of Skye.
First Traverse L. G. Shadbolt and A. C. McLaren, June 1911.
Map S.M.C. 3-inch map of the Black Cuillin; O.S. Tourist Map of the Black Cuillin and Torridon, 1–25,000 Sheet.
Guidebook S.M.C. District Guide, *The Isle of Skye* by C. G. M. Slesser.
Nearest Road An unclassified road at Glen Brittle, which leaves the B8009 at Merkadale.
Times Starting from Glen Brittle allow 3 hours to reach the summit of Gars-Bheinn, 10 hours to traverse the ridge to Sgurr nan Gillean and a further 2 hours to descend to Sligachan. A slightly shorter start can be made from the Coruisk Hut.
Campsites and Bunkhouses Campsite and B.M.C. Hut at Glen Brittle.
Good Conditions A clear dry day is recommended. Allow one dry day after heavy rain to enable all the technical sections to dry out.
Bibliography *The Cuillin of Skye* by B. H. Humble (Robert Hale, 1952); *Mountaineering in Scotland* by W. H. Murray (Dent, 1947); *One Man's Mountains* by Tom Patey (Gollancz, 1971); *The Magic of Skye* by W. A. Poucher (Chapman and Hall, 1949); *Scottish Climbs*, Vol. 2, by Hamish MacInnes (Constable, 1971); S.M.C. Journal Vol. XI; *The Main Cuillin Ridge* by L. G. Shadbolt, is a first ascent (traverse) account.

Few peaks in the British Isles call for rock climbing on their easiest routes. Most of those that do are located in the Black Cuillin of Skye. The main Cuillin Ridge extends from Gars-Bheinn, in the south, to Sgurr nan Gillean in the north. In a sigmoid sweep of six miles, it encompasses some ten peaks of over 3,000ft. and several others just below this height. Most sections of the ridge involve scrambling, often of quite a serious and exposed nature, and several involve rock climbing, two of them of up to Very Difficult standard. The ridge offers magnificent views of sea and loch, and at no point along its length does it drop below 2,500ft. This unique combination of attributes renders the traverse of the Cuillin Ridge one of the most sought-after mountaineering expeditions in the British Isles.

Many climbers traverse the ridge by sections. Each distinct section, such as the circuit of Coire Lagan or the four tops of Sgurr a'Mhadaidh, makes an excellent day in itself. Nevertheless, the logical appeal of the whole is inescapably greater than that of the sum of its parts. 'Expedition', therefore, means the complete traverse in a day. What is the history of the traverse? What does it entail? Is it worth it?

L. G. Shadbolt and A. C. McLaren made the traverse a reality on 10 June 1911. Leaving Glen Brittle at 3.35 a.m., they were on Gars-Bheinn by 6 a.m. They reached Sgurr nan Gillean 12½ hours later and arrived at Sligachan at 8.20 p.m. In 1914, T. Howard Somervell, later of Everest fame, made the solo traverse, Gars-Bheinn to Sgurr na'h-'Uamha, the final extension from Gillean, in 10½ hours. In 1932, Peter Bicknell reduced the Gars-Bheinn to Gillean time to 8 hours. The record is held by the late Eric Beard, who did it in an astonishing 4 hours and 9 minutes in 1966. The Greater Traverse, including Clach Glas and Blaven, was first done by I. G. Charleson and W. E. Forde in June 1939, and soon afterwards by R. G. Donaldson and W. H. Murray. This *tour de force* is not likely to become everyone's cup of tea, but Murray's account makes excellent classical reading. The winter traverse, from Gillean to Gars-Bheinn, was accomplished in two days by Patey, Robertson, MacInnes and Crabb, in the favourable February of 1965. The north to south direction was taken to enable several of the difficulties to be passed by abseil. Patey's exuberant account of this epic traverse abounds with such comments as: 'From here to Sgurr a'Mhadaidh was no more than a walk. That is to say, you could have fallen and escaped with your life.'

To do the ridge in summer you should be able to lead Severe. This gives a grade in hand and facilitates unroped movement at all but a few points. You also require good overall fitness and an adequate sense for route-finding. Only minimal gear need be carried – 120ft. of rope and a few slings for two climbers – but you do need plenty of food and water. The other desirable factors are ample daylight and reasonably fine weather, June and July being the favoured months. Prior experience of the ridge is not strictly necessary, given the above prerequisites, but you are in for a total of 10,000ft. of ascent and should generally allow some ten hours from Gars-Bheinn to Gillean.

Early in the morning the southern eminence of Gars-Bheinn, thrusting out between pale blue sky and darker blue sea, offers a supreme sense of isolation, and this provides sufficient aesthetic reason for starting at this end. There are also good technical reasons for a south to north traverse under normal, summer conditions. These relate to the configurations of the principal difficulties, the first of which is the renowned Thearlaich-Dubh Gap. This is a deep notch in the ridge at a point where cliffs drop for some hundreds of feet on either side into the flanking corries. Although the whole of this section *can* be bypassed on the south side, this involves quitting the ridge at one of its most impressive sections. The gap is attained via a short abseil down a vertical wall. The ascent of the other, 'long', side is up 100ft. of steep rock, of which the central feature is a chimney-crack with a good old-fashioned boot-wide cleft at the back. Traditionally this pitch is Difficult, but few would grudge it a V.Diff. grading and, because it is smooth, polished basalt rather than rough gabbro, it is diabolical when wet.

It is usual to make a small lateral diversion to include Sgurr Alasdair, the highest point in Skye. Then, coming off Sgurr Thearlaich, a corkscrew descent on the Coruisk side leads to the next difficulty, King's Chimney on Sgurr Mhic Coinnich. This V-shaped cleft looks steep and forbidding, but in fact provides a beautiful Difficult pitch with perfect holds and chock-

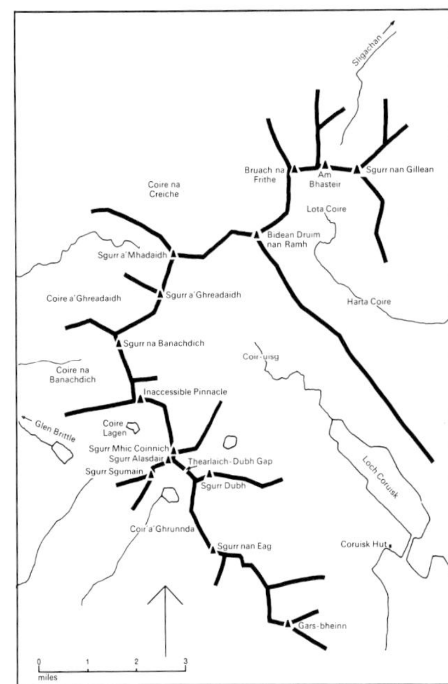

Chris Hall

Ian Fulton

Above: Looking down King's Chimney on Sgurr Mhic Coinnich – one of several technical sections on the Cuillin Ridge. *Climber: Ken Crocket*

Right: Naithsmith's Route on the Bhasteir Tooth. *Climber: Dan Stewart*

stones. The alternative, Collie's Ledge on the Coire Lagan side, is easier but spectacularly exposed.

In the interests of saving time, most aspiring ridge candidates will be happy, or at least prepared, to climb unroped up the long, easy ridge of the Inaccessible Pinnacle. The pinnacle, a huge basalt dyke which forms the second highest point in Skye, is defined by clean-cut vertical walls on either side. Thus the crest, though well provided with holds, is no place to miscalculate. A quick abseil down the blunt, short side of the 'In Pin' brings one to a right turn on Sgurr Dearg and the central section of the ridge. After a short, easy section, interest is then maintained to the end, with numerous minor obstacles and always the gaunt shadow of Naismith's Route on the Bhasteir Tooth over the final issue. This, the last major difficulty of the ridge, is fearsome to look at, but not too formidable in the ascent. It comprises two pitches, of which the second is Difficult by tradition: that is, perhaps Mild Very Difficult, and very exposed at the top.

So, anyway, I recall my one ascent in June 1956. Two of us set forth at dawn across the moor from Glen Brittle, our enthusiasm tempered with awe by the magnitude of the task ahead. In the event all went as smooth as clockwork: we had completed the ridge and were down at Sligachan for afternoon tea.

The ridge had always seemed a once-in-a-lifetime experience until, in spring 1976, BBC Television produced a film of the traverse. Soon afterwards, while England sweltered in a June heat-wave, three of us experienced the Thearlaich-Dubh Gap in the diabolical conditions mentioned above. The attempt fizzled out, to be reborn on 29 September, solo.

It was 6 a.m. and past the equinox. Conditions were unpromising in Glen Brittle in the gloomy pre-dawn. Gusts of easterly wind swept across the moor, and cloud clung at the 2,000ft. level. Daylight brought little immediate improvement. I was within minutes of abandoning the project at the foot of Gars-Bheinn when the clouds began to lift. I surprised myself by turning up the hill.

On the ridge the rocks were cold and wet after the previous day of torrential rain. This provided the unexpected luxury of puddles of drinking water, but boded ill for the Thearlaich-Dubh Gap. The first, easy section of the ridge was idyllic, however. The wind had moderated but had not completely dropped, visibility was now good, the more distant peaks were swathed in cotton-wool cloud and white mists occasionally welled up from the depths of Coruisk into the pale blue sky.

As I neared the gap, the rocks remained wet. Alone, not at all an aspiring hardman and with time a crucial factor, I felt obliged to bypass the difficulties. Rejoining the main ridge after traversing Alasdair, I balanced round the rim of Coire Lagan on to the 'In Pin' and Sgurr Dearg and a time check with a passerby. 1.30 p.m. already. Limited daylight began to intrude upon my thoughts.

The Banachdich section dragged, but interest revived on Sgurr a Ghreadaidh, a spectacular knife-edge between the gleaming Loch Coruisk on the right and wild corries on the left. The crenellated crest of Sgurr a'Mhadaidh provided real rock-climbing of Moderately Difficult standard in the ascents of the second and third peaks. The second peak presented a great prow which obviously had to be turned. A ledge led invitingly left but then into an invisible gully. A blind alley? Another track sloped down right but with more loss of height. Around here I was getting tired and could have done with company. What if there were a happening? The rocks were less steep on the right so I chose this way and found an easy route to the summit.

Below the third top was a smaller prow. I explored left along a scratched ledge. A little groove led up to the summit, but appeared to be holdless for a few feet above a good jug. A heave and a swarm would be necessary. I looked down between my feet over rocks which plunged for hundreds of feet to the screes. Stop! I recalled Robin Smith: 'I had no qualms about the swing, it was just that having swung I might not make the swarm, and I might not manage to swing back . . . and I shrank up into the Crack like a scared slug's horns.' I shrank back along the ledge to the prow direct, which yielded no bother at all: a short, steep pitch with magnificent holds.

The relief on passing the next peak, Bidean Druim nan Ramh, was enormous. This has three tops of which the central and highest presents a tricky descent to the north. The exposure is considerable and a slip or badly judged loose hold would be disastrous. Fortunately a new abseil sling had been left for the lower section, an abrupt drop into the col. Suddenly I could relax and look forward to the end.

I had completely forgotten the long distance which separates Bidean from Bruach na Frithe. The mist was now down and I could not see what lay ahead. I was unpleasantly surprised to encounter two peaks, a deep gash and much scrambling before reaching the latter summit. I drank my last half cup of lukewarm coffee, ate some biscuits and wondered what the time was. The light seemed slightly weaker, or was that my imagination? Despite much unnecessary climbing gear I had no watch, no torch. The wind was stronger. I was tired. I had done well enough for late September. I had left word that I would be back at the hut by nine. It was invitingly simple, eminently justifiable to play safe, to quit down the easy North-West Ridge of Bruach na Frithe to Bealach a'Mhaim, and so to Glen Brittle before dark.

Donald Bennet

Chris Hall

Above: Am Basteir and The Bhasteir Tooth from the west. Naismith's Route takes the obvious cracks to gain the shoulder on the right.

Top right: The northern peaks of the Black Cuillin. Sgurr nan Gillean can be seen on the left, with its Pinnacle and West Ridges in sharp profile, Sgurr a' Bhasteir is in the centre and Bruach na Frithe on the right.

Lower right: Sgurr nan Gillean from near Am Basteir. The Pinnacle Ridge (left of the summit) gives a worthwhile climb of Difficult standard, which can be added to the start of a north–south traverse to give extra effort and interest.

A gust of wind tore a hole in the mist. High flecks of cloud shone golden against the blue sky. They were not yet pink. The sun had not set; there might still be time. I turned up my coat against the wind and set off along the East Ridge. Yet another rocky peak loomed through the mist to provide another forgotten hurdle. A gully grovelled down to near the foot of the towering, primeval fang of the Bhasteir Tooth. In mist and doubtful daylight there could be no question of soloing Naismith's Route, and so I made a long downwards detour to the north under the great wall of Am Basteir. Dusk seemed to gather almost palpably as the path went down and down under the shadow of the crag. Should I cut my losses, and cover as much ground as possible towards Sligachan in the remaining light?

The descent beneath the cliffs ended and a track wound up into the mists. Out of the shadow of Am Basteir it was lighter. I might be in with a chance for the West Ridge of Gillean before nightfall. Screes led up to a level, easy crest. Rocks appeared and a cairn pointed the way up a damp little chimney. I emerged at a *brèche* to encounter the pinnacle known as the Policeman, which is traversed on its south-west side. There are only a couple of moves and the holds are large, but the drop below is steep. The rocks were slimy, and daylight was now fading even on the crest. Care was mandatory, but speed was essential if I was to avoid spending the night hugging the Policeman's belly. I safeguarded the moves with hand-jams, then pounded on up into the mist. After several false tops the summit cairn at last appeared, and was passed with a triumphant, breathless shriek into the deepening gloom. Without a pause I was already descending the Tourist Route. The light was so bad that route-finding errors were inevitable; at an abrupt step I relied on hand-holds, which I could still see, and let the feet scrabble for themselves. Eventually I was off the rocks and on to scree. I determined to get as far down as possible and, after a headlong descent over dim, lurching boulders, reached a little corrie halfway down, just below the mist, with shelter and water and a place to lie down, as darkness became complete.

I spent the night with my feet in my rucksack and my head in a cagoule, bawling songs into the darkness and glimpsing odd corners of the universe through shifting mists. And so this traverse, snatched from the very end of the season, and pushed despite the certainty of being benighted, had turned into an adventure, and that is what climbing is about.

Chris Hall

Donald Bennet

2 Cioch Direct and Integrity

by Paul Brian

Viewed objectively, Skye is a pretty unpleasant place. The pubs, like the people, are dour and unwelcoming. The midges in Glen Brittle, irksome at the best of times, reach unbelievable levels of malevolence in July and August. Even the petrol-dispensing machine in Broadford is of dubious morality and keeps the occasional coin for itself. The Cuillin is a ragged chaos of broken black rocks. Nobody could call it beautiful.

The black rocks, however, are gabbro and their magical properties of adhesion and friction give them a unique appeal to climbers.

These qualities were not long neglected by the gentlemen of the Alpine Club and the S.M.C., and the steep sides of Coire Lagan have attracted the attention of climbers since the beginnings of mountaineering history. By 1890, a score of high quality routes had been established on the island. Other, subsequently more popular, areas on the mainland had at that time received but cursory attention.

While the Pilkingtons and their Alpine Club colleagues had employed the conventional Alpine techniques of the age, the S.M.C. had displayed exemplary fortitude and ingenuity in overcoming the difficulties associated with the exploration of such a remote and inhospitable area. At Easter 1897 the *S.S. Erne* was employed as a floating base camp in Loch Scavaig, and in the summer of the same year an encampment of prefabricated 'Whillans Boxes' was erected at Loch Coruisk and served as a base for climbing on the ridge.

Inevitably the scene of such activity eventually attracted the remarkably talented Abraham brothers from Keswick, and during the period 1896–1907 they put up several routes which were subsequently to become classics. The Cioch Direct route on Cioch Buttress, put up by Ashley Abraham and H. Harland in 1907, is perhaps the finest and best known of these.

Not surprisingly, the line was not won easily and the account of the first ascent is packed with superlatives and near disasters in about equal quantities. By a curious coincidence, both Abraham and W. H. Murray, who climbed the route thirty years later, experienced serious rockfalls while making their ascents.

Although graded, probably correctly, at Severe, the route is not just another middle-grade excursion. It is in many ways a touchstone of a climber's mettle. For those whose skill is barely adequate, the route will be one of secure awkwardness, of squirming and wrestling, and they will bring away memories of torn clothing and skinned extremities. For the climber with some panache, or with a little adrenalin to invest, the route will be totally transformed.

In the initial groove the tiro will soon establish himself in the shadows wedged among the ancient boot marks and streaming boulders. Better by far to move on to the left wall and enjoy the small but excellent holds to be found there. Where the gully constricts, higher up, it is still possible to reject the gloomy confines of the gully bed and conserve a little energy and dignity.

The short walls above the chimney are generally at a fairly friendly angle, but they steepen occasionally. Once again the secret is confidence. A little boldness and alacrity will save much to-ing and fro-ing, with its attendant knee-jerking and palm-sweating. The crack above presents little difficulty, as the holds, though small, are positive and plentiful.

The crux is totally different. It is brutish, and requires moments of complete commitment. No amount of nervous pussy-footing beforehand is going to obscure the fundamental problem. Eventually the incut holds have to be relinquished for friction and side-holds and the fervent hope of something better to come.

After the crux the final pitches are pure pleasure, the rising leftward traverse is logical and satisfying, and the balance moves act as an antidote to the exertions below. The final 'twin cracks' pitch provides enough exposure to maintain interest and enough holds to maintain balance.

From the terrace to the Cioch itself a diversity of lines exists, but it would be inappropriate, at least on a first visit, to detract in any way from the character of the remarkable Cioch Slab. Set at a consistent angle of 50°, its ostensibly smooth surface bears such a variety of tiny holds of such perfect distribution and density as to suggest more than a passing interest in the affairs of mountaineers

Routes Cioch Direct, Severe, 500ft.; Integrity, Severe, 250ft.
Cliff Sron na Ciche, Coire Lagan, Isle of Skye.
First Ascents Cioch Direct – H. Harland and A. P. Abraham, 1907; Integrity – D. A. Haworth and I. E. Hughes, July 1949.
Map Reference O.S. 1–50,000 Sheet 32 (ref. 444204)
Guidebooks S.M.C. *Cuillin of Skye*, Vol. 1, by J. W. Simpson; *Scottish Climbs*, Vol. 2, by Hamish MacInnes.
Nearest Road An unclassified road at Glen Brittle, which leaves the B8009 at Merkadale.
Distance and time from cliff 2 miles/1,500ft. Boggy – allow 1½ hours.
Good Conditions The rock dries quickly but can be slippery when wet. The climb is not recommended in cold weather.
Campsites and Bunkhouses Campsite and B.M.C. Hut at Glen Brittle.
Bibliography *Rock Climbing in Skye* by A. P. Abraham (Longmans, Green, 1908; *The Cuillin of Skye* by B. H. Humble (Robert Hale, 1952); C. C. Journal, 1909; *June Days in the Coolins* by E. W. Steeple, has an account of an early ascent of Cioch Direct; *Mountaineering in Scotland* by W. H. Murray (Dent, 1947).

Note: Integrity was upgraded to Mild Very severe in the 1996 guidebook.

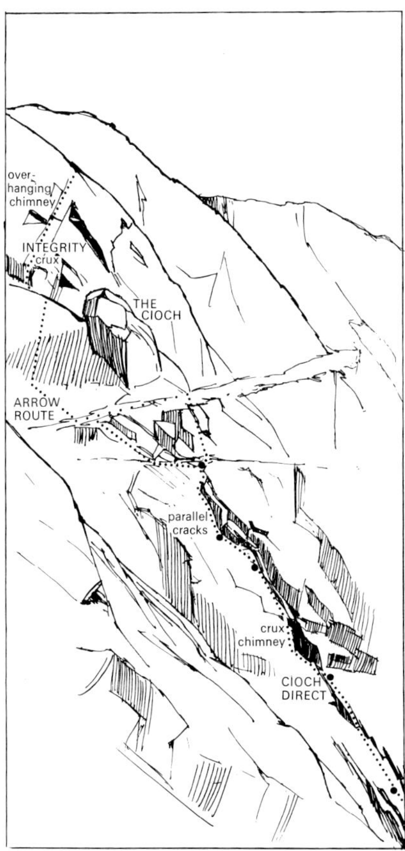

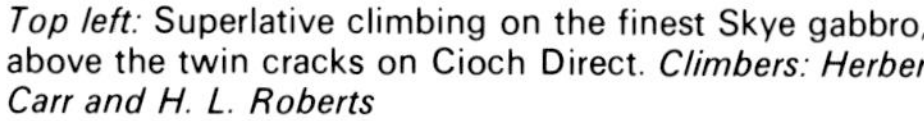

Top left: Superlative climbing on the finest Skye gabbro, above the twin cracks on Cioch Direct. *Climbers: Herbert Carr and H. L. Roberts*

Lower left: The Cioch from near the start of Integrity.

C. Douglas Milner

W. A. Poucher

by the Almighty. Arrow Route, then, is the inescapable choice and, despite its easy grading, it is not a route to be tackled in a condescending or lackadaisical manner. The total absence of protection and the vagueness of the line have given many a party pause in their headlong flight to the Cioch for lunch. Of course, for those wishing to conserve their energies for the afternoon, Cioch corner, on the west edge of the slab, retains some of the character of the slab and provides a pleasant solo.

The summit of the Cioch is a fabulous place! Surely it is the finest luncheon spot in the country. Apart from the exhilarating situation, the place reeks of history. The flat surface seems to have been designed for the concave bottoms of Bouvier bottles and tapping out Meerschaum pipes. How garish and tasteless are our coloured ropes and Mars Bars!

What a sensational viewpoint for the selection of one's post-prandial pleasures! Strangely, the upper Cioch Buttress presents a most belligerent and steep aspect when viewed from the Cioch. The cliff seems to overhang the spectator and even the easier graded routes take on an intimidating and impressive appearance. Only when one actually regains contact with the rocks does the angle relent and the gabbro reassume its previous properties.

For the middle-grade climber the choice quickly narrows: Crack of Doom or Integrity? The former has a fine appearance but little else to recommend it. It has an oppressive atmosphere and constricts at the crux to little more than a gully, damp and often odoriferous. It is, furthermore, an illogical line from the Cioch and involves a loose, abrasive traverse across awkward sloping ledges to gain the start.

Integrity, on the other hand, is the obvious finish and the rock is clean and sound. The steep open nature of the climbing provides a welcome contrast to the rather claustrophobic exertions of the morning.

Climbed first in 1949 by D. Haworth and I. Hughes, the route has become a post-war classic. There is a commonly held misconception to the effect that during that period all climbing development was in the hands of the Great Proletarian Movement centred in Manchester and Clydeside. In fact, the middle class was alive and well and living mostly in Edinburgh. The climbers of Scotland's capital have ever been an imaginative and resourceful group and this was particularly true in the 'forties and 'fifties. Of all the routes established by this group, none fires the imagination more than the stupendous Surgeon's Gully on the south-west flank of Ben Nevis. By far the longest climb in Britain, it still awaits its second complete ascent!

Of all this determined group none seems to have been more active than Derek Haworth. His Steeplejack Staircase on Salisbury Crags still retains a fierce reputation despite its proximity to the city centre. Another, more flamboyant, feat was his celebrated descent of the escarpment below the crag by motorcycle. It is not clear whether this was motivated by sheer *joie de vivre* or merely a desire to escape the attention of the ubiquitous park keepers!

The first pitch of Integrity embraces the crux which, though exposed, enjoys excellent protection, a characteristic incidentally of the entire climb. The crux moves bring one out on to a strange, corrugated slab, which provides good friction climbing to the first belay. The belays are all small and cramped, and other parties should be given as wide a berth as possible. The overhang above the belay is turned by the crack delineating its right edge, and again excellent protection

John Cleare

Above: Looking up Cioch Slab to Cioch Upper Buttress, with the Cioch itself on the right. Arrow Route takes a direct line up the centre of the slab to finish just right of the start of Integrity. A tiny figure can just be seen in an obvious sunlit groove high on the route. The parallel line to the right of Integrity is taken by Trophy Crack, one of Skye's hardest climbs, and Atropos weaves through slabs and overhangs just to the left of Integrity.

encourages the leader to make full use of the friction holds on the right wall. The final pitch makes a fitting climax to the day; the steep jumble of jammed blocks in the Chimney bed seems to overhang the Cioch Slab itself, and there is nothing between but space! Only the boldest and most flexible will be able to maintain their bridging position all the way to the top. Others will have to adopt more brutal methods to take them to the security of the sloping glacis above.

This loose and unpleasant ramp is no place to linger, as the Skye midge is the high altitude variety and by late afternoon has reached the apogee of its fury.

There is, unfortunately, no easy descent from the Upper Cioch Buttress. The least painful method perhaps is to descend the gully bounding the left edge of the Eastern Buttress. Alternatively, the more obvious descent of the Sgumain Stone Shoot gives the opportunity to swim in the Lochan in the upper corrie.

The three climbs described constitute a worthwhile itinerary for climbers of any standard. For the middle-grade exponent, the routes are sustained and testing. Even the more experienced party would do well to recognize that gabbro climbing requires a technique all of its own, and these routes provide a comprehensive and demanding introduction.

As to the quality of the routes, they are deservedly classics. They owe their popularity not only to their technical qualities and situation, but also to the inescapable nature of the lines.

Much is written about the aesthetic attraction of these direct, so-called natural, lines. To my mind their appeal is more practical than artistic.

The people I climb with rarely seem to know where they're going. The major part of any climbing day is spent in futile and heated argument in the most precarious and alarming positions. Recourse is made frequently to grubby and much reviled guidebooks. I have even known dissent to reach such a pitch that independently minded second men have pursued their own line, leaving the rope pinned in a great imbecile parabola by the runners of their desperate but misguided leader.

No one, particularly the middle-grade climber, wants to stick his neck out on an established route unless he knows that he's in exactly the right place. Most people have experienced that most frustrating of feelings when, having completed a series of particularly trouser-filling moves, the correct, much larger, holds appear a few feet to the side.

It is their total lack of ambiguity, along with their magnificent situation and historical associations with the past, that give these routes unique character and perennial appeal.

3 The Cioch Nose

by Donald Bennet

The Applecross peninsula can hardly be described as mountainous. For the most part, it is rough moorland on whose higher parts the heather clings only sparsely to the sheets of Torridonian Sandstone which form the backbone of this land. Only in the south-east are there high hills – Meall Gorm, Sgurr a' Chaorachain and Beinn Bhan – overlooking the head of Loch Kishorn. One feature that these hills have in common is their steep north-east faces, where sandstone cliffs enclose wild and impressive corries. The buttresses of Meall Gorm, in particular, are well seen by the traveller on the road to Applecross over the Beallach nam Bo.

The cliffs on the east side of Sgurr a' Chaorachain encircle the Coire nan Arr (the Giant's Corrie). This is well named, for it is easy to imagine some pre-Ice Age giant building the walls and towers of Sgurr a' Chaorachain with tier upon tier of Torridonian Sandstone, which has since been weathered by thousands of years of ice, wind and rain. The central feature of the corrie is A'Chioch, the terminal tower of a long ridge which juts out into the corrie, dividing it in two. The North-East Face of this tower rises in 1,000ft. of terraced sandstone, the finest feature of the mountain.

Not surprisingly, A'Chioch was the target of many early climbers. N. Collie, W. Ling and W. C. Slingsby all made early ascents of the South-East Face, but their routes avoided all difficulties and could hardly be described as direct. J. H. B. Bell, in the course of his many explorations in the Scottish Highlands, traversed along the ledge which encircles A'Chioch at mid-height in search of a more direct route, but without success. In 1952 Tom Patey led an Aberdonian party up a difficult route on the North Face, and in 1960 he returned with Chris Bonington.

Patey has related how they approached the climb late on an August evening after a long approach-march from Strome Ferry, and that as they traversed along the middle ledge to the start of the climb the clouds opened. Despite these unpromising circumstances (in which most climbers would have retreated to the nearest inn), they found a route up the almost vertical nose of A'Chioch, where, by the normal laws of Torridonian Sandstone, none should exist, unless of great difficulty. In fact, so good was the rock at the steepest part of the climb that Patey enthusiastically described it as 'the Diff to end all Diffs!' This remark, coming from Patey, could be taken to mean that the climb is a good V. Diff., and it is certainly now acknowledged to be one of the classic routes on Torridonian Sandstone.

The climb starts from the middle ledge where the narrow pathway goes round a projecting rock at a rowan sapling. (To continue along this ledge for another twenty or thirty yards takes one along what must surely be the most spectacular and exposed footpath in Scotland.) The first pitch is rather vegetated and leads more or less directly upwards by a series of short walls and grassy ledges. It is one of those deceptive pitches which look harmless enough from below, but turn out to be a lot more awkward on close acquaintance, as one pulls up on doubtfully rooted tufts of heather. There are those who say it is the hardest pitch of the climb, and there is certainly a feeling of relief when one reaches the broad grassy ledge at the top.

A short walk to the right along this ledge leads to the second pitch, an open chimney capped by a menacing overhang. Strenuous climbing for 30ft. leads to an exit on the right wall, and an escape is made from the chimney on to easy, open rocks leading to a splendid belay niche under another overhang. The key pitch follows; a traverse of a few feet to the right brings one to the foot of a vertical wall on the very nose of A'Chioch. Suddenly, the exposure becomes considerable and nerves become tense, but the holds are so plentiful and perfect that the steepness and exposure of this wall are exhilarating rather than intimidating; a truly remarkable pitch.

Above the next ledge the difficulties diminish and, after an awkward mantelshelf to get off the ledge, a rising traverse to the right leads to easy ground and a little rowan tree on a broad ledge. Finally, 200ft. of easier climbing leads directly to the top of A'Chioch. With the exception of the first pitch, the climb has been entirely on excellent rock with no vegetation, a rare pleasure for Torridonian Sandstone.

Route The Cioch Nose. Very Difficult. 450ft.
Cliff A'Chioch, Sgurr a' Chaorachain, Applecross.
First Ascents T. W. Patey and C. J. S. Bonington, August 1960; Variation Start and Direct Variation (Severe), T. W. Patey and H. MacInnes, 1968.
Map Reference O.S. 1–50,000 Sheet 24 (ref. 796427).
Guidebooks S.M.C. *Northern Highlands Area*, Vol. 2, by D. G. and R. W. L. Turnbull; *Scottish Climbs*, Vol. 2, by Hamish MacInnes.
Nearest Road The Applecross (Bealach nam Bo) road at a bend a few hundred yards west of the bridge over the Russel Burn (ref. 812414).
Distance and time from cliff 1½ miles/1,000ft. Allow 1 hour
Good Conditions The climb dries quickly after rain, the rock is good and the climb is best climbed in the morning to enjoy the sunshine.
Campsites and Bunkhouses Camping possible locally. S.M.C.'s Ling Hut in Glen Torridon (19 miles)
Bibliography *One Man's Mountains* by Tom Patey (Gollancz, 1972).

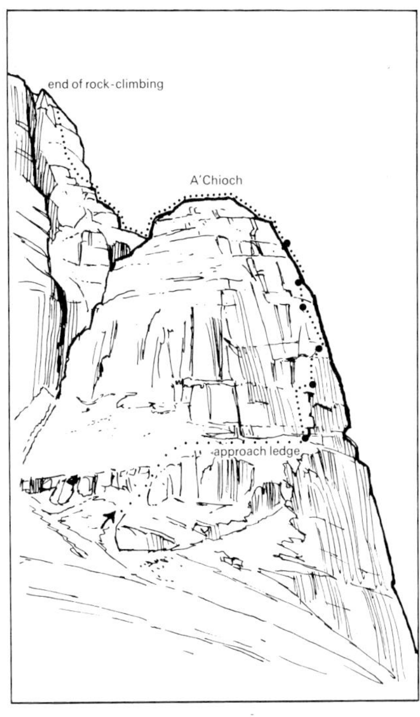

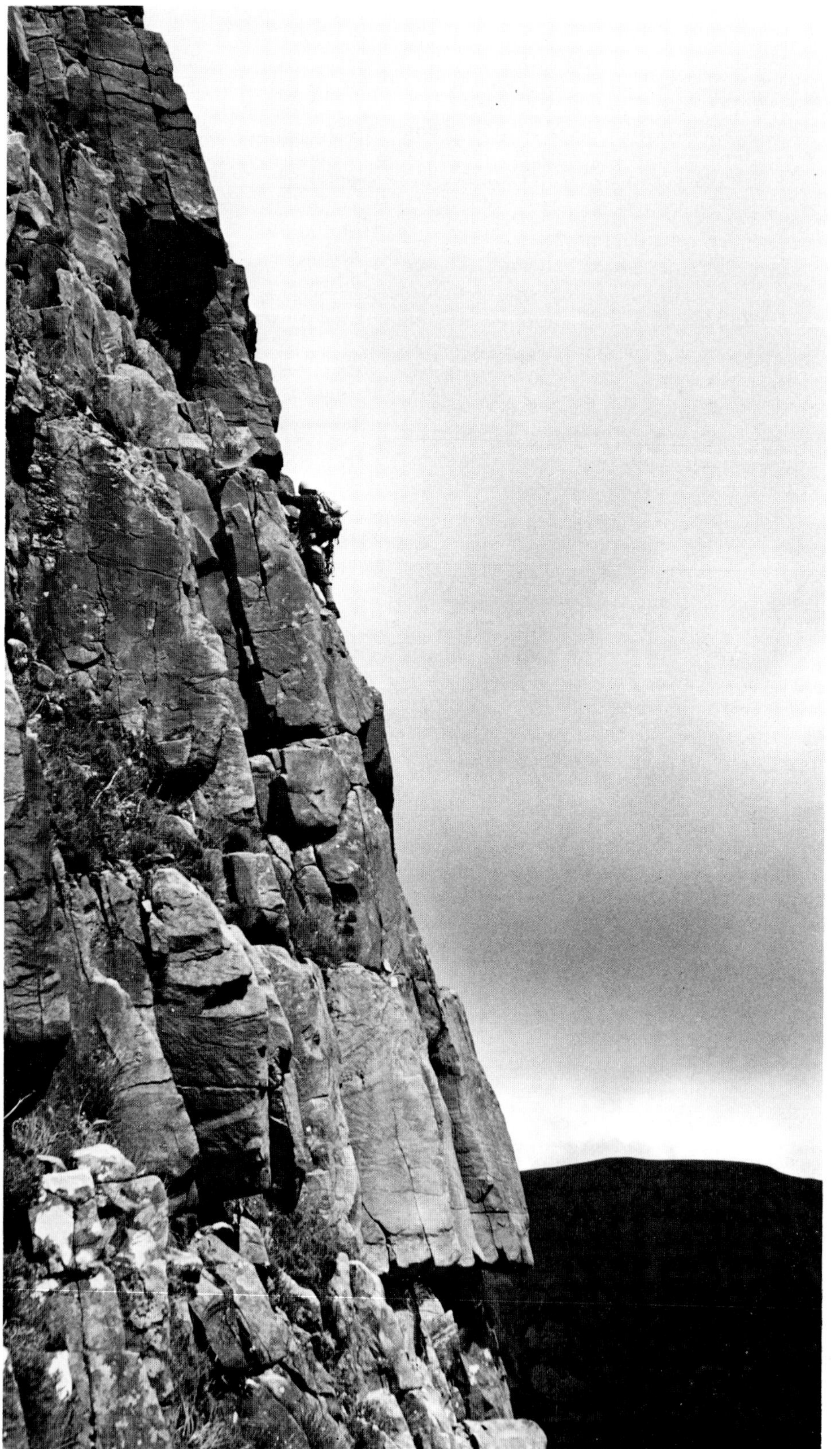
Donald Bennet

From the top of A'Chioch there is still a lot of climbing to reach the top of Sgurr a' Chaorachain (as every true mountaineer will want to do). The ridge above rises in two or three short steps, and is then girdled by a high and steep wall. This is best climbed directly up the front or near the left-hand end; another good pitch. Now only scrambling remains, but the ridge continues up and down over a succession of grassy towers and rocky gaps which seem to go on endlessly until at last the slope ahead broadens and becomes more level. Now, all the buttresses and towers of the Giant's Corrie are below, and in front there unfolds that uniquely West Highland panorama: seas and islands and mountains. There below is Raasay, lying across the Inner Sound, and beyond is Skye, with the Cuillin Ridge scratched across the horizon. For the purist (or the collector of Corbetts) there is still a walk of three-quarters of a mile to the topmost point of Sgurr a' Chaorachain; for others the temptation to find a sheltered spot among the rocks and gaze westwards is likely to be stronger. It is easy to be lazy after a great climb.

Left: The awkward first pitch of the Cioch Nose. *Climber: Lyn Jones*

Top Right: Sgurr a'Chaorachain from Loch Kishorn. The Cioch Nose can be seen in a dominating position above the right-hand corrie

Near right: The second 'open chimney' pitch of the Cioch Nose. *Climber: Iain Macleod*

Far right: The exposed 'key pitch' of the climb, giving excellent climbing on good rock in a fine position. *Climber: Klaus Schwartz*

Donald Bennet

4 The Long Climb

by Malcolm Slesser

Route The Long Climb, Severe, 1,400ft.
Cliff Orion Face, Ben Nevis.
First Ascent J. H. B. Bell and J. D. B. Wilson, June 1940.
Map Reference O.S. Tourist Map to Ben Nevis and Glencoe, 1–50,000 Sheet (ref. 168717).
Guidebooks S.M.C. *Ben Nevis* by J. R. Marshall; *Scottish Climbs* by Hamish MacInnes.
Nearest Road Park at the Golf Club on the Spean Bridge/Fort William road, one mile east of the distillery. A path leads across the golf course to a stile, and then up a steep, wooded hillside to the Allt a' Mhuilinn.
Distance and time from cliff 3½ miles/2,800ft. Allow 3 hours.
Good Conditions Allow three or four days of dry summer weather after prolonged rain.
Campsites and Bunkhouses S.M.C.'s C.I.C. Hut below the cliff. Campsites by the hut or in Glen Nevis.
Bibliography *A Progress in Mountaineering* by J. H. B. Bell (Oliver and Boyd, 1950) contains a detailed account of the exploration of the Orion Face, with diagrams and photographs.

Note: Upgraded to Very Severe in the 1994 guidebook with the Second Slab Rib given 4b.

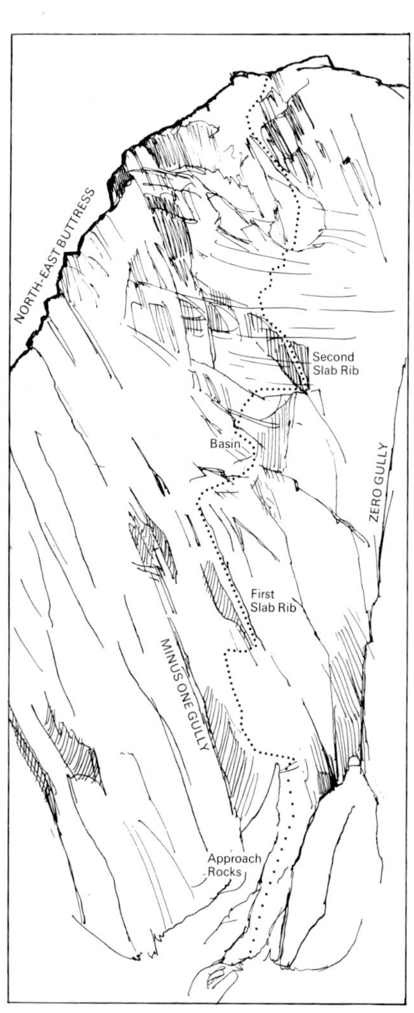

The Long Climb is certainly that: the longest climb in the British Isles – 1,400ft. But it is much more. For one thing it is the highest 1,400ft. in the land, for the climb finishes on the summit of Ben Nevis, 4,406ft. above sea level. For another thing it is the most alpine of the Scottish rock climbs, a route that works its way through the rock maze of the Orion Face, never seeking difficulty unnecessarily, but always maintaining an elegant line. For those of us who knew Jim Bell, who died in retirement in 1975, it will always be his climb – Bell's greatest. It was Bell, pawky, witty, resolute, who, with a number of different companions, opened up that vast amphitheatre of rock on the North Face of the mountain, bounded on the left by the North-East Buttress and on the right by Zero Gully. Although Sandy Wedderburn and two Yugoslavs had actually made the first ascent by way of Slav Route, it was Bell who worked out the line and gave it to them as a friendly gift. The face owes its name to Bell's desire for an all-embracing description for the network of routes that he had developed on the face. Not too fancifully he saw the stars of the Orion constellation as fitting his template. Orion's belt was the Basin and his sword the great slab rib.

The Long Climb was a two-part affair. Bell first broke through to the bowl of easier rock at mid-face – the Basin – in 1935 with Violet Roy, and, as he himself remarked in a later *S.M.C.J.* article, it was surprising that the group of young Glasgow climbers then exploring new lines like Rannoch Wall and Clachaig Gully in Glencoe should have failed to turn their attention to the superb rock of the then unnamed Orion Face. So Bell had the place to himself, and, with John Wilson, finally connected all the bits and pieces together on a fine June day in 1940, at the very moment that Paris was falling to the Germans.

In his own accounts Bell is habitually vague about difficulty and he classified his route as a 'Severe' or 'Difficult'. Certainly it says much for Bell's reputation and for the impressive atmosphere of the wall that in my young days we thought of the Long Climb as a VS, and only in recent years has it been downgraded to the hardest of the Nevis Severes.

To enjoy the Long Climb one should arrive early on a midsummer morning, when the sun reveals a series of steep undercut ribs leaning to the left. Above, at mid-height, the Basin will still contain a sizeable snow patch. High above, on the summit plateau, a haloed cornice will glow incandescently. The trudge up the lower snow slopes to the foot of the face gives way to a sense of wonderment that this is Scotland, not the Alps. Avalanche channels and a deep rimaye between snow and the final wall serve to give an Alpine sense of scale. Stop and listen. If all you can hear is the patter of dripping water and all the rock is glistening, turn back for Carnmore. The Orion Face is notoriously slippery after wet weather. But if your hand touches the lowest rocks and you can feel the pumice-like texture of the dry porphyry, then take your last drink and go.

The climb starts about 100ft. to the left of Zero Gully at the crest of the snow. The first objective is the foot of the Great Slab Rib. The easiest way requires some digression to the left before a return to the right. As one approaches it from the left, the Slab Rib has a lower slab to its left, which is tempting in its lower section. But this is strictly a winter route. Belay and traverse out to the right below the overhang of the rib. It is airy but full of holds. Ten feet and suddenly one is nose-to-nose with a narrow crack cleaving the rib. With PAs it is almost like ascending a staircase. Always there are just enough nugget-like holds, here and there a position for a chock runner and finally a widening to a belay stance of sorts, 100ft. up. Bell, one reflects, had neither PAs nor nuts. Almost certainly he was in his stocking soles.

The hardest part may be over, but now the route-finding starts. If you have not picked your line from below, you may well finish up away to the left, treadmilling on mossy grooves below overhanging ribs. But pick the right line and easier rocks lead into the Basin.

Several routes lead in and out of the Basin. The Long Climb simply takes the direct line to the summit, just left of the top of Zero Gully. The climbing is now mere scrambling, but the exposure makes it a place to be careful. Make rightwards to the natural continuation of the Great Slab Rib to reach a

J. D. B. Wilson

J. E. McEwan

Above left: J. H. B. Bell during the first ascent of Long Climb in 1940.

Above right: J. H. B. Bell and Mary Bell on the Great Slab Rib during an early ascent of Long Climb in 1947.

Right: Long Climb's Second Slab Rib, which gives climbing on 'peerless' rock with a problematic finish up the steeper walls above. *Climber: Reg Pillinger*

rib of peerless rock, the second slab rib. It is topped by a steep wall, whose negotiation is neither well protected nor favoured with holds, but the rock is so exquisite that few climbers will be thinking of salvation, but rather revelling in its texture.

Above, there is once again a choice, depending on your skill as a route-finder. If you find yourself on VS rock, then there are better lines. The climb ends abruptly, from vertical to horizontal in a single step, from shadow into sun.

Of course the great test of one's skill is the Orion Face in winter. Here the line of the Long Climb becomes irrelevant. Neither of the Slab Ribs provides the best line, although they are signposts. And it is the exit from the Basin, not reaching it, that tests the climber.

For a truly mountaineering route which combines fine rock, route-finding and some sensationally located pitches of Hard Severe, nothing can beat Bell's direct route of the Orion Face, the Long Climb.

Donald Bennet

5 Tower Ridge

by W. H. Murray

Route Tower Ridge, Difficult, 2,000ft.
Cliff The North Face of Ben Nevis.
First Descent The Hopkinsons – John, Edward, Bernard and Charles, September 1892. First Ascent – N. Collie, G. Solly and J. Collier, March 1894.
Map Reference O.S. Tourist Map to Ben Nevis and Glencoe, 1–50,000 Sheet (ref. 167718).
Guidebooks S.M.C. *Ben Nevis* by J. R. Marshall; *Scottish Climbs*, Vol. 1, by Hamish MacInnes.
Nearest Road Park at the Golf Club on the Spean Bridge/Fort William road, one mile east of the distillery. A path leads across the golf course to a stile, and then up a steep, wooded hillside to the Allt a' Mhuilinn.
Distance and time from cliff 3½ miles/2,800ft. Allow 3 hours.
Good Conditions Dries rapidly after rain, but can be slippery when wet.
Campsites and Bunkhouses S.M.C.'s C.I.C. Hut below the cliff. Campsites by the hut or in Glen Nevis.
Bibliography *Mountaineering in Britain* by R. W. Clark and E. C. Pyatt (Phoenix House Ltd/Dent, 1957) contains brief first ascent details; *Mountaineering in Scotland* by W. H. Murray (Dent, 1947) describes a trying winter ascent; S.M.C. Journal, Sept. 1894: *Divine Mysteries of the Oromaniacal Quest*, is a mystical description of the Collie/Solly/Collier ascent; S.M.C. Journal, Sept. 1899: *Four Days on Ben Nevis* by W. Inglis Clark.

Those happy few who enjoy rain and gales will enjoy Ben Nevis. It rises at the head of Loch Linnhe to 4,406ft., in the track of North Atlantic storms. Its persistent wooers are rewarded with days that stay indelibly in mind for one grim reason after another. Having said this, I must admit to days so clear that the Antrim hills can be seen from the summit, 120 miles to the south-west.

The Ben stands at the south end of the Great Glen, which is a crustal fault splitting Scotland from the North Sea to the Atlantic – earth tremors shake Ben and Glen to the present day. In shape, the Ben is a bottle-nosed whale, afloat on a sea of peaks covering 14,000 square miles. Its cliffs face north-east. They are Britain's biggest, for they form a two-mile arc, 2,000ft. high. They rise out of the glen of the Allt a Mhuilinn but, unlike the main mass of the mountain, which is granite, the cliffs are lavas, mainly andesite, formed 350 million years ago in a cauldron subsidence. The rock is hard-baked and sound.

The classic route on the cliff is the first one ever made. Unique for its time in Scotland, it was first climbed down instead of up. In 1892, when no railway had yet been built to Fort William, and the rough roads bore horse and foot traffic only, no exploration had ever been made up the cliff, which is not seen from below save from one angle, and then not too well. But rumour of it spread from the opening of the summit observatory in 1883. In September 1892, the four Hopkinsons (a North of England family of three brothers and a son, all alpinists) arrived at Fort William and, to view the cliffs, climbed 2,000ft. into the upper corrie of the Allt a Mhuilinn. Their astonishment and delight knew no bounds. A deeply curved array of ridges, buttresses, and pinnacles towered 2,000ft. overhead, some out of lingering snow-fields. And no climb had ever been attempted. They chose the most prominent central feature: a massive ridge whose broad base rose 700ft. to the first of three towers. Above this tower, now called the Douglas Boulder, the ridge narrowed lengthily to a second tower, and then more briefly to a third (the Great Tower) at 4,000ft. From a gap behind that, the summit plateau rose another 400ft.

The Hopkinsons climbed to the foot of the Great Tower, but retired in face of the late hour and unknown difficulties. Two days later they walked to the summit and found a way down the whole ridge, taking the Douglas Boulder on its short east flank. They had not made the first ascent – that was done two years later by Norman Collie's party under heavy snow – but they were the real pioneers. Despite the untold pleasure they must have had, they made no written record, save in a brief note sent three years later to the *Alpine Journal*.

Today, the climb is the most popular on

Ken Wilson

the Ben. Its classic qualities of length, definition, and splendid setting are best appreciated if the start on the Douglas Boulder is made from its lowest rocks up the direct face-route. While never more than Very Difficult, the rock is not for novices. The holds tend to slope out where high steps come in quick succession without easily seen belays; and if the leader has a nose for the best route he can save time when forced by smooth rock to deviate out of the direct line.

From the Douglas Gap (reached in winter from either flank), a chimney slants leftward

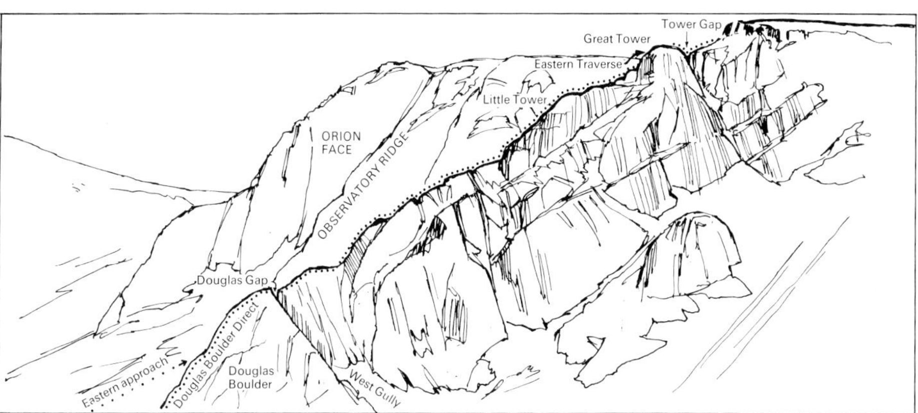

Donald Bennet

Left: The summit of the Great Tower from Tower Gap.

on to the true crest of Tower Ridge. The wider cliff-scene now opens out. On the right, above the rock-basin of Coire na Ciste, stand the Comb, the Trident, and Carn Dearg Buttress; on the left, across Observatory Gully, soar Observatory Buttress, Observatory Ridge, and North-East Buttress, all three split apart by the Zero and Point Five Gullies, which have deep snow-wreathes at their bases in mid-summer.

The ridge levels out for a space above the gap, then rears up several hundred feet in a series of steps to a second levelling. After crossing two shallow nicks, you will see on your left the top of the Great Chimney, cleaving the wall of the ridge. If you drop down a few feet on to a platform, you may inspect the chimney, with its big chockstone wedged surprisingly far out, and see the huge overhang of Echo Wall alongside. Less than 200ft. higher you reach the Little Tower and climb straight up its face. It has no gap beyond. The tower effect here is caused only by sudden steepening.

The Great Tower looms ahead. 'Looms', with its overtone of menace, is the right word if you arrive like the pioneers late in the day, or if the rock is encrusted with snow and ice, as it may be on any day between September and late May. Rising wind can be worse. I have twice reached Douglas Gap in a freshening breeze, to find the wind mounting with me to a gale at Tower Gap. The roar of wind on the tower and neighbouring crags, where cloud is shredded between the teeth of the Comb and Trident, can be frightening. The leader has to keep in mind that the tower should be climbable in any weather, if he knows the alternative routes and has daylight.

The best route from the easy rocks below the 100ft. tower is the natural one, by a level ledge called the Eastern Traverse. Snow banks up on this to a high angle; if clear, it is two feet wide. It leads round an easy corner above a long drop, and so through a tunnel under a huge block. Beyond that, climb a high wall on capacious holds to the tower's top, at 4,000ft. Its 20ft. link to the mountain is the top edge of a curtain-wall – a thin, horizontal ridge (knife-edged in snow). Where it abuts on the mountain, a deep cleft forms Tower Gap. When iced, this can be a

Ken Crocket

grim place in a big wind, for it is also the top of Glover's Chimney, which drops sheer beneath into Coire na Ciste. Once again, it should always be possible to get up, for the tooth-shaped wall on the far side has good holds. If these are thinly iced and hidden by hoar, try casting a doubled rope over the wall-top. The ridge beyond continues craggily but easily to the summit plateau. In mist, watch out for Tower Gully exit, close by to your left. It can be corniced in summer and bites deep into your direct line to the cairn.

Tower Ridge is the pre-eminent example of a mainly moderate route that must be called classic by virtue of its big cliff environment, its own great length, its clean sound rock, and the grand scale of its architecture. Whatever more ambitious plans one has on Ben Nevis, Tower Ridge is the first essential climb for the man who wants to know his mountain.

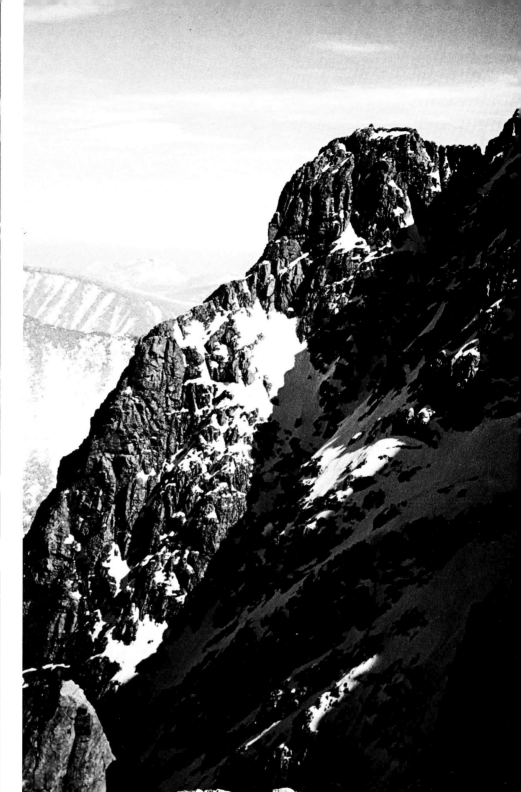

W. A. Poucher from Scottish Peaks

Above left: The 'tunnel' pitch on the Eastern Traverse of the Great Tower. *Climber: Aysel Crocket*

Above right: Tower Ridge in profile. The Great Tower and Tower Gap are the obvious features near the top of the photograph.

6 Clachaig Gully

by Allan Austin

Route Clachaig Gully, Severe (mild), 1,735ft.
Cliff West Face of Sgor nam Fiannaidh, Aonach Eagach Ridge.
First Ascent W. H. Murray, A. M. MacAlpine, J. K. W. Dunn and W. G. Marskell, May 1938.
Map Reference O.S. Tourist Map to Ben Nevis and Glencoe 1–50,000 Sheet (ref. 128575).
Guidebook S.M.C. *Glencoe and Ardgour*, Vol. 2, by L. S. Lovat.
Nearest Road A minor road at the foot of the hillside by the Clachaig Hotel. This leaves the A82 near the western end of Glencoe.
Distance and time from cliff 400yds/300ft. Allow 5 minutes.
Good Conditions The gully is usually wet, but unless particularly violent stream-bed struggles are sought it is wise to avoid it after prolonged wet weather.
Campsites and Bunkhouses Campsite near the entrance of the gully, bunkhouse and Youth Hostel a short distance down the minor road towards Glencoe village.
Bibliography *Mountaineering in Scotland* by W. H. Murray (Dent, 1947) contains a detailed account of the first ascent: *Call Out* by Hamish MacInnes (Hodder and Stoughton, 1973) contains accounts of various rescues from the gully; S.M.C. Journal 1970: *A Guided Tour* by Allan Austin (reproduced here by kind permission of the S.M.C.).

Note: Upgraded from VD to Severe in the 1992 guidebook which notes 'the grade is for dry conditions'. This gives the misleading impression that the climb might be VS in the more usual wet or greasy conditions, whereas a sporting Severe ability should overcome all obstacles.

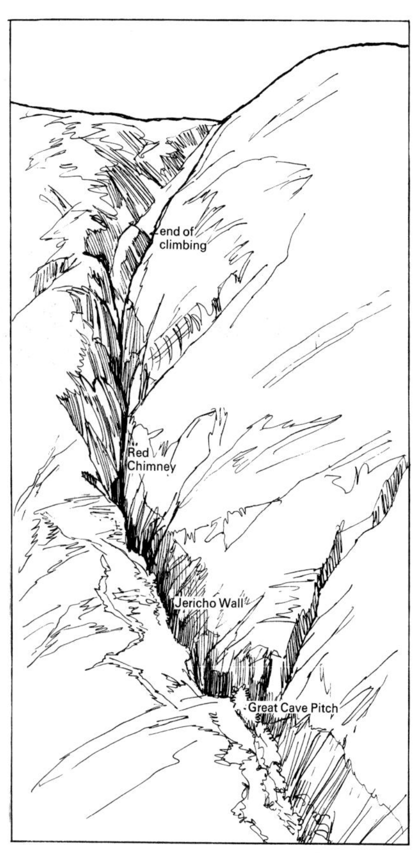

It was dark. Heavy rain was falling as we rattled across the bridge. The light in front glowing in the darkness meant warmth and comfort. Just what I needed. Matie was well ahead owing to the fact that someone had inadvertently left a plank off the bridge and I managed to put my foot on it. The rushing water sounded very near indeed, as I grovelled face down on the boards, nose pressed between the gaps, securely held by the heavy sack which had come to rest on the back of my neck. I sighed; it had been like this all day. I managed to reach a position of verticality without losing my gear over the side and set off in pursuit.

Matie had been ready to start first and, with practised smoothness, had picked up the torch and gone. I was still bemoaning the unfairness of it all and entirely failed to see the hole in the path down which I slid in the direction of the river. It could have been worse. At least I had stopped short of the water. My feet were still dry. This was soon remedied as I plodded dourly on towards the dancing light. It seemed the path had taken a detour over a small bridge; it felt like a drainage ditch. The light stopped. He was waiting for me! Maybe he wasn't so bad after all. But it seemed he was only waiting for moral support. He wanted to be two-up when we tried for a night's lodging.

A climber lounged in the doorway, propping up the doorpost. He was huge. The doorway was completely blocked. At the sight of this great black-visaged giant I resumed my rightful place at the rear; after all, Matie had the torch and anyway he was bigger than me. Then the incredible happened. The black visage cracked in a smile of welcome. A few words from Matie and the giant waved us inside. 'Be my guest,' he boomed. It seemed they had been on a rescue together in Chamonix.

They were just about to eat. There was a pale, thin-faced youth with shifty eyes who seemed incapable of telling the truth. There was a stocky, short-legged one with strange round eyes. A short, tubby one with thinning hair and an easy-going expression, and his brother, irreverently referred to as the 'Old Man'. The evil-looking curry on the table was for all. I was thankful that 'all' did not include me. Even this strange and motley crew were failing. But our friendly giant didn't seem to mind and ate the lot, emptying the dish and finishing with the pan. I lost a bet with him and he ate my biscuits. We retired to bed having lost a shilling at cards, two shillings in an electric meter that didn't work, and with the information that a climb called Hee-haw was a good one for wet weather.

We were up late the following day, sluicing pots of tea into a team of Scots idlers living it up in bed. A cunning ploy this. We needed a guide to show us the way. Alas, they all had elastic bladders. No amount of persuasion seemed able to move them from their beds. Appeals to their sense of decency, sportsmanship, etc., fell on deaf ears. They all slept. We offered to make their breakfast and at once the big man rolled over. 'Aye,' he announced, 'it's no fair to let ye go on your own; I'll come wi' ye.' He stood up and stretched and decided we needed a fourth member. With an easy, effortless movement he reached a hand under the next bunk and dragged forth a blinking, bleary-eyed youth, the short-legged one. We gave them grapefruit, porridge and bacon butties, and even cleared up for them. And finally, when they could prevaricate no longer, we set forth for the Clachaig.

I should make it clear at this point that we had entertained some doubts as to the usefulness of their recommendations and had decided on Clachaig Gully instead of some nebulous VS we had never heard of.

I stood there, aghast. 'That's it,' they assured me, indicating the foaming torrent rushing down the hill. 'That's the way, just follow the burn.' There was a certain amount of confusion when they found out I had no boots. I hadn't been able to wear any for a year, as a result of a wee miscalculation on a boulder. PAs wouldn't stand up to it, they insisted. Wouldn't stand up to it? They weren't the only ones. I could see right away that this wasn't the climb for me. I'd made a big mistake coming down here, but there was no point in compounding it. I put on a brave smile. 'Don't bother about me, chaps,' I said. 'You just go on ahead, I can always do it some other time.' 'Och, nae bother at a',' said the giant, dragging forth a pair of hut slippers from the depths of the van. They were Matie's old kletts, monstrously big with holes in the toes and one sole gaping. 'These'll dae fine.'

I blundered along in the wake of the giant as he ploughed his way up the stream bed, slipping and sliding on invisible boulders and eventually measuring my length in the water. I staggered to my feet to find my finger split across the end and opened out like an unzipped banana. The giant peered at it with interest, snapped it back into place and watched me spew in the burn. By this time, Matie and the short-legged one had come back to see what the hold-up was. 'I think you'd better climb with me,' the short-legged one announced, obviously fearing that the giant was too soft. 'Give him the rope.' And a dripping coil of rope was hung about my neck.

He stormed off up the stream, his short sturdy legs pounding the water to foam, while I vainly tried to instil some power into mine to keep up. Eventually he stopped below a particularly difficult waterfall which fell into a deep, evil-looking pool. 'We'll put the rope on here.' I breathed a heartfelt sigh of relief. I could just about second it, I thought.

'You'll have nae bother,' he announced, pointing to a red shelving wall on the right. 'There's a tree up there you can use as a runner.' The tree, a ridiculously immature sapling, sprouted from a grass sod about halfway up. If I should fall off, the life expectancy of the sapling would most certainly be severely reduced. I crawled up the wall using the maximum of friction offered by my voluminous ex-army breeches, rounded the unhappy little sapling and slithered across to a handy boulder at the top of the fall. It was all very insecure, but fortunately the rain lashing down on my spectacles effectively blinded me and the depths of the pool remained out of sight. The short-legged one followed without appearing to experience any difficulty and my hopes of fishing him out of the pool remained unfulfilled.

He disappeared upwards through some minor submerged boulder pitches, and when I eventually caught him up he was standing on the edge of a pool below a particularly intimidating fall. 'That's the way,' he announced, indicating the roaring torrent,

Ken Wilson

Klaus Schwartz

Above left: The Great Cave Pitch. The cave is actually turned on the right: the wall is climbed to the tree, and then a descending leftward traverse is made to regain the gully bed. *Climber: Alan Davis*

Above right: The pitch after the Great Cave is the crux, where a 30-ft. section of greasy and poorly protected slabs has to be climbed to reach the foot of Jericho Wall. *Climber: Klaus Schwartz*

Opposite page: Two views of Jericho Wall. Here the rock is still greasy but the holds are more positive and the difficulties soon relent. *Climber: Duncan Clarke*

which I now perceived was actually a chimney in disguise. I was beginning to suspect that perhaps this man wasn't a friend after all and it was some time before I was persuaded that salvation really did lie in that direction. Matie and the giant had caught up by this time and all three stood in a semicircle while I advanced, somewhat hesitantly, to battle with the great fall. The only possible way seemed to be to get in there and fight it out. Tentatively I poked my head in, but it was black as night. The weight of water had washed my balaclava down over my face and I was effectively blinded. Back I blundered, arms waving, tripped on an unseen boulder and measured my length in the pool. I surfaced to the sound of hoots of laughter from the ill-mannered throng, which had the effect of dredging up from somewhere a bit of determination. I felt a definite stiffening of my upper lip. Stuffing the offending balaclava into the short-legged one's hand, I stormed back into the fray.

Now I had been thinking about it and had decided on a plan. I would climb as far as I could in the water, then lean out backwards, take a couple of gulps of air and plough on. A reasonable enough theory, one would suppose. The moment arrived when I could hold

Ken Wilson

Ken Wilson

Above: A water-washed runnel high on the route, one of several tricky steps above the Red Wall pitch. *Climber: Bernard Newman*

my breath not a second longer, and so in accordance with the plan I headed out for the light and air. There was nothing wrong with the plan. Superman could have managed it, maybe even the giant below; but a bumbling Sassenach? More hoots of laughter as once again I was fished out of the pool.

This was the end. Whose idea was it anyway? I refused to go back into that maelstrom ever again, and indeed insisted that it was the short-legged one's turn. Whereupon he discovered that a little rib just on one side was a 'variation' . . . would I like to try? It was well scratched and about moderate in standard.

It will be appreciated that climbing in such conditions inevitably subjects one's equipment to undue stresses and strains, and my braces were showing every sign of falling down on their job. I was reluctant, therefore, to place further strain on them, but it seemed there was no way out; the only way was up. Fortunately, they showed an unsuspected tenacity for life, and though at times I seemed to be climbing with my knees tied together the worst did not happen and I was saved from an embarrassing situation. Eventually, in answer to my monotonous request, the short-legged one agreed: we could go home, this was the top, we could go no further. Joyously I passed this bit of information down to the next team. The last bit was a boulder pitch and, stimulated by the knowledge that he was almost there, Matie came sprinting up in a flying mantelshelf and with a vigorous heave crashed his head against a protruding boulder. This caused great amusement, and in no time at all Matie's face was all shades of red as blood blended with rain to run from his chin in an impressive flow. The two guides disappeared into the gloom, chortling and whooping, and leaving us to coil the ropes – our ropes – and follow them down.

We totally misjudged both their fitness and our own, however, for in spite of a five minutes' start we must have overtaken them somewhere on the hill, and when eventually I managed to stagger through the bar-room door, I found to my surprise I was the first arrival. 'I'll hae a wee dram,' said a voice from the rear.

And so help me! It's all true!

Note: This article, entitled 'A Guided Tour', was first published in the *Scottish Mountaineering Club Journal*, 1970. The Scottish members of the cast were Dougal Haston, Jimmy and Ronnie Marshall, James (Big Elly) Moriarty and Robin Smith.

7 Long Crack, Archer Ridge and Crypt Route

by John MacKenzie

One of the features of Glencoe is that several different medium-grade routes can be joined together, starting at the bottom outcrops and ending on the highest crags. Of course, it is equally possible to string together a series of hard climbs, but that does not concern us here. In fact, the following routes should prove suitably energetic for most, giving a tremendous day out, with interestingly varied rock climbs and pleasant and scenic ridge walking, all ending on the highest summit in Glencoe.

The itinerary is thus: crossing the River Coe by the bridge, walk up to the East Face of Aonach Dubh, to climb the Long Crack. Follow this with Archer Ridge, to gain the crest of Aonach Dubh and thence the summit at Stob Coire nan Lochan. From there, make a descending traverse to the foot of Church Door Buttress, before climbing Crypt Route to a finish on the summit of Bidean nam Bian. It makes a long day, but having the hardest climb first and the safest last should compensate for any lack of energy.

The climbs are varied. The Long Crack is a steep wall and crack, in the modern idiom. Archer Ridge is a fine and airy open rib, while Crypt Route is just the opposite: an enclosed series of chimneys and dark subterranean passages leading up the bowels of the Church Door. The rock types also differ, allowing the climber to savour both the rough rhyolite of the Aonach Dubh routes and the much smoother and more massive andesite of Bidean.

The East Face of Aonach Dubh is situated 1,000ft. above the road, and the climbs start from a fine grass ledge running along the base of the cliff. The cliff itself, 1,200ft. long and 600ft. high, is split mid-way by a terrace of grass and rock. The rock steepens above and below the terrace, and the foot of the cliff is bisected by a rowan-crowned outcrop, which makes a good landmark. The first climb, the Long Crack, starts near the middle of the Weeping Wall, which lies to the right of the Rowan Tree Wall. A large detached block at the base of the cliff forms a good point from which to launch off up the wall. Solid holds lead to a small ledge. A short traverse right, a steep cracked groove and an overhang lead to a steep wall, typical of this cliff, giving good hand-holds and protected by the occasional Moac. The wall leads to a broken ledge below the crux crack, with a belay on the left.

The climb now changes its character. Traverse back to the crack again, where another Moac protects the next few moves. The crack is rather awkward and somewhat stretchy, and for those used to tight jams it is a little threadbare. Thus careful footwork becomes important. Some delicate moves up, and a final mantelshelf, bring one to an excellent little ledge. Above, the angle lies back and the climb finishes easily to the terrace.

If Long Crack is thought too difficult, there is an easier alternative entry which takes the rough wall just right of the three cracks of Rowan Tree Wall. Both Long Crack and the Rowan Tree Wall approach end on the terrace, where two lines at once make their presence felt, merely by virtue of their appearance: the big rib of Archer Ridge, and the steep pillar of Quiver Rib on its left.

Archer Ridge is rather more complex than the guidebook makes out. It is open to considerable variation, often at a higher standard, and the rock is not as good as we are led to believe. However, it is certainly distinctive and gives 250ft. of V.Diff. climbing, although this grading should be treated flexibly: it is probably nearer Severe than V.Diff., as the easiest line on the 40ft. wall is hard to find. In many ways, the first pitch is the best: here, you climb good rock on excellent holds for some 110ft., without obvious protection, and in a fine airy position. From a small stance under some bulges, a straightforward traverse to the right (the direct route goes up through the bulges) leads to another stance below the 40ft. wall. The crux follows. The wall is a steep, reddish chunk of rock, equipped with an alarming number of blocky holds and wobbly spikes. It is quite steep and gives awkward, out-of-balance climbing. It is difficult to find the best line. The actual holds are big enough, if you can trust them, and it is partially the absence of runners and the hefty exposure which combine to make this feel more like Severe climbing. Above the wall, the angle relents and easier rock leads up and right to a big grassy niche.

Routes Long Crack, Severe, 300ft.; Archer Ridge, Very Difficult, 250ft.; Crypt Route/Flake Route, Very Difficult, 350ft.
Cliffs East Face of Aonach Dubh; Church Door Buttress on Bidean nam Bian.
First Ascents Long Crack – L. S. Lovat and J. M. Johnstone, June 1953; Archer Ridge – W. H. Murray and D. B. McIntyre, May 1947; Crypt Route – M. Wood, Wilding and A. S. Pigott, September 1920.
Map References O.S. Tourist Map to Ben Nevis and Glencoe 1–50,000 Sheet (ref. 158560 and 146542).
Guidebooks S.M.C. *Glencoe and Ardgour*, Vol. 2, by L. S. Lovat; *Scottish Climbs*, Vol. 1, by Hamish MacInnes.
Nearest Road The A82 at the Meeting of Three Waters (ref. 174567). There is a layby on the south side opposite the Lost Valley. A path leads down to a suspension bridge and thence diagonally up the hillside to the stream below the cliff.
Distance and time from cliff 1 mile/1,000ft. Allow 30 minutes.
Good Conditions Two days are needed for both cliffs to dry after heavy rain, but a strong wind will halve this time.
Campsites and Bunkhouses Campsites in Glencoe at various points. Youth Hostel and bunkhouse between the Clachaig Hotel and Glencoe village. Club huts near the parking place.
Bibliography *Undiscovered Scotland* by W. H. Murray (Dent, 1951) contains an account of the exploration of the East Face of Aonach Dubh; *Mountaineering in Scotland* by W. H. Murray (Dent, 1947) has a description of a summer ascent of Crypt Route; *The Central Highlands* by Campbell R. Steven (S.M.C., 1968).

Donald Bennet

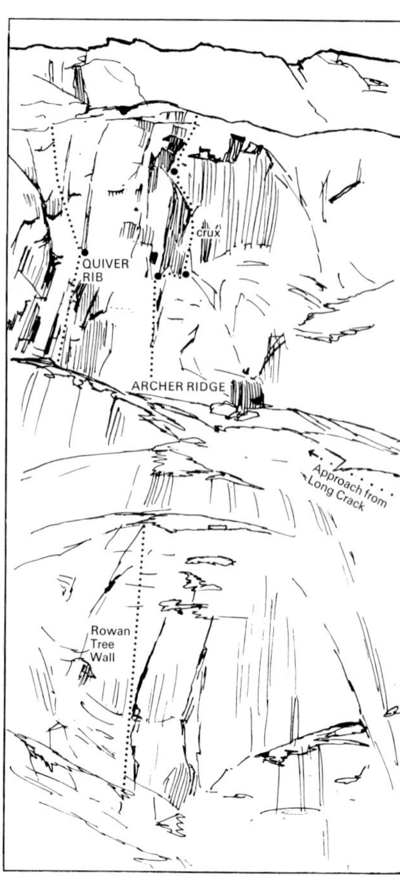

Above: The first pitch of Archer Ridge *Climber: Robin Chalmers*

Right: The East Face of Aonach Dubh

The guide suggests that the right side of the steep wall above should be climbed, but the slightly overhanging wall and corner directly overhead give an enjoyable Severe pitch, which is well protected and more logical than going to the right.

This pitch ends the climb, bringing one to the top of the cliff. Archer Ridge has a serious atmosphere for a V. Diff. and opinions vary as to its actual worth; but it is a good line, needing more thought than the average climb of its grade and is probably best suited to those whose climbing is above that standard.

Again, there are easier options, none better than one of the finest Diffs. in the country – Quiver Rib. This 200ft classic was a real discovery, as it has an impregnable appearance when viewed from below. Looking up, you see near verticality looming above: a line of holds running up an imposing 100ft pillar to end dramatically at a small ledge, where a seemingly impossible gangway slants up a sheer wall to the left.

But, though the eye may be deceived, the reality is different! Colossal holds appear as one climbs up the pillar: it is the ideal place to savour verticality without difficulty. A small spike serves as a rather apologetic belay on the cramped stance, and the gangway, now bristling with jugs, leads boldly upwards and involves only one difficult move. No runners are readily available, so the exposure can be fully savoured.

From the top of the cliff, the climber now has a short trudge to the crest of Aonach Dubh, past numerous little outcrops to level ground. After this the ridge rises gradually for another 1,000ft., to the summit of Stob Coire nan Lochan at 3,650ft. The Bidean's upper defences are now near to hand, in the form of two symmetrical buttresses, huddled together but separated by the easy central gully. An unstable scree approach leads up past Collie's Pinnacle, a blunt mass of rock,

W. A. Poucher from Scottish Peaks

Above: Bidean nam Bian and Church Door Buttress. Crypt Route ends at the top of the obvious sunlit shoulder half-way up the central cliff, and then finishes up the shadowy walls above. The sunny cliff facing the camera is climbed by the hard route Kingpin.

seamed with cracks, forming a barrier between Diamond Buttress on the left and Church Door Buttress, where Crypt Route lies, on the right. Viewed from below, these three masses of rock display a superb architecture, their fluted lines giving an impression of soaring verticality, especially on the Church Door.

Sacks can be left well below the start of Crypt Route, in a pleasantly sheltered cave formed by a huge boulder wedged between the pinnacle and the smaller rib to the right. The foot of the climb is reached by climbing easier ground to the right of the rib. Above, a vast arch spans the screes, with 180ft. of verticality beneath it. Daylight can be seen behind it in one or two places, and the atmosphere bears little similarity to the friendly rocks of Aonach Dubh's East Face, the andesite being a smooth slate grey and often completely holdless.

Some time in the past a huge rock fall must have occurred, leaving the arch suspended and forming the deep chimney and extraordinary subterranean passages of Crypt Route. The first pitch is in many ways the finest. After a short introductory scramble, the deep chimney is reached and excellent back-and-foot work is done past several chockstones, until, at 70ft. and just past a chock, a deep and darkening cleft is gained, the end shrouded in gloom and mystery.

> Stones of Old in high immortal verse,
> of dire chimneys and enchanted aisles
> And rifted rocks whose entrance leads,
> to Hell.

Here, a head-torch is useful, especially if the tunnel route is attempted. This rock corridor has two direct exits above, leading up and out sensationally over the chockstones. The situation is, to put it mildly, unusual.

Seekers of new sensations (provided that they are slim) should therefore try the tunnel route, taking a narrow passage at the left back of the corridor, with torches aglow. After a preliminary thrutch, a dank and dark chamber is reached. From here, another tunnel leads to a further slim chamber, where a misty light filters through from the end of a long, thin passage.

Below: In the depths of Crypt Route. *Climber: John MacKenzie*

Alan Craig

Ideally, the climber should be stripped of gear (none is needed). Facing left, he sidles crab-wise along to an upward step by a chockstone. Viewed from there, the chimney seems to plummet down 'to Hell', but the passage leads up to an ever-decreasing exit, where the climber might find it easier to turn several times. The final squeeze leads to an eighteen-inch exit hole. The hole seemed to us somewhat narrower than that, as a wretched edge of rock protrudes at the worst possible place, calling for awkward wriggles to gain the sunlight and welcome freedom on the spacious ledge outside.

Another chockstone now bars the way. You can either crawl through the hole, or exit left and follow easy cracks to gain another short, enclosed tunnel. Having walked through this, you step round some boulders and finally cross the 'gap' leading to the crest of the arch. Here, jammed boulders form a spacious ledge, while gaps between the boulders offer spectacular downward views. The arch seems a sound structure in spite of the gaps, but there is a feeling of insecurity compounded by the drop, which has an alarming downward perspective, with Collie's Pinnacle as its focus. Officially, Crypt Route has ended and Flake Route is joined on the arch to give one more pitch. The steep chimney crack is then climbed, facing right on good holds. This is the crux of the route, and there is plenty of protection available, if needed. Thereafter, scrambling over further short steep walls and cracks leads to an exit on screes forming the crest of a short spur.

Flake Route was climbed as early as 1898, but Crypt Route had to wait until 1920, when Wood, Wilding and Piggot snatched it from under Scots noses. Combined, they give about 400ft. of climbing. The rather meagre 180ft. of Crypt Route, given in the guide, does not take into account much of the traversing, but exact lengths are not important on a climb such as this.

A short walk up the rocky crest leads to the summit Bidean nan Bian, at 3,766ft. Here, one is rewarded with excellent views, particularly to the north and west, where range succeeds range until all is swallowed up in the grey ocean. It is a fitting end to a long and satisfying day.

8 North Face Route and Agag's Groove

by Tom Weir

Buachaille Etive Mòr was invisible, lost in a white helmet of mist pulled down to the rocks. We had agreed on the North Face Route, but first we had to find it, and I was glad I was with the editor of the S.M.C.'s *Climbers' Guide to Glencoe and Ardgour*. Len declared we were there. While I tied on the rope, he adjusted his boots, complaining of the drizzle and cold on the hands as he did so.

'Just push on,' he said, turning his back on me to sit down. I went round a short corner and was soon thirty feet up and facing a vertical corner such as you find in any room, the difference being that a finger-width crack split the meeting-point of the walls, and only pressure of one foot against the other held me on. Fingers were unpleasantly cold, and I didn't feel too happy about the greasy rock. I decided I must be off form, tried once again, and offered it to Len who was out of sight round the corner at the belay.

He didn't even start. One look was enough: 'That's Kinloss Corner.' I felt relieved and heartened when he added: 'We wouldn't stand a hope of getting up it today.' I was wondering if I was getting past even a V.Diff. in the rain. All we had to do now was go to the edge of the Central Buttress and start up the line of least resistance and we were away, up the exposed crack and easier rocks to the Heather Ledge.

This is where the real climbing begins, rightward round the steep edge of the buttress and up into a belay niche. Now you descend a bit, and attack a steep little wall on small holds to the 70ft. chimney. Both are high V. Diff. I led the first. Len made short work of the chimney, whose crux lies in getting from the left wall to the right wall across its gap.

Bell and Harrison pioneered the route to this point in 1929. The lead which was now mine was the airy 150ft. added by D. Scott in 1936. Going hard left from the chimney-top, it crosses a steep wall on balance holds to a soaring edge, exposed above the whole buttress and difficult enough to keep you literally on your toes.

I quickly lost sight of Lovat in the swallowing mist, but was enjoying myself, conscious of my situation even if my only dimension was space. Then, suddenly, my head went through a trapdoor in the clouds, and for a moment I was dazzled by the great ball of the sun reflecting light from the clouds as from a snowfield. I heard myself give a cry of pleasure, and in the same moment saw myself climbing, a shadow on a shimmering edge projected on the clouds.

The rocks were now warm to the touch, and, as I lifted my head, the top of the Buachaille was solidifying as a pink wedge against blue sky. Up at the belay point my shadow stood out on the clouds, ringed by a huge balloon of rainbow, a superb 'glory' or Brocken Spectre.

I said nothing to Len, but let him climb into the world of rainbows born on a glittering sea, where mountain peaks jostled in the silent world of sunshine.

He was silent for a moment, taking in the fantastic mixture of colours from the violet of the Mamores to the incredible red of Rannoch Wall. Then he spoke. 'Tom,' he said, 'I've been climbing on the Buachaille for over fifteen years, and I reckon this is the greatest moment I have ever had on it, or on any other mountain.'

In the genial warmth we traversed across to the 'Wall', to meet with other delighted climbers, some of them stripped to the waist, sunbathing on the Curved Ridge.

Now for Agag's Groove while it's warm and dry. P.A.s would have been nice, but the hard-edged holds of this trade route offer plenty for conventional boots. The first pitch contains the hardest technical moving, what we call the 'open-book' section, about 80ft. from the start. Holds are good, and runners can be fixed as you toe up the corner to a fine block belay.

'Marvellous,' says Lovat, carrying on up the next 100ft. of moderate climbing, so as to leave me the verticalities of the nose with the big drop below, which makes it one of the best VD pitches in Glencoe for situation.

The joy of Agag's is how swiftly it makes vertical height, even on the easier middle section. One can imagine the swinging *élan* and cries of joy when the ebullient Hamish Hamilton led the first ascent in 1936; how he must have enjoyed the steepness and big holds of what is still one of the best places for moving in Glencoe.

Routes North Face Route, Very Difficult, 500ft.; Agag's Groove, Very Difficult, 350ft.
Cliffs Central Buttress and Rannoch Wall, Buachaille Etive Mòr.
First Ascents North Face Route – J. H. B. Bell and A. Harrison, July 1929; Modern finish – D. Scott and party, September 1936; Agag's Groove – J. F. Hamilton, A. Anderson and A. C. D. Small, August 1936.
Map Reference O.S. Tourist Map to Ben Nevis and Glencoe 1–50,000 Sheet (ref. 227544).
Guidebooks S.M.C. *Glencoe and Ardgour*, Vol. 1, by L. S. Lovat; *Scottish Climbs* by Hamish MacInnes.
Nearest Road A82 at Altnafeadh (ref. 221563) or the Glen Etive road (ref. 242541).
Distance and time from cliff 1 mile/1,100ft. Allow 40 minutes.
Good Conditions Both routes dry quickly in the summer months.
Campsites and Bunkhouses S.M.C. Hut Lagangarbh (ref. 222560). Creagh Ohu Hut, Jacksonville; Campsites at The Kingshouse or in upper Glen Etive
Bibliography *A Progress in Mountaineering* by J. H. B. Bell (Oliver and Boyd, Edinburgh, 1950) contains an account of the first ascent of North Face Route; *Mountaineering in Scotland* by W. H. Murray (Dent, 1947) contains an interesting account of an ascent of Agag's Groove; S.M.C. Journal 1936; *Agag's Groove* by Alex C. D. Small.

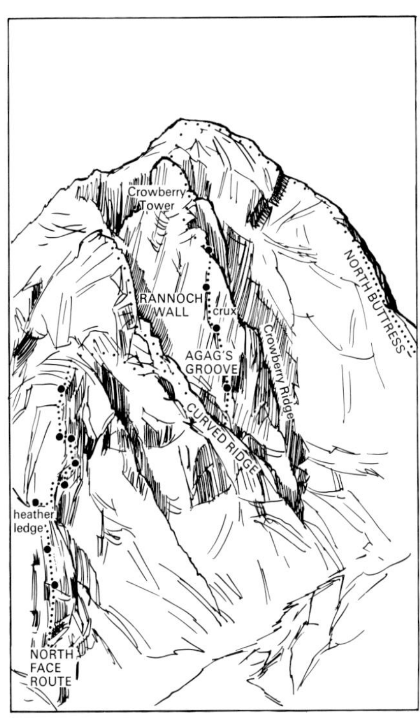

Below: The final pitch (Scott's variation) of North Face Route on the Central Buttress of Buachaille Etive Mòr. *Climber: Fred Mantz*

Right: The final pitch of Agag's Groove, which is tremendously exposed but has excellent holds. Glen Etive and the steep section of Curved Ridge can be seen in the background. *Climber: John Jones*

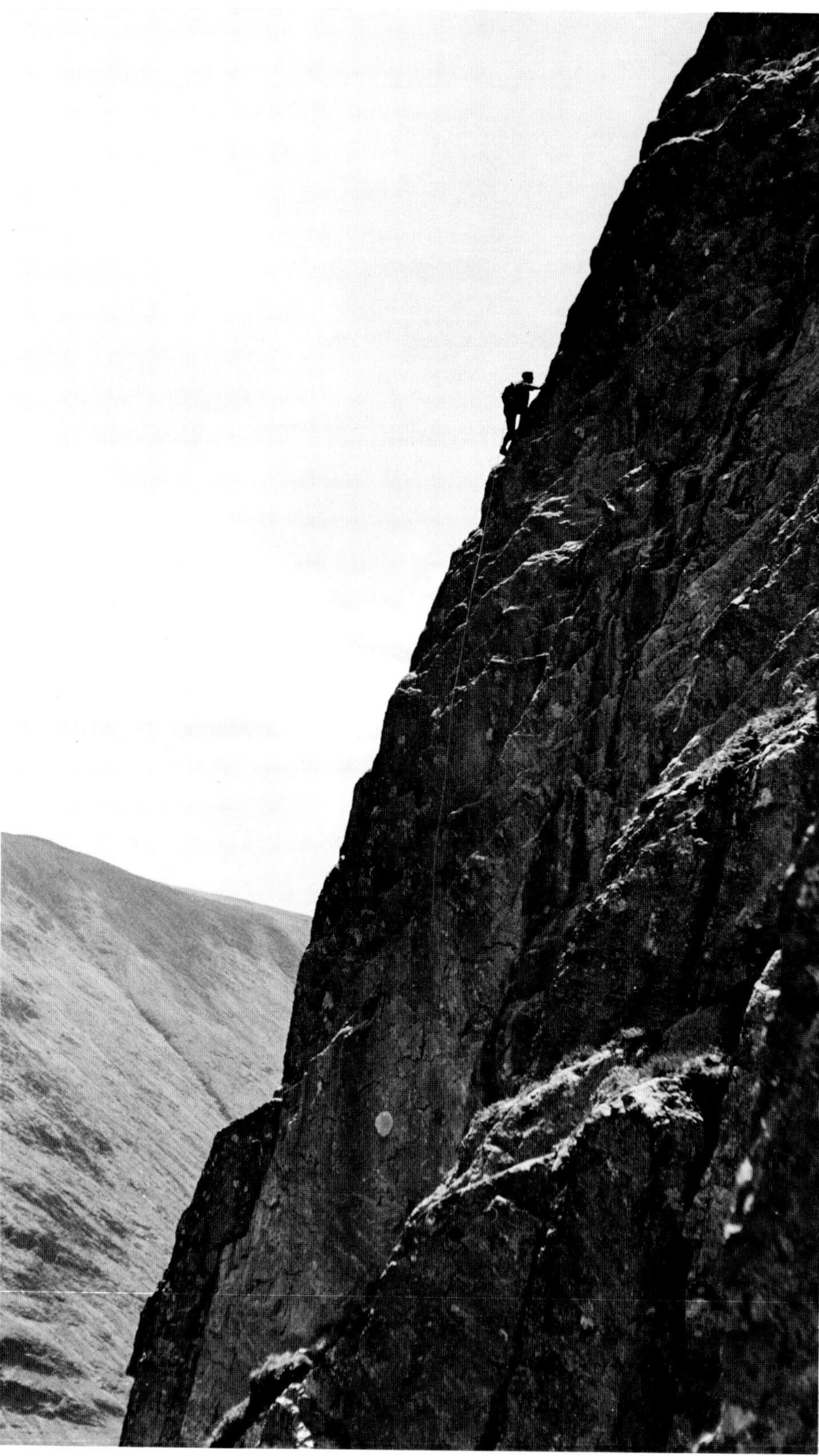

Donald Bennet

And there must have been plenty of underlying tension in his mind as he brought up his second, with the sheer plunge of the then unexplored wall below him, and a daunting vertical nose blocking the view of what lay above.

Many climbers find this nose the 'crux', but this can only be because of the exposure, the feeling of fresh air all the way to the bottom. There is an excellent hold once the first step-up has been made.

Undiluted pleasure lies all the way now, for a full 80ft. of clean-cut finger and toe-holds. Nor is it all over yet, since the last 70ft. to the Crowberry continues in the same vein, though great care must be exercised here, as the rock is that bit more shattered in the final pitch.

Lovat's face is wreathed in smiles as he joins me and treads up the last 70ft. We go on up the Crowberry Ridge to sit on the Tower, delighted to have this finest seat in Glencoe to ourselves. Then down the chimney and a straddle to get into the gap, and in 400ft. we are on the windless summit.

What a day for views, with the Cuillins of Skye and the Nevis range standing above a world where valleys and sea could only be guessed at. Below us was something I had never heard of anyone seeing before: the black silhouette of the Crowberry Tower echoed out on the clouds in shadow, with a halo of rainbow round it.

Len Lovat and I have often talked about that day of 10 October 1965; about the mystery of the Buachaille as we tried to find the North Face Route, and how challenging it was in the white-out. But most of all we have talked of that breathtaking dance of colour and light, as the particles of mist became prisms for the sun to throw our shadows on its ciné screen.

We never thought we would see anything so exciting again, but exactly ten years later, in October 1975, we had just arrived on the summit of Buachaille Etive Mòr, after a wet ascent of North Buttress, when the pale disc of the sun appeared. Within moments we were having Brocken Spectres, as the clouds dropped like milk going off the boil, and we sat in the sun surrounded by the black tips of mountain peaks.

Tom Weir

Normally we use the North Buttress as a route of descent rather than as a climb, but on that October day, by taking it on the steep eastern edge, we had 1,000ft. of good unroped fun. If I had to take a stranger to the Buachaille for just one day of rock-climbing in Scotland, I could offer him nothing better than an expedition up the North Face Route and by Agag's on Rannoch Wall to the summit of the mountain, then down by the North Buttress. That would be about 2,500ft. of rock-climbing, all of it exposed, but on perfect rock.

Left: The exposure enjoyed on all the Rannoch Wall Routes, and particularly on Agag's Groove, is emphasized by this photograph. Few cliffs of such unrelenting steepness and size offer lower-grade climbs; Agag's Groove and several other climbs on the cliff are therefore amongst the most rewarding lower-grade climbs in Britain. *Climber: Unknown*

Above: A cloud inversion from Bauchaille Etive Mòr. Ben Nevis and the Mamores are in the distance. *Climber: Len Lovat*

Ken Crocket

9 The Chasm

by Ken Crocket

The climbing careers of men echo the history of the sport: a brief adolescent scamper around various outcrops, short, brutal, but always educating, followed by an irresistible pull into the many dark and wet clefts which seam the hills of this country. A temporary retreat to the womb, perhaps. If the feckless climber survives this baptism, steep, holdless walls are next discovered, a phase best described as frightening. Finally, at least in Scotland, one can conceal declining powers in the mysticism of winter climbing. Some even write about it. But, at irregular intervals, the gullies call.

The attraction that gully climbing held for the Victorians – a fact well documented in the various journals – was part psychological and part practical. Gullies feel secure and, considering the equipment used by those pioneers, they probably were more secure than open face routes. The numerous ledges, caves, horizontal sections and large chockstones provided adequate belays for strong backs and simple rope loops. They also served as useful halts for enjoying refreshments and reading the barometer, a practice which extended into the 1920s. (This instrument, a vestige from the days when science was the *raison d'être*, was even more awkward on a route than the modern clutter of gear; it invariably broke during the day's outing, thereby explaining the anomalously high mercury content of some Highland rivers.) But, despite all handicaps, the technical standards achieved by the pioneers reached an early high.

The accidental marriage of geological faulting and high rainfall has provided Scotland with a rich endowment of gullies, and Glencoe has the lion's share, there being four major summer gullies in the area, no less than three of them on the Buachaille.

Towards the end of the last glaciation, the Rannoch Moor must have been a vast, glittering sheet of ice, with the broad, blunt bow of the Buachaille thrusting through like some primal ice-breaker. The scars can be seen today, as one drives north over the moor: with the sun full on the south flank of the Buachaille, individual crags soften and merge into one huge canvas of pinks and browns; but slashed down the middle, like the slip of a careless artist, is the deeply cut and enigmatic chasm.

There are harder gullies, even on the same hill; but for length, quality and scenery, together with a crescendo-like finish, few would dispute the regal position of The Chasm of Buachaille Etive Mòr.

The gully begins innocently enough; a section of porous river bed flanked by slowly rising green banks. A short tramp over rattling stones, a slight bend, and coyly the gully begins to reveal her goods. Obstacles appear, stolid chockstones unmoved by grunting climber and scraping boots.

The day that follows – and it might be a long one – is a day of contrasts. A strenuous pitch can be followed by a restful belay at a green pool, while you idly watch your own personal rainbow play on the spray from the next pitch, for the twin elements of the day are rock and water.

Excepting small problems there are sixteen pitches to be won, some of which are individually named, providing useful landmarks.

Pitch 5, The Red Slab, leads up to the blind south fork. In July 1976, a huge boulder completely blocked the gully below the fork, and the easiest bypass is by a Severe corner on the true right wall, approximately 50ft. back from the obstacle.

Pitch 8, The Hundred-foot Pitch, is spectacular, the line taking a steep rib just right of a large waterfall. The pitch following is called the Piano Pitch, after the antics of various unsung heroes, as it involves a traverse on rapidly diminishing holds above a beckoning pool.

Pitch 10, The Converging Walls, is a masterpiece, a touchstone of confidence. The gully narrows dramatically here, and a waterfall elbows one towards the exposed edge. On the left wall is a small ledge, polished, but not by water. The opposite wall is a few feet away, but the space between feels infinite, as crossing involves literally falling over!

Survivors of this are out of the frying-pan – and into the Devil's Cauldron. Three short pitches lead to the final awesome steepening above a rocky basin. Out of this claustrophobic bowl, after hours of climbing, escape seems hopeless, and yet there are three exits, two of which are on the left wall: the South Chimney and the South Wall.

Route The Chasm (with Direct Finish), Severe, 1,500ft.
Cliff The South Face of Buachaille Etive Mòr.
First Ascents By the South Chimney (Very Severe) – Mr and Mrs N. E. Odell and R. F. Stobart, April 1920; by the Direct Finish – R. G. Robinson and I. G. Jack, August 1931.
Map Reference O.S. Tourist Map to Ben Nevis and Glencoe 1–50,000 Sheet (ref. 227547).
Guidebooks S.M.C. *Glencoe and Ardgour*, Vol. 1, by L. S. Lovat; *Scottish Climbs*, Vol. 1, by Hamish MacInnes.
Nearest Road Minor road down Glen Etive about one mile from the junction with the A82.
Distance and time from cliff ½ **mile/700ft** Allow 20 minutes.
Good Conditions The climb requires one week of dry weather to be in reasonable condition, and it is best to allow two weeks for the Direct Finish to dry out.
Campsites and Bunkhouses Camping in Glen Etive or near The Kingshouse. S.M.C. Hut Lagangarbh (ref. 222560) Creagh Dhu Hut, Jacksonville; and Grampian Club Hut at Inbhirfhaolain (ref. 158508).
Bibliography *Always a Little Further* by Alastair Borthwick (Eneas Craig Ltd, 1947) gives an amusing account of an early ascent; *A Progress in Mountaineering* by J. H. B. Bell (Oliver and Boyd, 1950) contains accounts of several ascents, with line illustrations; S.M.C. Journals of 1921 and 1931.

Note: Regraded to Very Severe in the 1980 guidebook for the difficulties on the Converging Walls when wet. The Severe grade applies only in dry conditions which are rare.

Left: Approaching the Converging Walls pitch of The Chasm. The torrent roars down the back of the cleft forcing the climber to bridge up the front. *Climber: Ian Fulton*

Ken Crocket

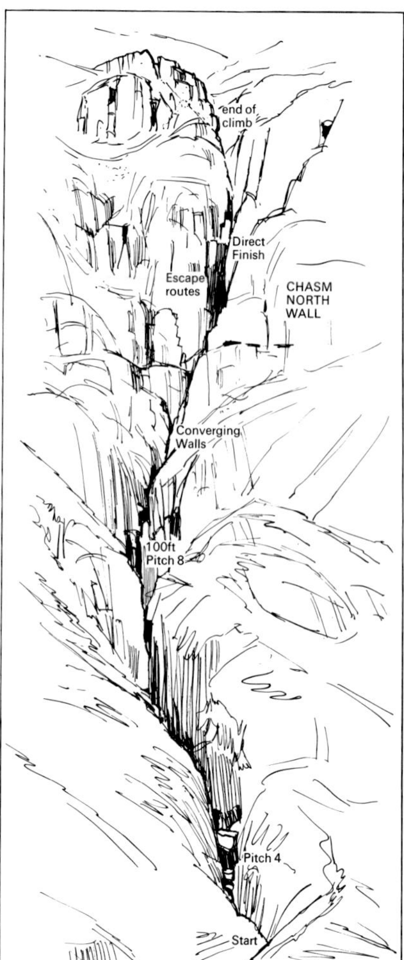

Above: The Chasm, a 1,500-ft. river gorge cleaving the south-eastern slopes of Buachaille Etive Mòr and giving one of the finest gully climbs in Scotland.

Right: Three photographs of the water-sprayed Converging Walls pitch. *Climber: Ian Fulton*

The line which rivets the eye, however, is the Direct Finish, soaring up from the bubbling Cauldron. This pitch is longer and more serious than anything previous, and may give a good soaking to the hopeful pilgrim. Due to its position and obvious difficulty it was not climbed until 1931, after a long, dry summer, and thirty-six years after the first attempt on the gully.

It was first overcome, appropriately, by a group of determined young climbers from Glasgow, one of the ripples from the new wave of enthusiasts spreading north from the cities at weekends. Earlier exploration in 1930, and several attempts in 1931 finally saw J. G. Robinson and I. G. Jack above the pitch, wet, tired, but presumably happy after a desperate struggle of seven hours over all, three on the last pitch alone.

Early estimates of the pitch were understandably exaggerated; some putting it at over 200ft. The true length is just over 110ft., but subjective feelings are more important, and the exposure, atmosphere, and a general feeling of being very small all add up. A crack of 50ft. or so leads through the watercourse to a small cave and stance. The next section is the crux: almost certainly wet and shivering, trying to ignore the drop below, one takes a short, brutal chimney crack, until a long step right can be made to a foothold. Savour the moment as you work up courage to move off this towards the finishing chockstones, for the Chasm demands more than mere ability and strong arms.

After the climax, coda and conclusion, one last small pitch brings release on to easy ground. But to travel hopefully is better than to arrive, and it matters not which finish is taken; for you will return to explore the Chasm again and again.

Ken Crocket

10 Squareface

by Martin Burrows Smith

Route Squareface, Very Difficult, 330ft.
Cliff An Garbh Choire, Beinn a'Bhuird.
First Ascent T. W. Patey and J. M. Taylor, July 1953.
Map Reference O.S. Tourist Map to the Cairngorms, 1–50,000 Sheet (ref. 107015).
Guidebook S.M.C. *Cairngorms Area*, Vol. 2, by G. S. Strange.
Nearest Road At Keiloch by the Invercauld Bridge on the A93, two miles east of Braemar. The alternative route starts from Linn of Quoich (ref. 114911). Other very long approaches are possible from Glenmore and Tomintoul.
Distance and time from cliff 10 miles/ 2,000ft. Allow 5 hours. The approaches up Glen Slugain and Glen Quoich pass through deer forests and should be avoided in August, September and early October, unless permission is given. Individual militancy is not recommended.
Good Conditions In the summer months. The crag is high and north-facing, and though well drained, should be given a day to dry.
Campsites and Bunkhouses Discreet camping and bivouac boulders in the corrie below the crag. The Cairngorm Club Hut at Muir of Inverey (ref. 077896) is the best valley base.
Bibliography *One Man's Mountains* by Tom Patey (Gollancz, 1972).

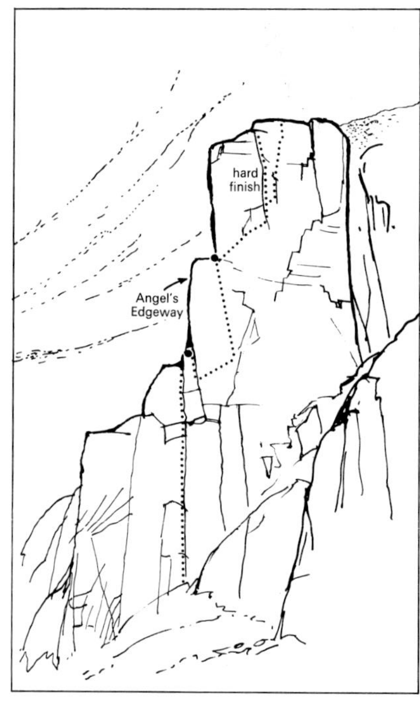

Cairngorm rock-climbing has many contrasts. The visitor is naturally attracted to the accessible and superbly exposed Shelter Stone Crag, or perhaps to the fine and highly underrated climbs on Hell's Lum. However, deep in the heart of these mountains are many hidden gems whose secrets will only be revealed to the ardent explorer or dedicated escapist. Soloing in distant corries can give one's climbing a new dimension; none of the trappings of modern climbing, just glorious rough granite, the rushing of a water-slide, the croak of a ptarmigan, the soaring of an eagle, and plenty of time to soak up the atmosphere of these beautiful surroundings. One of the remotest and finest corries in Scotland is the splendid Garbh Choire, on Beinn a'Bhuird. That such an isolated corrie can match its unique environment with excellent rock-climbing is irresistible to the mountaineer.

Given good weather, the instructor working from Speyside is in a fortunate position. On days off he can be climbing on the Loch Avon cliffs soon after leaving the valley, while on the long summer expeditions he can conveniently seek out and explore such esoteric classics as the Garbh Choire climbs.

It was on such an occasion that I made my first visit. The approach from Glenmore is unusually long: too far, thank goodness, for the crag to become popular. At least, on this hazy, windless day the chairlift was working, so the vulgar Coire Cas was soon behind us. From the summit of Cairngorm the whole approach along and above the vast wastes of Glen Avon could be seen. A long day was spent navigating between tiny lochans, ring contours and Gaelic obscurities. The monotony of these tedious slopes was relieved only by a solitary eagle and a herd of deer, and it seemed inconceivable that the terrain would ever change. However, as Stob an t-Sluichd on the north-east shoulder of Beinn a'Bhuird was reached, there was a feeling that all would change, a feeling soon realized as a convex ridge was crossed and the ground suddenly dropped into the great cavern of the Garbh Choire. The massive Mitre Ridge dominated the back wall, but high up on the left was the clean-cut buttress of Squareface, a climb I really wanted to do, and one that was ideal for late evening activity.

We set up camp beneath the cliffs and viewed the north-facing corrie walls. The Mitre Ridge, and its right flank in particular, stood out impressively, while between this and Squareface was an undistinguished area of rock giving typical steep winter ground. A long scree-rake cut up rightwards beneath Squareface to the top of the crag, giving convenient access to it. The buttress itself faced west up the rake, so that it could not be seen from the floor of the corrie. Rather than scramble up the rake, we decided to approach the climb from above, so we climbed the Mitre Ridge and then traversed left along the lip of the corrie to the top of the rake. From here, the route is seen from above and face on, and very impressive it looks. Seemingly smooth and holdless, its left edge leans out formidably, high above the corrie, in a series of steps, forming two ledges on the sharp arête at the junction of the north and west walls.

As we scrambled down the rake, I was relieved to have a companion with me, for the face loomed ever more imposingly above. The first pitch hinted at what was to come. Wonderful climbing up cracks and grooves in the granite slabs, and an awkward step over a bulge, led up to the first platform. At this point the seriousness and exposure are realized, as the appalling drop of the north wall becomes apparent. I followed a ridge to a smaller stance beneath the undercut crest of the arête. From here, the appropriately named Angels' Edgeway takes the sharp edge direct to the second ledge, with obvious delicacy. However, it was a big boot day, so, without shame, we could follow the original route which launches out right on to the huge slab, climbs it delightfully by steep cracks and then traverses back left to gain the next ledge, which forms an airy stance poised spectacularly on the arête. The final pitch gives a fine climax: more difficulty, exposure and great climbing. On perfect rock, a delicate traverse back on to the slab is followed by steepening, deep-cut, jamming cracks, horizontal and vertical (those who can't jam will have problems with many Cairngorm V.Diffs.), until a gangway provides easy escape to the right. But it was impossible to ignore the winking final crack, the very best of all, which gives a satisfying gritstone-like struggle to an abrupt finish on large granite blocks.

As I belayed on the summit I had an intense feeling of well-being; the sun's last rays glowed on the final towers of the Mitre Ridge and, far below, amidst the boulders on the corrie floor, I could just make out my tent, where I would soon be eating my tea.

So that's Squareface: a secluded jewel, typical of Patey's discoveries of the early 'fifties. Those who make the effort to go there will not regret it.

Right: Climbers on the second pitch of Squareface.

Greg Strange

Left: The well-positioned stance between the second and third pitches of Squareface.

Right: The superb final pitch of Squareface with the remote corrie of An Slochd Mòr in the background. *Climbers: Iain Brooker and Willie Munro*

Greg Strange

11 Mitre Ridge: Cumming/Crofton Route

by Robin Campbell

Despite the intruding ski-lift (which has devalued the Loch Avon crags) and many ugly bulldozed roads, the Cairngorm Mountains still offer the climber a chance to savour what Robinson Jeffers called 'the dignity of room, the value of rareness'. Their broad valleys and high plateaux ensure a constant canopy of sky (usually a clear, bright blue) whose generous light strikes rich harmonies of colour from every quarter. There are few fussy ridges to irritate the eye; even the rude, black crags are tucked away in deep bowl-like corries, and, something to be treasured above all, the grim geometries of the Forestry Commission have not everywhere superseded the natural forest, an organic trinity of pine, birch and juniper which is the outstanding feature of the range.

Rock-climbing on the black granite of the central Cairngorms enjoyed a poor reputation until quite recently. In the formative years of Scottish climbing, it was largely ignored by the Cairngorm Club of Aberdeen and by the Scottish Mountaineering Club, until Harold Raeburn discovered its attractions in the 1900s. However, thanks to the advocacy of James Bell before the Second World War, and Mac Smith, Bill Brooker and Tom Patey since then, it is now widely recognized as a unique and worthy climbing ground, offering fine natural lines and highly concentrated climbing, often on big crags in beautiful and remote corries.

The Mitre Ridge conforms exactly to this recipe. It lies in the great corrie at the head of An Slochd Mór, the great pit which divides the northern sections of the Beinn a'Bhuird and Ben Avon ranges. To reach it you must walk ten miles or more and, if your approach is from the south, cross the Sneck, a 3,200ft. col. Once there, you may count yourself unlucky if you see or hear another person all day. Although the walk is long, this is classic deer forest, so the paths are excellent and the gradients always gentle. From the south you may go by Glen Quoich or Glen Slugain: both are beautiful, and in the gorge of Glen Slugain there are perfect campsites. The Ridge itself is obvious enough once you have crossed the Sneck and begun the long and jarring traverse to its foot. It juts out into the corrie in a succession of three striking towers, before swooping 600ft. to the boulder field.

James Parker, who named the ridge in 1921, fancied that he saw some resemblance between these towers – seen from low in the corrie – and the twin peaks of a bishop's mitre. Parker, one of the original members of the S.M.C. and well known for his part in the early exploration of the Northern Highlands, could make little of the steep central section of the ridge, but noted it as a possible climb and published photographs. Then, in 1930, A. C. Hutchison and A. Rusk, co-founders of the newly formed J.M.C.S., made an attempt. They fared no better than Parker and felt that the 'Mit-not-re' would have been a better name. However, in 1933 a J.M.C.S. party of five, most of them from Cambridge University, made a carefully planned ascent. They climbed the ridge by two routes: E. A. M. Wedderburn, P. D. Baird and E. J. Leslie followed a line which avoided the impossible sections of the crest by minor deviations, mainly on the left, while M. S. Cumming and J. W. Crofton took an obvious line of weakness just to the right of the crest. Later in the same year, in ignorance of the J.M.C.S. ascent, the ridge was climbed by D. Dawson and C. Ludwig from Aberdeen. Ludwig was a strange man: although he made many worthy climbs in Scotland, his descriptions were always perfectly incomprehensible, so none have survived into modern guidebooks. His route on the Mitre Ridge was no exception: it is most unlikely, however, that he followed a line distinct from the two earlier ascents.

Of the two routes, the Cumming/Crofton is the more sustained and takes an arguably better line. At any rate, local consensus seems to favour it. If the rocks are wet, however, it might be better to opt for the Wedderburn route. On the right flank of the ridge, about 100ft. above the lowest rocks, there is a bay from which two long chimneys spring up to the crest. The right-hand chimney divides at a nose, and its right wall lies back and slants off right, forming an enormous groove which rises parallel to the ridge crest. This is the line of the Cumming/Crofton route. The climb begins with a puzzle: the chimney soaring up to meet the ridge is obvious, but how to enter it is not.

Route Mitre Ridge (Cumming/Crofton Route), Severe, 550ft.
Cliff An Garbh Choire, Beinn a'Bhuird.
First Ascent M. S. Cumming and J. W. Crofton, July 1933.
Map Reference O.S. Tourist Map to the Cairngorms, 1–50,000 Sheet (ref. 107015).
Guidebook S.M.C. *Cairngorms Area*, Vol. 2, by G. S. Strange.
Nearest Road At Keiloch by the Invercauld Bridge on the A93, two miles east of Braemar. The alternative route starts from Linn of Quoich (ref. 114911). Other very long approaches are possible from Glenmore and Tomintoul.
Distance and time from cliff 10 miles/2,000ft. Allow 5 hours. The approaches up Glen Slugain and Glen Quoich pass through deer forests and should be avoided in August, September and early October unless permission is given. Individual militancy is not recommended.
Good Conditions In the summer months. The crag is high and north-facing, and though well drained, should be given a day or two to dry.
Campsites and Bunkhouses Discreet camping and bivouac boulders in the corrie below the crag. The Cairngorm Club Hut at Muir of Inverey (ref. 077896) is the best valley base.
Bibliography The S.M.C. Journals of 1921 and 1933 contain references; *One Man's Mountains* by Tom Patey (Gollancz, 1972); *A Progress In Mountaineering* by J. H. B. Bell (Oliver and Boyd, 1950).

John Higham

Bill Brooker

When I climbed the route last year, we found a solution well over to the left and worked back to the chimney. This goes in the straightforwardly strenuous way that chimneys do, squeezing awkwardly past a jammed flake halfway up by the left, to reach a comfortable perch on top of a small pinnacle flanking the ridge. Another puzzle then looms: entry to the huge groove system on the right is barred by a short, steep wall. This gives 50ft. of concentrated climbing: a holdless groove dips outward over the deepening abyss of the chimney and leads out rightwards to a point where holds on the top edge of the wall can be grasped and followed airily back left to an easement at the base of the groove system. The first few feet of this are awkward but then it relents slightly and unrolls majestically for a full hundred feet before dying and circling left into a simple gully, which leads to the col between the first and second towers. On our ascent I found

Top left: Entering the chimney on the first pitch of the Cumming/Crofton route. *Climber: Alison Higham*

Lower left: The crucial third pitch of the Cumming/Crofton Route, at the start of the long groove. *Climber: Greg Strange*

Right: Traversing round to the West Face of the Second Tower – Bell's Variation. *Climber: Ken Grassick*

the initial holdless groove perplexing. The steep left wall was crowding me all the way: the holdless, out-dipping slab up which I must make my way suggested a steady, nail-splintering slither, followed by a sweeping pendulum down and across the chimney into the opposite wall. A good inch or two, perhaps. I dithered and swithered until the solution finally came to me. Cairngorm climbers know their sugary black granite well: writers of climbing textbooks seldom do. So, a knee, a deliberate and precise knee, shod in good hairy tweed, was applied to a roughish patch near the outer edge of the slab and suddenly what seemed impossible became easy. To me, this was a revelation; to a Cairngormer, it would have been a matter of course. It is one of the small pleasures of Scottish rock-climbing that we have major crags of gneiss, quartzite, sandstone, schist, granite and gabbro, as well as the familiar and classical lavas, and that each of these rocks requires its own peculiar adaptations of technique. On Cairngorm granite you need an open mind and a closed textbook.

The col between the first and second towers is one of the several points on the route from which the so-called Direct Route may be joined, and indeed Cumming and Crofton went that way, round on to the left flank of the ridge. However, it would be illogical not to finish with a variation made by J. H. B. Bell which keeps faith with the right flank. A narrow groove and crack lead to a pedestal from which, poised over everything, a mighty heave-up left leads to the narrowing arête, which is followed over the final tower. The plateau is just a short scramble away, there is a refreshing spring a little beyond that and then, to show that you are a real Cairngormer and not just a miserable cragrat, you can walk a gentle mile to the summit and then work south round the rim of the three corries before dropping back down the Quoich.

Donald Bennet

SCOTLAND Coire an Lochain, Cairngorms

12 Savage Slit

by Doug Lang

Route Savage Slit, Very Difficult, 180ft.
Cliff Number 4 Buttress, Coire an Lochain, Cairngorms.
First Ascents R. B. Frere and J. D. Walker, July 1945; First Winter Ascent: G. Adams, J. White and F. Henderson, April 1957.
Map Reference O.S. Tourist Map to the Cairngorms, 1–50,000 Sheet (ref. 982027).
Guidebooks S.M.C. *Cairngorms Area*, Vol. 1, by W. March; *Scottish Climbs* by Hamish MacInnes.
Nearest Road Cairngorm car park below the chair lift (ref. 996053).
Distance and time from cliff 2 miles/ 1,400ft. Allow $1\frac{1}{4}$ hours.
Good Conditions Although the climb is both high and north-facing, it is climbable in most conditions.
Campsites and Bunkhouses Jean's Hut is below the cliff. There is a Youth Hostel and large odious campsite in Glen More.
Bibliography *Thoughts of a Mountaineer* by R. B. Frere (Oliver and Boyd, 1952) contains a first-ascent account; *Rock Climbs* (near Inverness) by Richard Frere (*Northern Chronicle*, Inverness, 1938).

At last, the road signpost reads 'Cairngorm'. The tortuous A9 is now eliminated by crossing the bridge over the River Spey. The drive through the picturesque Rothiemurchus Forest provides a magnificent setting, while to the south the northern corries of Cairngorm form the skyline. Winter's snow still lingers in the gullies; the blue buttresses appear to be unattainable.

I wonder how Messrs Frere and Walker approached these bastions in the last summer of the Second World War. Their pleasure must have been real, unspoilt by the now prevalent commercialism bordering Loch Morlich. What with 'No Camping' signs, parking ticket machines, hot-dog vendors and the like, tourism is rife. An overcrowded, vulgar, official camp-site hastens a continuation up the ski road, complete with parking control. This final intrusion is avoidable by returning at an hour when most plebeians are under alcoholic sedation. After ascending a series of 'S' bends to an altitude of 2,150ft., one comes across a large car park resplendent with tourist facilities. A well-trod path, starting below and west of the establishments, leads to the resited Jean's Hut – an ideal base, free from the humdrum of the valley. It is then only a short boulder hop to the coire floor.

Full of majestic features, Coire an Lochain is a little gem. Number 1 buttress forms the eastern-retaining wall. Numbers 2 and 3 buttresses provide the backbone, with huge boiler-plate slabs sweeping down from their base towards the tiny green lochan. Number 3 or Ewen Buttress has a most impressive right flank, then cuts back to the 'Y' gullies. Finally, Number 4 buttress thrusts out to form the west-retaining wall. This east-facing wall is ravaged by spectacular *dièdres*, the most impressive of which is fissured from top to near bottom by a savage slit. Since the slit cannot be detected from the coire floor, padding up the great slab gives a sporting approach along with a view of the Foray.

As I looked into the dark slit I wondered whether Richard Frere realized he was initiating a surge of climbing activity. Prior to his ascent there were only forty recognized rock-climbs in the whole of the Cairngorms, excluding Sgoran Dubh and Lochnagar. These climbs were mainly in gullies. The grades indicated that climbing development in this region was dormant. There were only five routes of Very Difficult category, one Mild Severe and two Severes, one of which, Raeburns Buttress, is said to be dangerous. The immediate area of Loch Avon Horseshoe and the Northern Corries now boasts upwards of 115 routes, many of which are among the finest and most technically

Right: Looking down the symmetrical corner of Savage Slit. *Climber:* Rebecca Schwartz

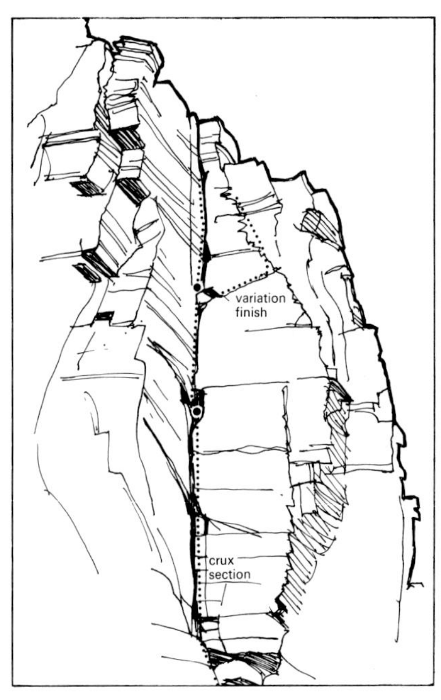

demanding on these islands. To the right and left of the slit a further eight routes have been claimed.

Belaying after 30ft. of moderate climbing, the slit proper is not easily embarked upon. As on most granite cliffs, an acute awareness of lack of holds ensues. The slit offers only small finger-pulls in its innards, while feet are too clumsy for any wrinkles that are available. The pillared formation to the immediate right provides the solution to this crux section, while the thin crack, half a metre from the slit, provides a placement for a nut runner. Horizontal 'ledges' run between slit and crack to give the impression of gigantic masonry. Combining effort and genuflexion, toes can be placed on the ledges until good hand-holds are found, permitting a pull on to a platform some 20ft. up.

It is advisable to ignore the guidebook instructions in gaining the next chockstone. Make use of the shallow crack on the left wall for the feet. The opposite wall provides support for the body, while upward movement is made over the chockstone. A belay can be arranged at this point if so desired. The most continuous section of the slit looms steeply above. This will dismay many a leader, as it appears to be devoid of holds. To climb the slit internally would be masochistic. Falling into it would prove fatal, either through asphyxiation or hypothermia, since the slit at this point is so deep it holds ice even as late as August.

Start by easy bridging moves until the holds on the right wall dwindle. The position is spectacular, but progress can be made safely and simply by 'walking' the feet up the crack on the left wall while using the right wall for support as in the previous pitch. The final boulder of a chockstone usually receives a 'dunt' from one's helmet. It is now easy to reach the top of the slit without bothering about the creased right wall.

The obvious pinnacle at the cap is worth a visit for the view over to Glen Einich. The scree-tracked slopes can be avoided by climbing the wall behind the pinnacle, then the deep 'V' groove, which is full of jugs. It is a pity the guidebook's 350ft. is so inaccurate, as the climbing is confined to a classic 180ft. pitch. It must be a 'wow' in winter!

Klaus Schwartz

13 Clean Sweep

by Allen Fyffe

Martin and I, each with a minimum of gear, met in Coire Domhain and followed the stream down from the rolling Cairngorm plateau into the deep cleft of Loch Avon. We were heading for Hell's Lum Crag, a superb, flat-faced granite cliff, named after the dark slot of the Lum itself, a smokeless satanic chimney which defines the left side.

'Got your P.A.s?' I asked.

'No,' Marty replied, holding up a foot clad in something resembling a green suède slipper, with a vaguely vibram sole.

'You can climb up to V.S. in these.'

I said nothing, being suitably impressed by the ultimate bendy boot.

Reaching the foot of the cliff we were faced with our first problem. As it was only the beginning of June, a wave of snow still lapped the lower rocks. Getting on to the crag involved a less than impressive display of mountaineering competence. Wet-footed and cold-toed, we eventually perched on a ledge by our chosen route, Clean Sweep.

Although I had done the climb previously and knew it was a great route, I could remember little of the detail. The line is a superb, logical whole, not a collection of bits. It starts up a green slab pillar; then, by slabs and corners, it reaches the foot of a pink, tapered corner above and right of the obvious 'Hellfire Corner'. This corner in turns fades out into cracks, followed by a rounded pillar of steeper grey rock. It is a climb of classic correctitude, gradually steepening from bottom to top, and running up from the lowest to the highest rocks in the centre of the cliff.

I sat on the ledge, while Marty went right to join the route. The idea was to gain the crest of the green whale-back, by a groove running up out of the main left-bounding corner. Ten minutes and one poor runner later, we had changed places, Marty conceding that his boots were more suitable for climbing on real holds. I could see his problem: leaving the little groove and its one hold, you friction right to a hairline crack, pad breathlessly up that till at last holds arrive, then go up the widening crack joyfully to a huge stance on the pillar's top. I volunteered to take the next pitch, as I wanted photographs of the corner above. Marty agreed, so I led off across a short, steep wall, where a diagonal fault runs up from right to left, then up slabs and ledges to a series of small corners leading up to the main pink corner: 150ft. of interesting climbing with good protection where needed. It was very wet, but the rock was so clean that it mattered little. At the top is a textbook belay: a huge block and a perfect nut for an upward pull.

Martin soon appeared. Having led the first two pitches, I had manoeuvred him into a position where he had to lead the corner. It is the crux and was running with water.

'Are there holds?' he asked.

'Sure,' I said, neglecting to mention that they appeared every 15ft. or so, and usually sloped outwards. That they were wet was obvious.

From where I sat I could look out on to the boulder bleakness of the plateau, with the remnants of the winter snows hugging the hollows. The Garbh Uisge and Feith Buidhe roared in white torrents down the slabs and steps of the headwall, to join and meander through the lochan-dotted moraine below, into Loch Avon. On the left, Stag Rocks were in profile; opposite, Carn Etchachan sat scarred, shadowed and squat; its neighbour, the Shelter Stone Crag, loomed above its enormous screes. Towering and massive, the top corners of 'Needle' and 'Steeple' caught the last of the evening's sun. All that rock, wild scenery, solitude and space puts climbs in this area out of the realm of mere routes.

Back to reality: about 20ft. up, Marty was in the corner, his right arm and leg stuck in a wide crack. Water could be seen falling steadily from the top edge of the corner. As the whole thing leans to the left, the water fell where Marty wanted to climb. What didn't hit the rock, hit him. His right elbow and knee produced water like faulty taps. He was unhappy and wet, but unlikely to retreat unless under the influence of gravity. Above him the wide crack closed, then, at 40ft. a small roof cut the corner. His meagre supply of nuts had already dwindled significantly. He tried to edge on a crack to the left. The foot edged but the boot crept. He went up and down, fought and cursed and struggled with his conscience, but eventually got lodged on ledges below the roof. Crossing

Route Clean Sweep, Hard Severe, 500ft.
Cliff Hell's Lum Crag, Loch Avon Horseshoe.
First Ascent R. Smith and G. Tiso, September 1961.
Map Reference O.S. Tourist Map to the Cairngorms, 1–50,000 Sheet (ref. 996017).
Guidebook S.M.C. *Cairngorms Area*, Vol. 1, by W. March.
Nearest Road Cairngorm car park below the chair lift (ref. 989062).
Distance and time from cliff 2 miles/600ft. of descent. Allow 1 hour from top of chair lift. Allow a further hour if walking from car park. The best approach is to contour round above Loch Avon and drop down to the cliff by Coire Domhain.
Good Conditions The cliff is usually fit for rock-climbing between May and October but needs two or three days to dry after bad weather. Melt water can sometimes keep the route wet as late as June.
Campsites and Bunkhouses Camping at the head of Loch Avon and bivouac under the Shelter Stone (ref. 002016).

Note: Regraded to Very Severe in the 1985 guidebook with pitches of 4c, 4a, 4c and 4a.

Left: The crux corner of Clean Sweep *Climber: Martin Burrows Smith*

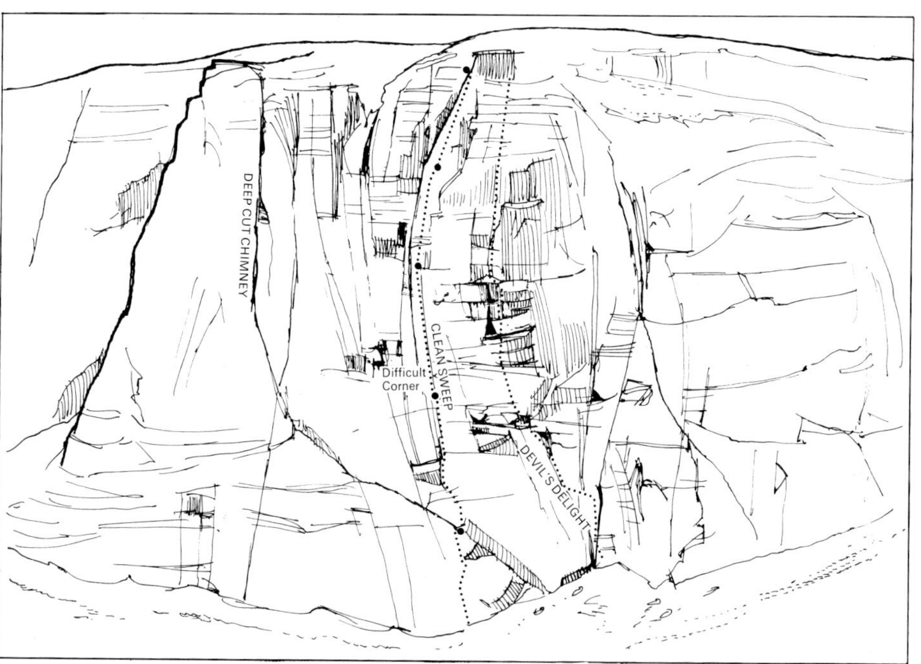

it went fairly smoothly, then the crack and corner continued to another steepening. Again, sporadic movement and noises, until he disappeared. The rope trickled out slowly, till there was no more and it was my turn. I tried to move fast to stay dry – easy to be brave with a rope straight above. The crack still wept winter's slime, but the slab was clean and smooth after centuries of dripping from above. The climbing was sustained Severe, the moves interesting and varied. Resting places arrived fairly regularly and there was better protection than is usual for Cairngorm granite. After the steepening, at about 90ft., the corner faded out, to be replaced by a very shallow chimney, followed by cracks. The climbing was similar to that below, but slightly easier. At last it was dry, and the pitch ended with superb, slabby climbing on perfect, pink granite.

And there was a shivering, dripping Martin with big, white, wet, swollen fingers. I led through up the broad rib of rough rock, which stands slightly proud of the surroundings. Now there is no single way but a variety of similar possibilities. Up cracks, over bulges, across walls, round corners, picking a line and revelling in its freedom. The view down reveals the whole length of the route below, growing longer, but not as long as you would like. Another similar pitch follows, but then it's finished.

Hell's Lum has a number of similar routes to offer, all in the Severe grade and all offering excellent climbing: Devil's Delight, Hell's Lumps and Auld Nick, for example. But none are quite as good as Clean Sweep. When you treat yourself to this, however, make sure you wait until it's dry, and wear your rock boots.

Brian Lawrie

Right: The delicate traverse on the second pitch of Talisman (see following chapter). *Climber: John Moreland*

14 The Talisman

by Brian Lawrie

Sleep comes slowly. Outside the hut, the elements are stalking each other in their endless war of attrition. Inside . . . inside my head the memory of a long walk struggles to escape. Sleep, mind. Sleep.

Must have dropped off. The bad weather has retreated with the night. The subterfuge of wind and rain has abated and the sun, I feel, is up.

Breakfast arrives from the frying-pan of an early riser. Sausages crammed into bread make their greasy way to my stomach. Tea, and that little sacrificial ceremony with a cigarette do something to remove the jaded feeling.

I remember other times when enthusiasm sparkled at breakfast. In the flush of youth, we would walk miles. A few pegs and slings, and off up the hill. After climbing on Etchachan, we would walk over to Sputan Dearg or the Shelter Stone. Long leads with little thought of falling off. Today, the fear-gear will clank around me, each piece identifiable by its own particular twang, making me feel slightly absurd. A cacophony of noise, embarrassingly rich in variety.

In the 'fifties Etchachan began to be explored, mostly by Aberdonians. Few climbers approached the crag from the Aviemore side, but this has been made more possible now with the development of the ski chair-lift on Cairngorm. Despite the lift it is still a long way to the crag, but a very fine one, traversing the wild scenery surrounding Loch Avon.

Meanwhile, the addicted Cairngormer from the east wasn't deterred by the seven-mile hike up Glen Derry. This is a more placid approach, but longer than the Aviemore one, passing in its initial stages through fine scatterings of ancient pine.

The Cairngormer took all this as a fact of life. Only later, much later, when the motor-car broke down his insularity and took him beyond the confines of his own back garden, did he realize how lucky he was. He still had peace and quiet.

Etchachan became a great favourite.

Dagger and Djibangi on the Crimson Slabs, and The Talisman, were the high-points of the exploration of the 'fifties, and are still among the best routes on the cliff. Their originators were mysterious men to us later lot, and it was to Tom Patey's *Cairngorm Commentary* that we turned to gain insight into the doings of Aberdeen's first generation of serious climbers. Today, Stilleto on the Crimson Slabs, without its pegs, is the test piece.

Often, however, the Crimson Slabs are wet, whereas The Talisman dries quickly after rain. This factor, plus its superbly challenging line boldly plunging down the edge of the Bastion, should be enough to whet any appetite. The climb begins in the lower reaches of the Corridor.

Gazing upwards, I tell myself once again that these walls of the Bastion belong to the future. A magnificent 300ft. chunk of grey granite, diamond hard, compromising very little. Proudly it rears out of the decaying rubble of the Corridor, as if flaunting the forces that will render it to dust.

Better move on and leave the gloomy restrictions of the gully.

A short crack leads to a ledge at the foot of a large slab, the Great Slab. Some climbers have been tempted beyond their original modest plans by this beguilingly easy slab. Today we are in no mood to be misled. The impending walls above, and our not-so-warm hands, have cast a shadow on our spirit. Sunshine and known qualities, that happy combination, await us on the edge. Delicate horizontal cracks at mid-height on the slab show us the way. Not hard, but with the gully dropping away steeply at your feet there is increasing exposure with little protection. The winter pioneers must have trembled as they edged their way over on crampons.

Fine, steep climbing follows, up the rib on grand holds to a short overhanging corner. In times gone by, climbers belayed here, at the end of the second pitch, lashed to their soft metal pegs, remnants of which remain: an exposed and often windswept perch. Modern boldness has deposed such old-fashioned fiddling, and it is usual to find a belay above the corner.

Bridge up and pull out of the corner. This is not a dainty move. Ugly, in fact, the way I'm doing it. Suddenly, on the edge of the corner, it's delicate, and remembering the holds isn't helping a great deal. Old skills

Route The Talisman, Hard Severe, 320ft.
Cliff Creagan a Choire Etchachan, Cairngorms.
First Ascent W. D. Brooker and K. A. Grassick, June 1956.
Map Reference O.S. Tourist Map to the Cairngorms, 1–50,000 Sheet (ref. 017997).
Guidebooks S.M.C. *Cairngorms Area*, Vol. 2, by G. S. Strange; *Scottish Climbs*, Vol. 2, by Hamish MacInnes.
Nearest Road Car park at Linn of Dee, six miles from Braemar (ref. 062897). It is also possible to approach from the Cairngorm Ski Lift – by a shorter but more complex route.
Distance and time from cliff 7 miles/3 hours from Linn of Dee, 3 miles/2 hours from Cairngorm.
Good Conditions Between May and September this route takes no more than a day to dry out after bad weather. Other routes on the cliff take longer.
Campsites and Bunkhouses The Hutchison Memorial Hut is in Choire Etchachan, just below the crag.
Bibliography *One Man's Mountains* by Tom Patey (Gollancz, 1971); S.M.C. District Guide *The Cairngorms* by Sir Henry Alexander.

Left: The traverse on Talisman with the climber just beyond the point in the previous picture. *Climber: David Avens*

degenerate into an ungainly scrabble for the finishing holds. Quite a pitch!

Sheer delight up the long, last pitch on the lip of the abyss. Sustained, but always easier than the corner. A pitch to linger on. Painfully undercut granite drops away from the edge into space, giving rise to further speculations. Happy not to be there.

So it ends. High up on the Cairngorm Plateau. Miles from nowhere and hard to get at. A lonely place, but cherished.

Left: Talisman's third pitch. The difficult corner is directly above the leader. *Climbers: Michael Hawkins and David Avens*

Above: Grappling with the difficult corner on Talisman. *Climber: Ian Fulton*

SCOTLAND Lochnagar, Cairngorms

15 Eagle Ridge

by Bill Brooker

The claim that Eagle Ridge is 'the finest of all Lochnagar climbs' is open to question, as there are certainly others with as distinctive a character, more continuous difficulty and equally good rock. Nevertheless, Eagle Ridge is deservedly the best-known route on the mountain and, although not without blemish, having occasional loose rock and points where the direct line can be avoided, it is worthy of its popularity. J. H. B. Bell, that great explorer of Scottish rock, was the first to attempt it, diverging below the tower at just short of mid-height to make his Eagle Buttress route in 1936. A Dundee rope climbed the tower in 1940, but abandoned the crest before the second vertical section. Bell returned a year later to complete the direct ascent and his enthusiasm for the ridge established its reputation 'for difficulty, narrowness and steepness'.

Like many other classics, what was once a test piece is now a trade route, but it remains a climb of memorable character. Delicate balances are few, but satisfying physical moves abound: heaves on splendid holds, permitting secure enjoyment of the many airy situations. Although exposed, the protection is excellent almost everywhere and the rocks dry out quickly. When wet, the ridge can be much more difficult and in winter conditions it still presents a formidable challenge.

Situated hard against Douglas Gully, into which overlapping walls and slabs plunge from the ridge crest, the broken right flank forms the steepening mass of Eagle Buttress. The toe of the ridge forms a sheaf of slab ribs and turfy grooves, but, a little way up the Douglas side, a 60ft. V-cleft, often greasy and awkward, provides entry. Higher up, the skyline is gained by a short chimney-crack, which can prove an effective rucksack trap unless climbed well out. On the other side, 150ft. of grooves and fractured blocks lead to a carapace of slabs, curving up toward the first tower. These slabs created a considerable impression when I first climbed Eagle Ridge with Doug Sutherland, back in 1949.

We started the climb with apprehension, since as far as we knew, no one had climbed it since Bell's original ascent eight years earlier,* and we were well aware of at least two unsuccessful attempts, one of which had resulted in a party of leading Aberdeen climbers being benighted. By misinterpreting the route description, we mistook the slabby wall for the first tower and spent the best part of an hour trying to force a route. Even in stocking soles we were unable to gain more than 15ft., and it was a very despondent pair of young aspirants that resumed their boots and moved right in search of an easier way. In a few feet we had reached the right-angled 40ft. chimney which, well furnished with holds, leads back to the crest. Doubtful hopes were rekindled as we mounted the shattered, tapering ridgeway which sweeps up to the base of the tower, and confidence was finally restored when we saw the rusty piton, relic of the original Dundee ascent in 1940, which was to remain irremovably in place for over twenty years.

The tower is about 50ft. high and easier than it looks. The first move is a swing up into a groove, sloping and insecure until one can gain a lodgement at its head. Thereafter good holds lead straight up to the right corner of the tower, with a leftward step near the top and a final pull up into the Sentry Box. This perfect haven has been thankfully greeted by many a winter climber at his last gasp, for the first tower can be a formidable obstacle in winter conditions and usually constitutes the crux. There are far more crampon scratches on the key holds at the foot of the tower than at its top.

The crest now falls back, takes a twist and, after a short slabby scoop, rears up in the Whaleback, a monolothic fin of rock which can be avoided by traversing its base to the right; better, however, to scale its flank and then proceed along its holdless spine. An impending mass of rock now bars the way, turned on its right by a narrow ledge leading into an inset 30ft. corner, with a superb stance and belay halfway up its slabby left wall. This is an ideal spot for the second man to watch his leader as he tackles the crux above. The top of the slab up which one climbs forms a short knife-edge below a 10ft. wall leading to the next level crest above. Here the situation is superb, with the void of Douglas Gully yawning beneath as the climber cautiously stands erect, feet poised on the

*Eagle Ridge in fact had a second ascent in 1948.

Route Eagle Ridge Direct, Severe, 650ft.
Cliff N. E. Corrie of Lochnagar.
First Ascent J. H. B. Bell and Nancy Forsyth, July 1941.
Map Reference O.S. Tourist Map to the Cairngorms, 1–50,000 Sheet (ref. 248856).
Guidebooks S.M.C. *Cairngorms Area* Vol. 4, by G. S. Strange; *Scottish Climbs*, Vol. 2, by Hamish MacInnes.
Nearest Road Car park at head of Glen Muick (ref. 310851).
Distance and time from cliff 5½ miles/1,800ft. Allow 2–3 hours.
Good Conditions Between May and September. The route dries quickly except for two or three points but is slippery when wet. It is often damp after September, and in true winter conditions provides a superb Grade 5 climb.
Campsites and Bunkhouses Discreet camping possible in Glen Muick. Aberdeen University Hut at Alltnaguibhsaich (ref. 298858).
Bibliography *A Progress in Mountaineering* by J. H. B. Bell (Oliver and Boyd, 1950) contains an account of the first ascent; S.M.C. Journals of 1949, 1950, 1951 and 1969 (account of winter ascent).

Left: On the crest of Eagle Ridge at the end of the projecting block pitch. This point marks the end of the major difficulties, and easier slab climbing leads to the top of the climb. *Climber: Bill Brooker*

Left: The initial groove pitch of Eagle Ridge. Such grooves on Cairngorm granite often lack a definite crack at the junction, and the cracks on the walls are often blind and flared, making the climbing far more difficult than it would appear. *Climber: Iain Brooker*

Bill Brooker

flake below and the right hand gratefully pulling against a helpful undercut crack in the wall. The creaking spike which originally projected like a bowsprit above the wall has long since gone, but the slot it occupied is furnished with a good hold at its rear. To reach it one has to swing up on sloping foot-holds, reach to the left, grasp an edge and so pull up over the top. When wet it can be an awkward move, especially for those with a short reach. It is not surprising that Bell used stocking soles and a piton on the original ascent.

From a short arête, the ridge now rears upwards in a final 50ft. step. At its base a delicate traverse right regains the easier broken chimney line of the Dundee Route, 20ft. away, but although this may prove a welcome winter alternative it is a pity to miss the continuing interest and difficulty of the direct line. This takes the precise crest up a short, curving scoop to some cracked blocks topped by a square-cut, projecting overhang. The ensuing move is vintage Lochnagar, an up-and-over roll on to a narrow coping slab to the left of the projection. The slab slopes and there is a strong impression that the roll may develop into a slide down into Douglas Gully. Plenty of body friction and a quick grab for the top edge of the slab provide the solution. Above lies a short V-shaped recess from which one steps back on to the airy ridge crest. This point is the threshold of the upper landing, and it is worth a pause to appreciate the successive step and arête formation of the ridge plunging downwards beneath one's feet, before proceeding up the last 100ft. of easy-angled slabs to the plateau.

Recently, after an absence of over ten years, I climbed the ridge to try and get some photographs for this book. I enjoyed it so much that I returned and climbed it again a week later. That must surely prove something.

Bill Brooker

Above: The Lochnagar cliffs from the northerly, Gelder Sheil, approach. Eagle Ridge is the prominent central buttress.

Near right: Starting the First Tower. The leader is moving right out of the recess. A little higher the route moves back to the left to gain the sentry box, which can be seen as a cleft on the skyline. *Climbers: Bill Brooker and Iain Brooker*

John Moore

Bill Brooker

Top left: Emerging from the Sentry Box on to the crest of Eagle Ridge, at a point where it becomes less steep and takes a twist. *Climber: Dave Wallace*

Lower left and below: Two views of the projecting block pitch with the leaders in virtually the same position. A mantelshelf move follows to gain the crest and the projecting block is then turned by means of a bold swing to the left. In winter it is usual to avoid this obstacle by traversing to the right to gain the wide chimney that can be seen on the right (lower left photo). *Climbers: Iain and Bill Brooker*

Bill Marshall

16 Ardverikie Wall

by Bill Skidmore

Route Ardverikie Wall, Severe, 550ft.
Cliff The South Face of Binnein Shuas.
First Ascent D. F. Lang and G. N. Hunter, June 1967.
Map Reference O.S. 1–50,000 Sheet 34 (ref. 468826).
Guidebook *Scottish Climbs*, Vol. 2, by Hamish MacInnes.
Nearest Road At a concrete bridge just off the A86 at the west end of Loch Laggen. There is a good parking place a short distance along the unmetalled road that crosses the bridge.
Distance and time from cliff 3½ miles/ 1,600ft. Allow 2 hours. The route goes directly across the moor towards Binnein Shuas until an estate road is reached. This is taken to the side of Lochan na h-Earba from where the crag can be seen. A rapid beeline descent can be made back to the road from the summit of Binnein Shuas.
Good Conditions The crag dries quickly in spring, summer and autumn, but the stalking season can restrict access in the late summer.
Campsites and Bunkhouses Camping is possible at the west end of Lochan na h-Earba but prior permission should be sought.
Bibliography S.M.C. Journal 1968 contains a diagram and route descriptions of most of the Binnein Shuas routes.

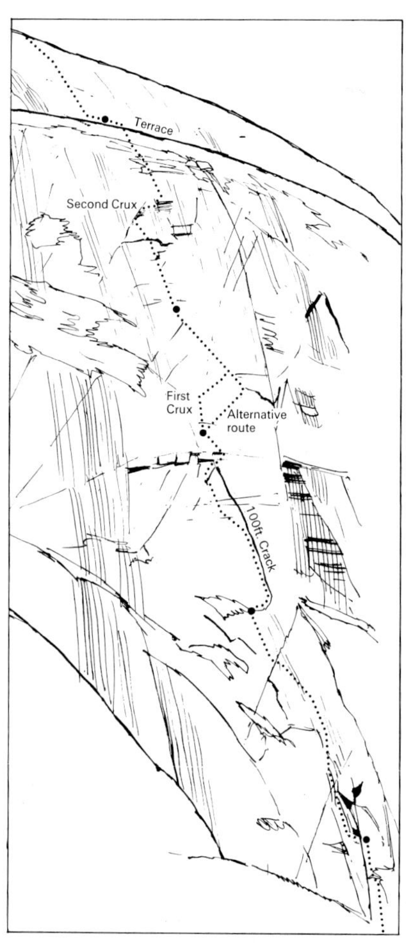

The great thing to experience is a special rock climb in an equally special place. Separately, the ingredients are common enough, but the happy combination of the two is harder to find. Ardverikie Wall (even the name sounds right), in Ardverikie Estate or 'Forest', is just such a rare blend, made all the more enticing by the fact that it is tucked away from the sight of casual eyes on the dreary Laggan road.

There is, without doubt, something 'different' about Ardverikie that cannot easily be pinned down. Perhaps integrated beauty is the factor at work here, rather than wildness or grandeur. The heart of the estate is at its east end, on the south bank of Loch Laggan, where Ardverikie House, built in 1840, stands in a magnificent setting. Queen Victoria considered taking it as her 'Highland House', but during her stay there the rain was said to have 'come down in sheets', so she made do with Balmoral instead.

True, the area continues to be rained on today, but less so than the Cairngorms to the east or Ben Nevis to the west. This is perhaps the main attraction of the climb: it is the ideal place to break a journey in either direction between bigger and harder expeditions. Climbed before or after more serious routes elsewhere, Ardverikie Wall will be remembered and savoured for its own special merit. But make sure you choose a sunny day outside the stalking and midge seasons, or you risk the indignity of being chased, shot or eaten alive!

As classic climbs go, Ardverikie Wall is young. It was first climbed in 1967, by Doug Lang and Graham Hunter, during a memorable (and secret) summer in which they camped and climbed themselves to a standstill, before publishing the all but finished details in the *S.M.C. Journal*. The late Tom Patey had actually explored the crag three years earlier, but his visit (like Queen Victoria's) coincided with bad weather and he failed to appreciate the potential. Later, when it was all over, Patey acknowledged with customary good-humoured chagrin that Ardverikie Wall was the finest route he had ever walked past!

The approach walk over plain concrete bridge, dug-up moor and tedious estate road is uninspiring, to say the least, but relatively brief. The final bend in the road changes everything, when the scene opens out with such impact that a change of mood is irresistible. Lochan na h-Earba stretches away eastwards from an idyllic little sandy bay (good campsite this) to the woods of the inhabited part of the estate, while up on the left appears your objective, the cliffs of Binnein Shuas. This hitherto uninteresting hill takes on a new dimension and at last becomes obvious as the main barrier, the protector, cutting off easy access to the hidden place.

Apart from some alarming overhangs, the cliff does not at first appear very impressive, yet a certain atmosphere pulls you onwards to explore this area of silent rock. The wall lies near the far end, beyond the overhangs, really the outer, right edge of the so-called 'Hidden Gully'. It is obvious as the narrow, 500ft. ribbon of pale, grey micro-granite, dropping straight down to the hillside. The whole thing appears somewhat featureless and a bit frightening, until the initial steep unwelcoming rib is climbed; at once the rock becomes rough and solid and leans back enough to dispel any real worries. Above, there are four long pitches of delight over slabs, ribs, cracks and grooves, with considerable exposure all the way, made more enjoyable by virtue of good stances and belays. A veritable feast of classic rock. For maximum effect, wear big boots, hide the guidebook and carry the sack. No need for the paraphernalia of hard rock or blow-by-blow descriptions. If climbing really is a search for 'alternative realities' – this is it. Relax and simply do it.

The penultimate pitch (below the terrace) is the guidebook crux. It involves a long, rising traverse, poorly protected and exposed, but on superb rock. The fact that this pitch is so fine and exciting probably explains why many climbers experience palpitations on the next and final pitch to the terrace: they drop their guard. The pitch looks, and is, innocuous enough, if the correct break-out point is taken, but opinions vary as to the exact spot. Some traverse a long way, some don't; others climb straight up. Be ready for some kind of dilemma, lest you be stung by this exposed and poorly protected exit.

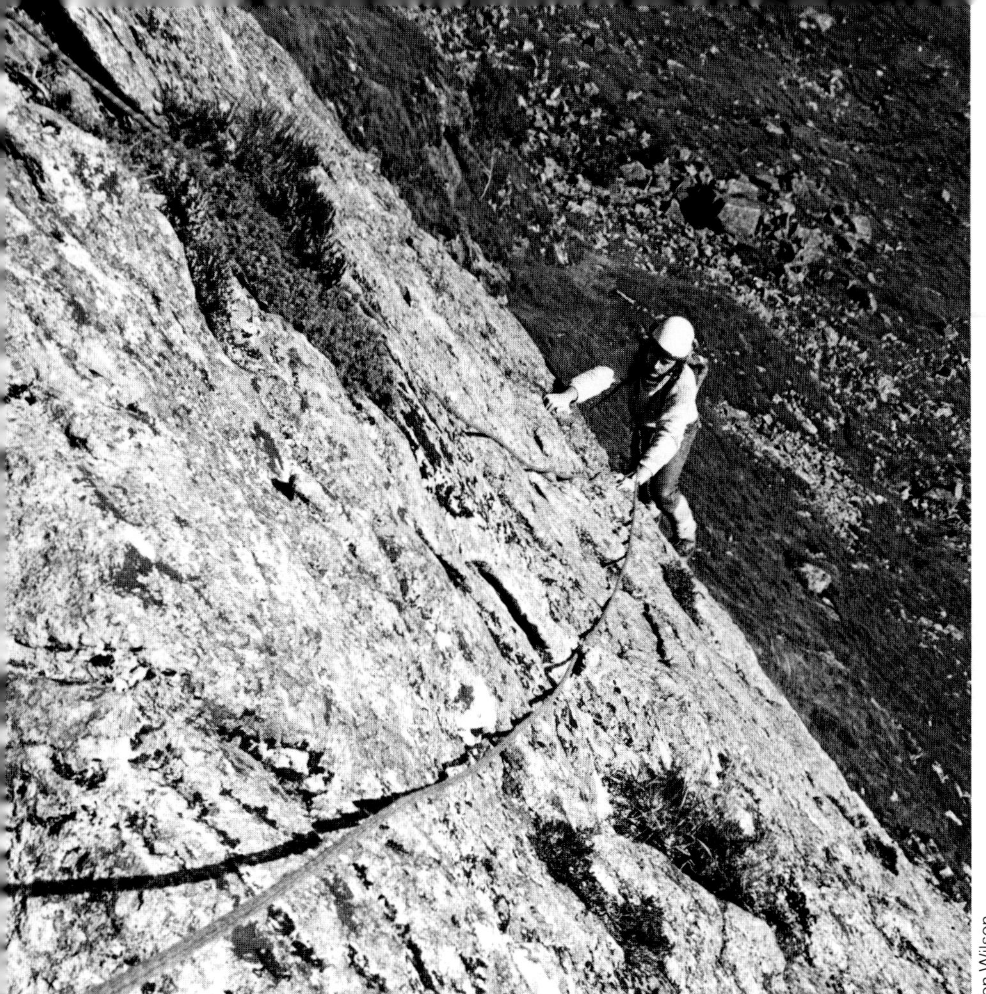

Ken Wilson

Top left: The final section of the second pitch of Ardverikie Wall. *Climber: John Jones*

Top right: Looking up the third pitch. The route either follows the crack on the right or takes a line directly up the slab. Either way gives excellent climbing. Steeper moves lead through a break in the overhangs to the third stance at the foot of a groove. *Climber: John Jones*

Once on the terrace the main climbing is over, but the slabby wall above is a pleasant finish and can be made more difficult, if desired, by taking a line further left. This is where carrying everything on the route pays off, because a short stroll leads to the summit of Binnein Shuas, with its magnificent outlook over Loch Laggan to Creag Meaghaidh. Forget about other routes here, they are all shorter or harder and come nowhere near Ardverikie Wall for excellence: a unique case of the classic climb for the area being the best, and not merely the best in its grade. Instead, wander back along the broad ridge and thence directly to the road, to make your way east or west from this, the watershed of Scotland and, perhaps, your climbing too.

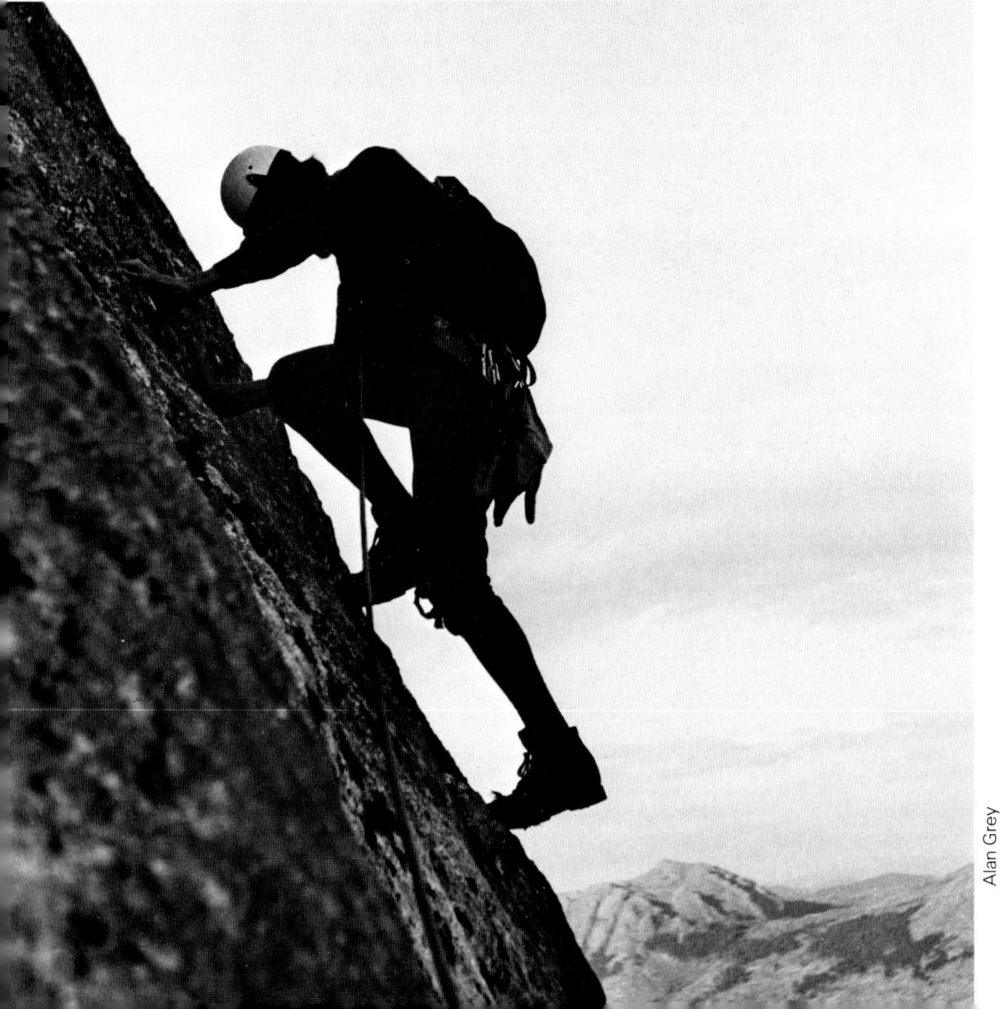

Alan Grey

Left: Moving out on to the difficult section of the fourth pitch. The route-finding at this point is tricky. One can either work directly upwards, trending a little to the left, or make a long ascending traverse to the right until a line of holds leads back up to the left. *Climber: Alan Kimber*

Right: Looking down the fourth pitch. The climber is just starting the difficult moves to leave the stance. *Climber: John Jones*

17 Recess Route, Punster's Crack and Ardgarten Arête

by John MacKenzie

Routes Recess Route, Very Difficult, 250ft.; Punster's Crack, Severe, 160ft.; Ardgarten Arête, Severe, 200ft.
Cliffs South and North Peaks, The Cobbler, Arrochar.
First Ascents Recess Route – J. B. Nimlin, J. Fox and R. Ewing, May 1935; Punster's Crack – J. Cunningham and W. Smith, August 1949; Ardgarten Arête – J. Cunningham, June 1948.
Map Reference O.S. Tourist Map Loch Lomond and the Trossachs, 1–50,000 Sheet (ref. 259059).
Guidebooks S.M.C. *Arrochar* by J. R. Houston; *Scottish Climbs*, Vol. 1, by Hamish MacInnes.
Nearest Road The A83 at Succoth Farm, 1 mile beyond Arrochar. There are laybys on either side of the road at this point. A well-marked path leads up the hill and soon joins a concrete stepped ramp. The ramp leads to a path which leads diagonally across to the left to join the Allt a'Bhalachain.
Distance and time from cliff 3 miles/ 2,500ft. Allow 2 hours.
Good Conditions Allow three days after rain in winter; the cliff dries rapidly in summer. The rock is very slippery when wet.
Campsites and Bunkhouses Ardgarten Campsite (ref. 275030) and hotels at Arrochar.
Bibliography *The Southern Highlands* by J. D. B. Wilson contains a rock-climbing section of historical interest, by B. H. Humble and J. B. Nimlin; S.M.C. Journal 1938; *Cobbler Calling* by B. H. Humble contains a brief description of the events leading to the first ascent of Recess Route.

Note: Recess Route was upgraded from HD to VD in the 1988 guidebook which also recorded that Harold Raeburn had climbed the crux pitch in 1904 having traversed the Halfway Terrace from Ramshead Gully. It is now believed that he climbed the complete route.

Ardgarten Arête was upgraded to VS in the 1997 guidebook based on a totally direct approach at the start – a short and difficult section of climbing before easier ground is reached.

Right: The cliffs of the North Peak of the Cobbler. The top section of Recess Route links the two obvious shadowy chimney/grooves on the lower cliff. Whither Whether, a fine route, rather undergraded at severe, takes the right edge of the spectacular jutting arête on the upper bastion in one long poorly-protected pitch.

As far as the English climber is concerned, the Cobbler is something of an unknown quantity. Being near Arrochar and off the A80, it is all too often bypassed for the greater attractions of Glencoe and the Ben.

It is not generally realized that the Cobbler was the birthplace of hard Scottish rock-climbing (as opposed to mountaineering), and that fierce routes such as Club Crack were being done here when Scottish rock-climbing was still thought to be in the gully stage. Apart from the hard routes, some of the finest Severes in the country are to be found here, if length alone is discounted. Due to the nature of schist, however, some might find the grading rather lax, as the rock is essentially a smooth matrix inundated with an amazing profusion of quartz knobs, which a newcomer will find sufficiently different, delicate, and even dubious, to make Severes into Very Severes at the merest hint of moisture.

The Cobbler, a gnarled rocky peak, has three summits – North, Central and South – separated by a bowl-like corrie. The best climbs lie on the North and South Peaks, on dramatically shaped rocks. On a fine summer's day, the 2,500ft. climb to reach them is an enjoyable walk, firstly via the concrete ramp beyond Succoth and then by a path which leads pleasantly into the wide corrie and so to the rocks; but if the cloud is down and wetness is in the air, it is just not worth it: schist is more like soap in those conditions.

The city of Glasgow has the advantage of being easy to get out of, and, having a young female eager to grasp the rock, the North Peak's Recess Route seemed a natural choice. At 250ft., this is one of the Cobbler's longest. Graded at V.Diff., it follows a line of cracks and chimneys directly up the main face of the crag and gives pleasantly varied climbing to the top of North Peak.

So up we went, first up the cracked slab – all very reasonable – and then into the short slanting crack on its left, which leads to the foot of the deep chimney. Unfortunately the cloud, which had been progressively lowering, now issued forth a torrent, and the chimney rapidly assumed the quality of the Eiger exit cracks.

Being innocent, she really had no idea that rock could be so greasy, but she straddled the chimney, overhang and all, and arrived wet and somewhat puzzled on the halfway terrace. After a short psychological boost, we walked to the right end and stood beneath the crux pitch, the Fold. This was first climbed by Raeburn, back in 1896, on one of his numerous lone sorties. It consists of a steep groove with a slabby left wall and small, incut holds. Fortunately, it was bone dry and, with the lower pitches so greasy, it proved to be the easiest pitch of the day.

Above is another open groove whose capping overhang can normally be bypassed on left or right; but now it resembled a budding waterfall and had to be climbed direct. While she struggled, the water poured down, rapidly washing away her climbing career. A hefty tug landed her, spent, on the spacious platform below the short last pitch, a cave-like recess, climbed by the left wall. It had now stopped raining, but the schist was still glistening and the pitch had to be climbed mainly on the hands until the sloping summit rubble was reached.

She declined an offer to try Whither Whether, now drying nicely in the sun, and vowed never to return. In one day she had completed the process of initiation and enthusiasm, experience and caution, and finally the realization of terror, that most climbers take forty years to undergo.

Though Recess is good, Punster's Crack above and to the left is finer and, at Medium Severe, gives some very exposed climbing in its upper reaches. This time it was a hot sultry day, the walk up had been purgatory, and we had expended considerable energy on Direct Direct before the heat called a stop to hard climbing. Punster's starts left of Right Angle Gully and right of Direct Direct and, unlike Recess Route, is composed of steep slabs and airy traverses with a fine exposed top pitch.

There were three of us and there was plenty of time for leisurely photography and Punster's is certainly photogenic, more so than many of the harder routes. As far as the climbing goes, the first pitch takes a steep slab which eases into a corner on the left and then ascends without much trouble to beneath an overhang at 50ft. A rather fine right traverse then follows, across a line of holds to

Near right: The initial pitch of Recess Route.

Far right: The second pitch – a deep chimney.

Below: The last main pitch of the climb, which gives steep bridging over a chockstone to gain the top. *Climber: John Jones*

Ken W

an obvious gap. This poses an unusual problem, and probably constitutes the crux. It an be approached in a variety of ways. You ave to step right and across, but an awkward bulge seems to throw the matter out of all proportion, despite the security of a fine ut. It is easy for gnomes, but normal people will need time to sort it out. Though exposed, it is only a 'one mover', and the raverse finishes soon after at a rather ramped little stance on the edge of the cliff, ucked securely away from the void beneath.

Undoubtedly the next pitch constituted the meat of the climb and the guidebook's ration of 30ft. seemed a little meagre. It looks really quite hard and must have been exciting for John Cunningham and Bill Smith, who made the first ascent in 1949. Like several other Cobbler Severes, the appearance is far worse than the reality: fine holds on a steep wall, following a shallow crack which can be protected by a judicious nut or two, soon ease anxieties. Though only 160ft., Punster's Crack packs a fine punch and has the added advantage of ending abruptly near the top of the mountain.

One overlooked attraction of the Cobbler is the possibility of soloing these spectacular routes and, due to their shortness, a climber can get a dozen or more climbed in a day.

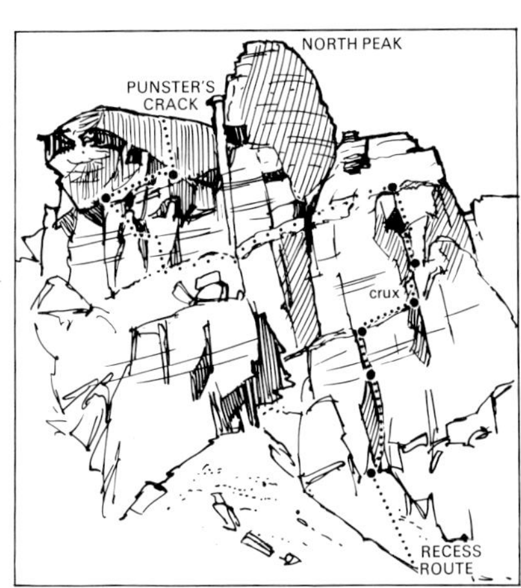

Donald Bennet

Ken Wilson

Donald Bennet

On a very fine Friday, some years ago, I was up without a partner and, apart from two other climbers, the mountain was deserted. Not being a solo climber by nature, I started a rather cautious programme with a quick warm-up on Jughandle, followed by Ardgarten Arête, and then a series of routes of Diff. and V.Diff. standard, of which the best were Right Angled Chimney and North Rib Route.

However, it was Ardgarten Arête that made the day. This Cunningham solo route of 1948 has a wonderful delicacy. About 200ft. long, and Severe, it lies on the angle between the West and South Faces of South Peak. It starts as a steep slab which has the advantage for the solo climber of having the crux (a small bulge) at around 20ft.! This is followed by easier delicate climbing up the arête, past various flakes and possible 'ways off' to the right. Like Punster's, however, it keeps the real stuff to the end: a steep, cracked, 30ft. groove, right on the edge. With a rope it must feel airy; ropeless it felt much nearer to the true essence of the sport and it was good to linger on the last few moves, looking down the sweep of the West Face and the slabs below. It is not technical difficulty, so much as the combination of position and atmosphere at the top of a mountain, that makes these classic routes of the Cobbler so rewarding.

Above: The Cobbler from the lower part of the Allt a Bhalachain. North Peak is on the right.

Opposite page: The traverse on the second pitch of Punster's Crack; the leader is at the difficult section of the pitch, where awkward moves allow access to the upper wall. *Climbers: Unknown*

Left: The steep final pitch of Punster's Crack. *Climber: Dan Stewart*

18 Sou'wester Slabs and Labyrinth

by Graham Little

Routes Sou'wester Slabs, Very Difficult, 340ft.; Labyrinth, Very Difficult (Hard Severe), 400ft.
Cliffs South Face and Upper East Face of Cir Mhor, Arran.
First Ascents Sou'wester Slabs – G. H. Townend, G. C. Curtis, H. Hore and M. J. H. Hawkins, September 1944; Labyrinth – G. C. Curtis and H. K. Moneypenny, September 1943; Direct Finish – J. S. Orr and J. C. MacLaurin, May 1951.
Map Reference O.S. 1–50,000 Sheet 69 (ref. 975429).
Guidebooks S.M.C. *Arran* by W. M. M. Wallace; *Scottish Climbs*, Vol. 1, by Hamish MacInnes.
Nearest Road Steamer from either Fairlie or Ardrossan to Brodick. Cycles can be hired here and taken some way up Glen Rosa.
Distance and time from cliff From Brodick – 7 miles/2,000ft. Allow 3–4 hours.
Good Conditions The cliff dries quickly. Any sunny day should be adequate.
Campsites and Bunkhouses Good campsites in Glen Rosa.
Bibliography S.M.C. Journal 1945: *Arran 1944* by G. C. Curtis and G. H. Townend.

In retrospect, many of one's early climbs seem glorious affairs, as gripping and fulfilling as any of the hard routes done in later years. On deeper reflection, it becomes apparent that a few routes formed keystones in one's climbing development, heralding a differing outlook or an improvement in standard and ability. The demands that Sou'wester/Labyrinth made on me and the lessons they taught, during my solo ascent many years ago, stood me in good stead for the future and gave me a strong affinity for granite climbing. My gripping experience on that occasion imprinted on my mind an indelible impression of mist-swathed slabs and overhangs, which, instead of serving as a deterrent, gave me an insatiable appetite, for the ultimate in rock. To return to such routes after many years may seem like wallowing in nostalgia, yet it is a fascinating and illuminating experience, with many surprises.

Arran climbing has much to offer at every standard, but its real strength perhaps lies in the quality of its middle-grade climbs. Scenically, the island has a great deal to commend it: the ordered lushness of Brodick and lower Glen Rosa contrasting markedly with the massive bare structure of the interior, whose peaks thrust skyward with a grandeur totally disproportionate to their modest height.

The talents of Curtis and Townend were responsible for many fine Arran routes in the 1940s, but few would disagree that Sou'wester and Labyrinth rank as their finest, the combination giving over 700ft. of superb and varied climbing, at a sustained

Right: A long-focus view of the Rosa Pinnacle – the S and Y Cracks of the South Ridge Direct and the traverse section of Sou'wester Slabs (upper groups). The South Ridge Original (HS), a climb of comparable quality to the Direct, takes the obvious slanting crack right of the Y Crack. *Climbers: Unknown*

Below: Looking steeply up to Sou'wester Slabs (see topo on page 88). The blanker lower slabs offer some outstanding climbs in the harder grades – The Sickle (HVS), Vanishing Point (E4) and West Flank Route (HVS).

Graham Little

Klaus Schwartz

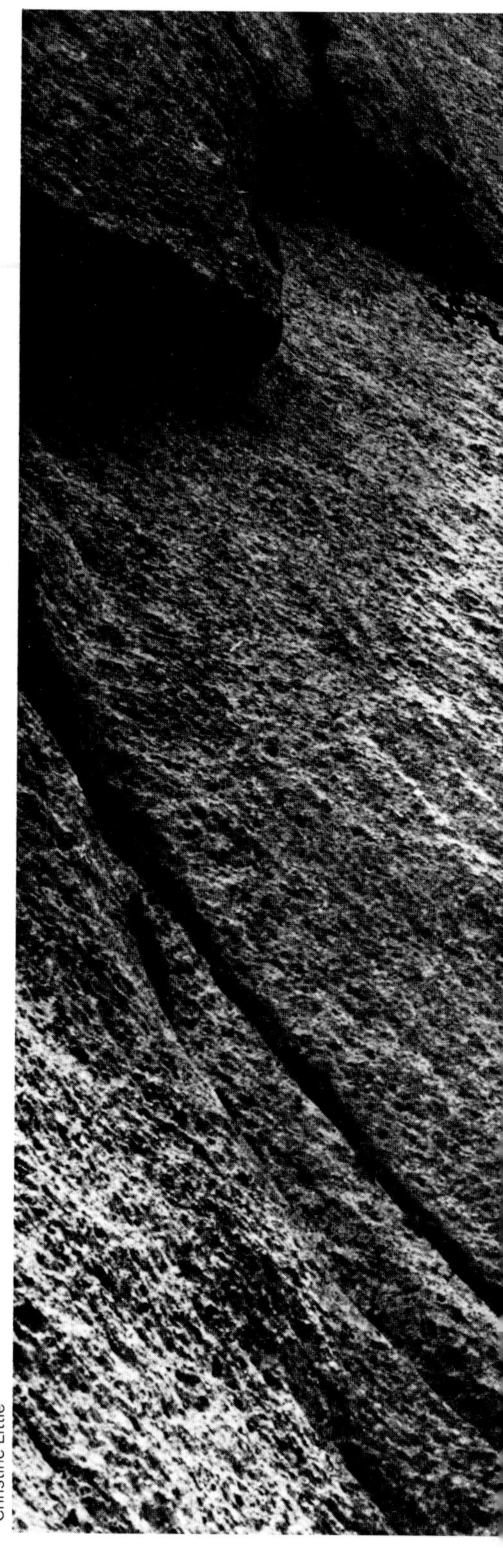

Christine Little

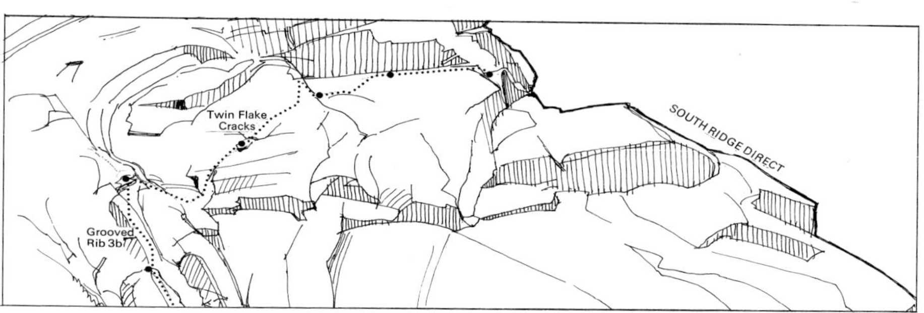

standard, on rough grey granite. Excellent routes on which to cut one's teeth (and any other part of one's anatomy that comes into contact with the rock).

After the rigours and bog-trotting of Glen Rosa, rest your sweaty body and admire the sweeping symmetry of the Rosa Pinnacle, the lower west wall of which comprises a vast sea of overlapping slabs. Stroll through the boulder field, then up to the base of an

obvious groove system, where the slabs begin to merge into the broken rock of the green hollow to the left.

The first two pitches up grooves and ribs, though very fine in themselves, are merely the *hors-d'oeuvres*, bringing you to an obvious rightwards traverse line. The main course begins: please don't rush it! Savour the perfect slabs, delight in the rough, textured grooves and sharp-edged flakes, pause a while now and then to gulp the full rich panorama and contemplate the incomparable positions.

A magnificent corner and cracks bring you to a small stance below the twin flake cracks. The grade of this pitch is immaterial; it is pure climbing poetry, giving a graceful, flowing layback. Enthuse openly; sing to the world: 'Thank you for the Arran granite'. Onward to the square-cut edge, then drop

Above left: Moving down to the lower slab prior to the traverse under the overhangs where Sou'wester slabs moves across to join the South Ridge. *Climber: Rebecca Schwartz*

Above right: On the slabs above the Twin Flake Cracks. *Climber: Graham Little*

Graham Rowe

down to a lower slab on the right. Another superb cracked slab brings you to a scoop. Traverse right under the overhang and, alas, the feast of slabs is over.

A melancholy creeps over you: all else must be an anticlimax. But despair not: there is more to come.

For the purist, I suppose, the upper part of South Ridge Direct is now the only way to go, but for those fond of a skirmish, follow me and I'll show you a more devious way. A way not without its moments. Come tangle with the multifarious delights of the Labyrinth. Down the Old East highway we go, via big jugs and heather, and then sneak round into Sub Rosa Gully below the bold East Face.

Now for something completely different. Labyrinth is a route in a separate class; it may not have quite the quality of Sou'wester, but it certainly has considerable character and interest. It is not, however, advisable for the squeamish or those bothered by a little vegetation. Enter the

Gordon Gadsby

Above: The view north-east from A'Chir across the head of Glen Rosa to Cir Mhor with its Rosa Pinnacle sharply etched in the afternoon sun. The smaller sunlit buttress to its left is taken by 500ft Caliban's Creep (D) an easy climb of high quality. The main climb on the rather ill-defined Prospero Buttress, emerging from the shadows to the right of the Rosa Pinnacle, is Prospero's Peril (HS) – described in the S.M.C. guidebook as 'a very good route giving varied climbing on excellent rock'.

Right: The East Face of Rosa Pinnacle.

Left: On the 'Small Corner' of Labyrinth. *Climber: Chris Schiller*

Christine Little

Christine Little

shadowy, sloping 'close' below a huge, firmly jammed (I hope) flake and grovel hastily leftwards towards the light, then up to the base of a steep wall. Throw yourself with determination at the chimney above and fall off (I did) ... curse profusely, then try again with more success, and on into the groove. With the surreptitious aid of several heather holds, gain a grassy stance. Traverse left into a small corner (supposedly the crux). Up the corner on straddling friction holds to a turf cap. Beware of Minotaurs crossing from the left! A long chimney soon confronts you and there's the rub. Wedge and grapple upwards, passing over both groups of chockstones, and slump your grazed carcass into the Eyrie. Emaciated climbers, and those with masochistic tendencies, should follow the guidebook's advice and go behind the second chockstone group (I still have nightmares about it). Take a short rest; you deserve it.

The grassy ledges of the normal route tempt you rightwards, but the brave of heart should spurn such deviousness (we've been devious enough already) and climb straight up over massive blocks to the base of a right-angled corner capped by an enormous roof. Above you the Prow projects, all else plummets below. Take a deep breath, gain the 'weird flange', do a wee layback, a hasty footjam, and finally an 'interesting' (always a thought-provoking word) traverse left, leading you round a smooth bulge. A short slab and you're up (thank God!). Drift with the thermals up the final cracks of South Ridge Direct, which give a grand finale to an intriguing climb and bring you close to the summit of Cir Mhor.

Despite today's higher climbing standards, my return to these routes of the past impressed upon me the fact that quality is no respecter of grade, and that enjoyment and achievement are purely relative factors.

Take my advice: hop on a steamer to Arran and treat yourself to some great climbing.

Left: The easy lower chimney on Labyrinth – passing behind the jammed flake on the first pitch. The Prow, grossly foreshortened, looms overhead. The climb deviates to the right on the second pitch and rejoins the crack line at the obvious slot. *Climber: Graham Little*

19 Little Chamonix

by Angela Faller

Once upon a time, we learned of Lakeland climbing from a postcard. I have it here, showing Abraham's photographs of Napes Needle, Scafell Pinnacle, Amen Corner and . . . a route on Shepherd's Crag. We hitched to the Lakes for autumn half-term, armed with postcard and enthusiasm, and made Borrowdale our base. Autumn comes late to the Lake District and the woods of Rogue Herries country were in all their glory, but more rugged scenery drew us away. Alas, we failed on Napes Needle and frightened ourselves. A postcard doesn't show how greasy high mountain rock can be. We were tired and not too sure of ourselves when we settled down by Derwentwater.

Sleep didn't come easily. Those ex-W.D. sleeping-bags were never warm, and frost was in the air. The moon cast creepy shadows, the trees rustled, ripples lapped the shore. An owl hooted. We dozed, shivering from cold and anticipation of steepness. In the morning we ate biscuits till the sun came over, then put on our pumps and walked to Shepherd's. It seemed a long crag. Luckily, two proper climbers (wearing magic boots) came along and reassured us; we really were at Shepherd's and the overhanging wall on the postcard obscured a V.Diff. ridge. Be careful, they warned, noticing our all-purpose footwear and minimal equipment. So it was we came to start Little Chamonix.

Thinking of Almscliff V.Diffs., I trembled inside. But this route looked feasible at first, with a choice of ways. The rock felt very smooth compared with gritstone, the only rock we knew, but there were spikes and tree belays at convenient intervals for our stiff 100ft. rope. After about 100ft. we could have scrambled; not wishing to cheat, we made a short traverse round a bulge on the right and climbed a little wall. We were worried; things must now get hard and, although in theory we could abseil, we hadn't much experience, or for that matter very much rope.

Now the character of the route began to show. The only way was up a groove capped by an overhang. My friend bridged neatly up it and emerged in a crouching position on a block. He shuffled about, trying to step across another bottomless groove on to a steep slab, succeeded eventually and disappeared up and right. Confident tones announced that he could see the top and would soon be there. By the time he had belayed, there was little rope left. I wondered what to do if I found myself dangling. Putting aside such unhelpful thoughts, I too launched up the groove to the block. Leaving it was difficult. My head was in the way and hands and feet wouldn't both reach the slab. The footholds were small and shallow for floppy-toed pumps and the fingerholds sharp but tiny. This won't do! At last, perched on the very edge of the block, I just made contact with both hands and feet. The slab formed the left side of an arête on which I was soon sitting comfortably, *à cheval*, in a very exposed position. Now I was in the postcard view, with the overhanging wall on my left. Everything above was steep. Spikes and pinnacles abounded; I hoped they weren't loose. I warmed my hands and considered which side to climb round the biggest pinnacle of all. The holds were good, but sideways, so the rock seemed to be pushing me off. As I tentatively leaned right, the sequence came to me and I bounded to the top, thinking: 'Great! We've done a famous Lakeland climb.'

Now that beginners have magic boots, lots of slings, and guidebooks correct to the last detail, do they still feel the thrill that we felt then? Watching a modern youngster finish Little Chamonix, his first lead, I feel sure they do. Perhaps the latest generation, better informed than we were, soon progress from here to real Chamonix and beyond. The future of the climbers is predictable, but what of the future of the climb? A classic like Little Chamonix, accessible, quick to dry, is highly vulnerable. Thirty years after Bentley Beetham first soloed it, the holds are very polished, far worse than in our postcard days, and the route gets harder with the passage of yet more feet. I'm as responsible as most, having repeated this classic many times. I sit at the top, gaze at the reflections in the peaceful lake, and wonder what it all was like, before it was like this. If there's nobody about, I might take a very dog-eared postcard out of my pocket, look back on many years of climbing that started here, and be glad that the rocks remain.

Route Little Chamonix, Very Difficult, 200ft.
Cliff Shepherd's Crag, Borrowdale.
First Ascent B. Beetham, May 1946.
Map Reference O.S. Lake District Tourist Map, 1–50,000 Sheet (ref. 264185).
Guidebooks F.R.C.C. *Borrowdale* by P. Nunn and O. Woolcock: *Rock Climbing in the Lake District* by Geoff Cram, Chris Eilbeck and Ian Roper.
Nearest Road The B5289 Keswick to Buttermere road, directly below the crag. It is best to park a short distance to the south near the High Lodore Hotel, as parking below the crag is now restricted.
Distance and time from cliff 5 minutes.
Good Conditions The cliff dries quickly after rain in all but the most humid conditions.
Campsites and Bunkhouses Superb campsites by the River Derwent at Grange ($1\frac{1}{2}$ miles). Youth Hostels at Keswick and Borrowdale. F.R.C.C. Hut, Salving House, at Rosthwaite.
Bibliography F.R.C.C. *Borrowdale* (1953) by Bentley Beetham, gives a good illustration of Beetham's climbing philosophy.

.eft: The exposed final
›itch of Little Chamonix.
Climbers: Unknown

Right: The right-hand buttress of Shepherd's Crag.

Ken Wilson

20 Gillercombe Buttress

by Joann Greenhow

Route Gillercombe Buttress, Severe (mild), 360ft.
Cliff The South East Face of Grey Knotts, Borrowdale.
First Ascent H. B. Lyon and W. A. Woodsend, May 1912.
Map Reference O.S. Lake District Tourist Map, 1–50,000 Sheet (ref. 223125).
Guidebooks F.R.C.C. *Borrowdale* by P. Nunn and O. Woolcock; *Rock Climbing in the Lake District* by Geoff Cram, Chris Eilbeck and Ian Roper.
Nearest Road Honister Pass (ref. 225135) or Seathwaite Farm (ref. 235121).
Distance and time from cliff 1 mile/600ft from Honister Pass. Allow 20 minutes; 1 mile/1,300ft. from Seathwaite. Allow 1 hour.
Good Conditions The climb dries quickly after rain but is rather smooth and slimy when wet.
Campsites and Bunkhouses F.R.C.C. Hut, Salving House, at Rosthwaite; 'K' Hut at Seathwaite. Camping at Seatoller. Youth Hostels in Borrowdale and on the Honister Pass.
Bibliography F.R.C.C. Journal 1925 has a description of the climb by H. S. Gross.

Right: Two views of the first pitch of Gillercombe Buttress. The square recess is obvious in both pictures. *Climbers: Andy Cairns and Dave Hancock*

The van squiggles through the Borrowdale narrows, up through the Jaws and round down the hill, bringing into view the several combes which hem in the valley head. Our normal wet weather haunt, Combe Gill, is passed and the last mile of bumpy tarmac ends in Seathwaite.

Sudden gusts of wind splosh the tea in our flask tops and splodges of sleet dash the windscreen. 'Gillercombe Buttress', the man said, so we gear up – he in the eternal blue polar suit, me in longjohn combinations of red, white and blue. Through the farmyard and under the barn-arch to be channelled, like so many 'yows', by dry-stone walls leading across the valley floor to the bridge. The path grinds up alongside Sour Milk Gill, short but steep. Today the ground is stone-hard. Knotted, ice-blue veins and gleaming knuckles twist and turn in the subdued falls. Impressions at the stile-top: of the patchwork valley, of my pumping heart slowing, of a chandelier birch tree tinklingly rimed in frozen spray. Soloing on up the rough Upper Slabs, so delightfully different from their bland sisters below, we are greeted with a fine view of the buttress. Across the boggy combe, past bivi boulders, to the grey rock tongue running from buttress to fence.

As a rock climb, Gillercombe Buttress is not the finest Severe in Britain, but, as a mountain way from soggy combe to springy turf and weathered summit rocks, it's as good as they come. Clean, grey rock up the gully arête gives steep, varied climbing with good ledges and belays.

Hellies and 'Steptoe' mitts are donned and, in a shower of hail, Colin heads on a leftwards traverse up into a smooth square recess. I hesitate on reaching it, but the wind insistently plucks on the rope. Height is essential, I decide, and reach up awkwardly left before stepping across the right wall and up to a sloping stance with a good Moac. The rock is damp in patches, with the odd jug hiding a finger-numbing pool. Blow and suck the fingers – a strong taste of sheep! My lead now, up steep steps to a deceptively neat slab. An undercut hold and a 'soft-shoe-shuffle' across to the ledge. A shelf breaks left but 'no, those are not good flakes', after all. The secret is to keep low, stepping up by one's ear to exit left to another Moac belay. Colin shuffles out into the neat slab before realizing his boots are 'wrang yan forad'. A hurried reshuffle and relieved grin. Once bitten, twice shy. He enters the traverse left with caution, his 6ft. height against him as he crouches down to stomach-traverse the flake. (The guidebooks suggests belaying after a 60ft. scramble, but this leaves the poor second on his own – often with a slack back rope.) Colin scrambles up bilberry, across rock to an open chimney and belay. Some good bridging moves up this to catch up with a party ahead. They're avoiding the next pitch, a small 'Amen Corner', by frozen sods on the left, but, preferring rock and with a comforting Moac runner just where it's needed, I make an awkward move to a hidden hold on top and pull over. Colin again gets the easy rock and scrambles to the large flake belay below the final rock step. From the flake I step boldly up left to find the groove smooth and holdless. A second move brings no ease, but third time lucky and my heart stops fluttering. The groove gives on to a delightful stepped slab; an alpine pitch, pleasant climbing, spectacular downward view, and that feeling of nearing the summit.

The gale lifts me across and up a shallow chimney. I care not for the suggested belay, visualizing its downward plummet with me attached, and find a sounder nose 15ft. higher. Colin grins as the wind cuffs him. 150ft. of easier climbing leads to the top.

Aspirant alpinists should now stride out for Great Gable, via Green Gable and Windy Gap, or climb one of the Gable North Face routes. The almost level ridge broadens and falls away to Buttermere and Crummock, then to Ennerdale; Pillar Rock juts out nobly, defying the threatening forest plucking her skirts. Ahead is wonderful Gable, the sombre North Face brown-damp and lichen-green – a forbidding place. Patches of snow cling to Great End; Scafell and Lingmell stand behind. Rounding Green Gable the Langdale Pikes spin into view and I see why Colin likens this centre of the Lakes to a great wheel, with valleys radiating like spokes.

But today the light is fading fast. Coil up and head south-west to clatter down the easy descent gully. Sheep, bivied for the night, scatter wildly. Gear is thrust into sacks, then, laying on the wind, we plunge through the icy gloom, past the tinkling chandelier tree, to the cheery lights and welcoming byre-warmth of Seathwaite and a flat van tyre!

21 Troutdale Pinnacle

by Anthony Greenbank

Troutdale Pinnacle (or Black Crag Buttress, as it is also known) is one of the greatest Lakeland climbs, regardless of grade. Black Crag stands a good twenty minutes from the Borrowdale road, but you can still trace the line of Troutdale Pinnacle from there, by picking out the most Vector-ish looking sector. The climb goes right up the middle of the crag, where slabs and overhangs leap into focus at the lift of an eyebrow. And you'll be raising that eyebrow in surprise, because Troutdale Pinnacle is only a Mild Severe.

Hand it to Mayson and Mallinson, the Borrowdale cragsmen who, in 1914, made the first ascent, producing a route that has been a byword in British climbing ever since. Overhangs like the roof of a football ground Kop, hooding a high terrace of slabs that has supported thousands, are pierced by the goal – the pinnacle. This is linked to the face Siamese-twin style, and was piled higher with blocks on the first ascent. Above it is the epic-making last pitch, where your last real reach in anger finishes the climb right on the summit – at least, it should do. For there was once a leader who ran out of rope on the last five feet (a bulge); he untied his waist loop, knotted the rope to his belt, slipped and fell, landing in the trees far below – unhurt. On another occasion a *Daily Express* photographer boned off with a mighty swing, and Chris Bonington got a great shot of him doing it.

But it is another anecdote that really sums up the nature of this marvellous climb. Ganny Barber – the only man to fall off C.B.'s Flake in a heatwave, because of *verglas* – was evacuating a broken ankle injury from Black Crag to Keswick, on the pillion of his A.J. Making an emergency stop for a medicinal double scotch at the Lake Hotel, he left the patient to prop up the bike with his good leg (the kick-start had broken, so the engine had to be kept running, and there was no stand . . .). Collecting his change in the hotel, Ganny was startled to hear roars and screams coming from the road. Rushing outside, he found that patient and bike had overturned; the hot exhaust pipe was further compounding the unfortunate victim's injuries by branding his good leg. Result: *both* legs shattered.

The point of this apocryphal little tale (for, indeed, the crag might have been Shepherd's, the bike a Gold Star and the original injury a cracked femur) is that Troutdale Pinnacle, like Ganny's steed that day, is inescapable once you are established on its ramparts. You either reach your destination or go down.

Not that the first pitch, an old-style off-width crack, cannot be bypassed, for the first-ascent team did just that. But those first three pitches let you in easily, anyway. It is only after following their terrace-cracklet-slablet-groovelet-and-slab sequence that you face the reckoning proper, in the form of the fourth pitch.

Once it had good holds; rock-fall has sheared them. Once a tree grew beneath; this, too, has gone. What remains is an open passage via a thin slab and a rightwards stride into a steep corner, where the nervous find a turnstile: the one in the brain that locks if the Kop-end-like crag above looks too hectic, and only clicks open if you are ready to commit yourself to definite aggro above. So you runner the rocking tree that tops the pitch (and that may have gone, as well, by the time this is published), and step up and over and out of sight, to belay.

Out of sight! The slabs traverse beyond tips into space, its far end blocked by a bulging wall. For decades, the ceiling overhead has baffled the roar of the crowd – generations of seconds telling leader after leader not to pull so bloody hard. And this is because leader after leader takes that old familiar diagonal line down the slabs, leaving a couple of runners *in situ* (particularly one on the jug at the base of the bulging wall), then swings smartly up the bulge to the stance above, glances back with pride at his handiwork and sees . . . the rope curving, Golden Gate style, straight across space from his waist to the second's fists, with all runners hanging free. And that unfortunate second, way down over there, is now subjected to a hawser-like pull normally experienced only by tugs towing the *Q.E. II.* The problem of combating it and keeping in balance at the same time is the reason why inexperienced seconds find the traverse so much harder than it actually is.

There follows 50ft. of easy wall. Only this is also a shocker, and few realize it until –

Route Troutdale Pinnacle (Black Crag Buttress), Severe (mild), 375ft.
Cliff Black Crag, Borrowdale.
First Ascent F. Mallinson and R. Mayson, May 1914.
Map Reference O.S. Lake District Tourist Map, 1–50,000 Sheet, (ref. 263174).
Guidebooks F.R.C.C. *Borrowdale* by P. Nunn and O. Woolcock; *Rock Climbing in the Lake District* by Geoff Cram, Chris Eilbeck and Ian Roper.
Nearest Road The B5289 ½ mile north of Grange (ref. 255177). There is a small layby on the east side of the road at this point.
Distance and time from cliff 1 mile/800ft. Allow 20 minutes. Take the private road to Troutdale Cottages and then follow a path through fields and up the steep hillside to the cliff.
Good Conditions Allow one day of dry weather after heavy rain.
Campsites and Bunkhouses Superb campsites by the River Derwent at Grange (1½ miles). Youth Hostels at Keswick and Borrowdale. F.R.C.C. Hut, Salving House, at Rosthwaite.
Bibliography Mountain 7: *The Classics* by Tony Greenbank; F.R.C.C. Journal 1914 contains a short description by Mayson and a photograph of the old pinnacle.

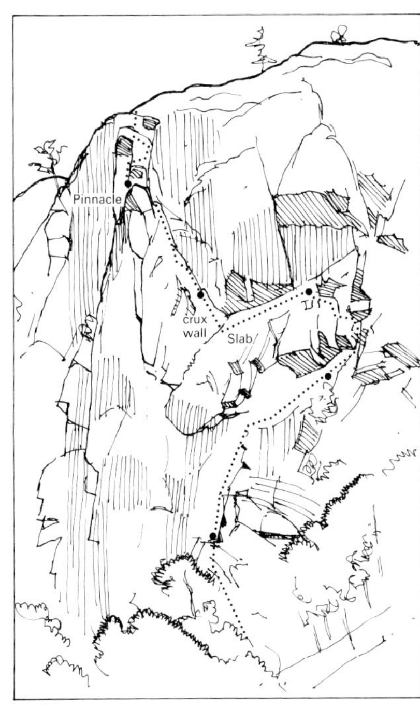

Above: Starting the traverse across the bulging wall which forms the crux of Troutdale Pinnacle. *Climber: Tony Greenbank*

wow! – they finally chin-up on what is actually the lip of Troutdale Pinnacle itself, to see Derwentwater straight ahead, total space below down the far side, no stance other than this leg-over wafer, and, jogging their right shoulder, a 50ft. final pitch which also looks amazing.

Which is nothing to how it feels. You are protected by nuts in the neat crack backing the steep corner, but your right fingers fail to cotton on to the sideways yank on the very edge which will drag you out on to the rib, and anyway the holds seem no more than solder smears as you begin to struggle. On your own on this pitch (the Shroud/ Vertigo/Coffin panel are grim round the corner), you know you are into something that's 'the best'. And then your sixth sense sounds a warning: you look up in time and the topmost bulge is there, eyeball to oddball, loose runner spike and all. It is at this point, as you work out the next move, that the 369ft. of climbing you have just done nutshells into one reach of the left arm, one high throw of the left leg, and every scrap of nervous energy you can muster. And even when you've hit the secret button and done it, and are belaying for the last time 10ft. higher, you are still revving. At the foot of the pitch, all you thought was: 'Can I do it?' Now, it's 'Can they?'

Climbing instructors, who have cajoled, threatened or muscled their charges up to this point, begin to see visions of public enquiries and nasty headlines, as the final pitch proves too much for the fat boy and rain begins to fall; the crag-rat (the phrase originated in Borrowdale), trying to keep pace with the sun, space-oddity-wise, by rising as fast as it falls behind Maiden Moor, fears missing the pint of the evening as the crinklie who would have bought it falters on the bulge; the guy with the chick in tears below the bulge – and who only persuaded her on to this route because he knew she would know any soft option at the top – begins to panic as she sags once more on the rope, while the wind blows his entreaties away; and even the VS man, who has been using pegs on the route as snowploughs and ice-chippers, can feel the stirrings of anxiety as darkness falls and with it his second. 'Are they up to it?' is on his mind as never before.

They always are, of course. They always make it. It's just that there has to be a first time. And many a leader up there has thought: 'This is it!'

Right: With the second man belayed at the neck of the Pinnacle, the leader begins the tricky final pitch of the climb. *Climbers: Rick Sagar and Willie Parkes*

Chris Hall

22 Bracket and Slab

by Tom Price

To the hill-farmer, 'Gimmer' means a two-year-old ewe-lamb, but to the Lakeland climber it spells exposure, small holds, open climbing, quick-drying rock and a sunny aspect. It is the Belle Vue Bastion of the Lakes, a place to take a gramophone, as they used to on Terrace Wall, a crag for sybarites.

It lies high up above the Old Dungeon Ghyll Hotel, and it emerges from the steep fellside in a single clean buttress, pink rock weathered to a pale grey, one of the durable compact lavas that denudation has laid bare in central Lakeland. George Basterfield, among the most prominent of the climbers of the 'twenties, wrote that it provided maximum exposure with minimum risk, but added: 'The writer would advise careful attention to belays, for, apart from Amen Corner, Gimmer holds out no saving interception to the unfortunate climber who has once lost contact!'

As you approach from Langdale, the most prominent feature on the crag is Gimmer Chimney, with its twin cracks extending right up the crag. Bracket and Slab is just to the left. It starts well down at the foot of the Bilberry Chute, and thus gives the longest route on this flank of the crag, and one of the most varied.

You start by climbing what Basterfield described as a small minaret, from the top of which you make a move on to a smooth slab, one of the hardest bits of the climb in my view. From halfway up the first pitch there are fine open situations and a variety of moves. The climb trends right in a series of upward traverses, over the Bracket (providentially situated to get you through a steepness), then by a zigzag course up to the summit rocks.

My own first brush with Bracket and Slab was years ago, in days when many climbers thought that to tackle a Severe was to have ideas above one's station. Accordingly, I was on Gimmer Chimney. I made the mistake, however, of following the direct line, which led me in my iron clinkers up a very hostile chimney, from which I emerged uttering the familiar refrain: 'That's no V.Diff!' I had strayed on to the sixth pitch of Bracket and Slab, but I was in good company: H. M. Kelly made the same mistake in 1918, during the chimney's first recorded ascent. On the misty, drizzly summer day when the definitive first ascent of Bracket and Slab was accomplished, the leader, H. B. Lyon, devoted an hour to this chimney, and afterwards a whole page of description. 'In its ratio of difficulty,' he commented, 'it is to Amen Corner what Amen Corner is to Broad Stand,' and concluded, 'Amen Chimney may be a better name for it.'

H. B. Lyon was one of the pioneers of Gimmer, a crag which began to claim attention only when climbers had emerged from the cracks and chimneys on to the open faces. He had already reconnoitred Lyon's Crawl, and put up the fine 'B' route in 1907. Sixteen years later he spent a particularly rewarding few days in Langdale. First he explored most of what was to become Bracket and Slab. Then he went off and made the first ascent of White Ghyll Chimney, thereby opening up a whole new climbing area. And the following day, 12 August 1923, he made the first ascent of Bracket and Slab in its entirety, leading a rope of five, including that very good local woman climber, Mabel Barker.

In the initial exploration of the route, with J. Herbert, he was attracted by a 'bracket-shaped outcrop of rock beneath an overhang'. He reached its edge, 'to find it occupied by a large loose flake of rock which had first to be dislodged by hitching the rope behind and hauling. This done I again approached the bracket, crawled along its flat top and regained the upright position.' The bracket gave access to a difficult ten-foot groove, which was the way ahead. It was a novel and interesting pitch.

The next notable pitch was the Neat Bit, a delightful slabby section. Lyon found it already nail-scratched, and assumed it had been used to circumvent Amen Corner on 'B' Route. Though it is a pity to miss the Neat Bit, Amen Corner can easily be taken as a variant on Bracket and Slab, by those who long to exert a little brute force and submit themselves to this ancient test of virtue. It is a 12ft. vertical crack in a right-angled corner, rising from a flat ledge large enough to accommodate several jeering companions. It is a stern lay-back, and the furious pedalling in nailed boots that its left wall has endured over the years has not im-

Route Bracket and Slab, Severe, 295ft.
Cliff South-East Face of Gimmer Crag, Great Langdale.
First Ascent H. B. Lyon, J. Herbert and party, August 1923; the Amen Corner on B Route was led by H. B. Lyon in April 1907.
Map Reference O.S. Lake District Tourist Map, 1–50,000 Sheet (ref. 273071).
Guidebooks F.R.C.C. *Great Langdale* by J. A. Austin and R. Valentine; *Rock Climbing in the Lake District* by Geoff Cram, Chris Eilbeck and Ian Roper.
Nearest Road Car park at Old Dungeon Ghyll Hotel at the end of the B5343 Great Langdale road (ref. 285060).
Distance and time from cliff 1 mile/1,200ft. Allow 1 hour. A direct ascent from the valley is only recommended in the spring as bracken complicates progress later in the year. At other times a rising, stony track leading directly from the O.D.G. is the best way, and this can be improved by starting up Middlefell Buttress, and then traversing round to rejoin the track.
Good Conditions The cliff dries rapidly after rain in most seasons.
Campsites and Bunkhouses Large campsite at the head of Great Langdale; F.R.C.C., Wayfarers' and Achille Ratti Huts (3 miles).
Bibliography F.R.C.C. Journal 1923 contains a first-ascent account by H. B. Lyon.

proved the friction. By modern standards it is hardly fierce, but one must remember that at the time it was first climbed, 1907, there were two techniques regarded as supremely strenuous and committing, the hand traverse and the lay-back. And it is certainly a great feeling as you haul yourself out at the top.

Above the Corner you traverse easily right to the redoubtable chimney. Climbers on pleasure bent, rather than conquest, can traverse a bit further and ascend an easier chimney. Thereafter a leftwards traverse and 80ft. of easy climbing take you to the top.

Gimmer abounds with good things. The Neat Bit is not the only neat bit on the crag, nor, for that matter, is it the neatest. But Bracket and Slab is a good sample, and is very popular, especially without the chimney. It has the wonder ingredient, of course; that is, it is a Severe that everybody can do. But it has much more than that. It has a peculiarly Lake District quality of originality and charm. In good conditions, it flatters the climber, and persuades him he is on form. It does much to sustain the fallacy that rocks were made to be climbed on.

Above: The celebrated Amen Corner, a vicious 12 ft. layback crack first climbed in 1907, can easily be included in the Bracket and Slab climb to add extra tradition and difficulty. Modern protection takes away some of its original bite, but it still stops its fair quota of aspiring leaders. *Climber: John Evans*

Left: Getting established on the Bracket, the jutting block that gives the climb its name. Some leaders tiptoe delicately across small holds below the bracket, but most, especially if conditions are greasy, swarm unashamedly on to the bracket at the first opportunity and crawl along it. *Climber: John Evans*

John Evans

Above left: For those not attracted by the lure of Amen Corner, the Neat Bit provides an exposed and enjoyable alternative. *Climber: Ken Wilson*

Above right: The Neat Bit emerges on to this smooth slab which also forms a welcome landing for those emerging from Amen Corner (the crack of which is obvious at the top of the slab). From this point a delicate traverse leads across to the foot of the crux chimney. *Climber: John Evans*

Right: The crucial chimney of Bracket and Slab involves an entertaining and thrutchy struggle that has defeated many a leader. A soft-option alternative exists to the right, but the route has not been properly accomplished unless the chimney is climbed. *Climber: John Evans*

Chris Hall

23 Ash Tree Slabs and 'C' Route

by Lord Hunt

One of the compensations of getting older is that memory holds the door wide open to the past. You have only to mention a person, a place, or a combination of the two, for a scene and its surrounding circumstances to spring up in sharp relief, complete with sounds and smells. Certainly this is true of my own store of mountain memories. Unlike facts fed into computers, memories remain private to oneself unless one wishes to share them. And this is precisely what I have been persuaded to do in this chapter.

Gimmer Crag, whatever its limitations in stature, looms large in my recollections of pre-war days, when I was climbing in the Lake District more frequently than I have been able to do since; what with various expeditions, to say nothing of the Western Alps, the attractions of North Wales and incidental jobs of work which have claimed my attention elsewhere.

My memories of Gimmer go back to 1933, the year I started climbing in Britain after serving a six-year apprenticeship in the Alps. With A. W. (Bill) Osborne, Donald Murray, Norman Slack and Stewart Mitchell, I had climbed several of the Severes on the West and South-East Faces, but do not recollect having ventured round the corner on to the North-West Face, or having climbed 'C' at that time. But I had enjoyed the experience well enough to make the crag a first port of call three years later, on my honeymoon, when I put young love to a severe test by initiating my wife, Joy, to rock climbing, with Gimmer 'C' and Ash Tree Slabs in the repertoire. If the merit of a climb were to be judged by the criterion of a life-long married partnership, I would strongly recommend Gimmer, and these two climbs in particular, on this score alone.

So I recall those sunny days in September 1936 with tender emotion, and with the added delight of discovering that I had acquired a wife who took naturally to steep rock. I remember that she evoked the admiration of one Sutcliffe, who was there with a client. He was one of the few professionals in those days, and a stickler for style: he collected sixpenny fines from his clients for using knees. Watching Joy leading up Main Wall with balanced ease, he said, and it is a measure of the change that has taken place: 'Fancy a girl leading! And she's good, too.' Gimmer was also a lurking shadow in that hot and sultry August of 1939, when the clouds of war were gathering over Europe, before the storm finally broke into war in early September. We were staying in Grasmere at the time and, abandoning my studies for the Army Staff College, we went climbing every day, with a desperate, unspoken wish to hold on to things we loved while the world threatened to fall apart. It was at Old Dungeon Ghyll, after a glorious day climbing on Gimmer, which included, I think, both Ash Tree Slabs and 'C', that I received a fateful telegram recalling me to military duty. Three days later, I sailed from Greenock in the first convoy of the war, a copy of Heaton Cooper's *The Hills of Lakeland* in my kitbag.

But I really must stop reminiscing and introduce these two routes. One of the advantages of combining them is that by doing so you can sample two faces of Gimmer; another is that this produces a reasonably long and varied climb of 355ft. It is undoubtedly the best combination of climbs (albeit not the most logical one) at this standard hereabouts, and has the merit of taking you from the bottom to the top of the crag.

The Slabs are easy to identify. After skirting the toe of the buttress to start up North-West Gully, a big detached flake is passed; 40ft. higher there is a notable corner on your right, with the Slabs forming its left flank; their left edge is demarcated by a vertical wall falling into the gully bed. The first pitch provides the most enjoyable move on this route, which is later capped by the splendid final pitch of 'C': a rising traverse from the corner to the left edge, with a delicate move upwards when you get there, in order to reach a stance overlooking the gully. Last year, when taking a beginner on this climb, with my wife also on the rope, I committed the cardinal folly of running out of available rope just before making this upwards move. There followed a protracted period of rearranging our 120ft. of nylon before I was free to proceed to the security of the ledge.

The climb continues pleasantly and, for a beginner, in a spectacular manner up the edge, enters a groove which, after a further 50ft. or so, is abandoned, before it becomes

Routes Ash Tree Slabs, Very Difficult, 155ft.; 'C' Route, Severe, 200ft.
Cliff West Face of Gimmer Crag, Great Langdale.
First Ascents Ash Tree Slabs – G. S. Bower and A. W. Wakefield, June 1920; 'C' Route – A. P. Wilson, G. H. Jackson and A. Brundritt, August 1918.
Map Reference O.S. Lake District Tourist Map, 1–50,000 Sheet (ref. 273071).
Guidebooks F.R.C.C. *Great Langdale* by J. A. Austin and R. Valentine; *Rock Climbing in the Lake District* by Geoff Cram, Chris Eilbeck and Ian Roper.
Nearest Road Car park at Old Dungeon Ghyll Hotel at the end of the B5343 Great Langdale road (ref. 285060).
Distance and time from cliff 1 mile/1,200ft. Allow 1 hour. A direct ascent from the valley is only recommended in the spring as the bracken complicates progress later in the year. At other times a rising, stony track leading directly from the O.D.G. is the best way, and this can be improved by starting up Middlefell Buttress, and then traversing round to rejoin the track.
Good Conditions The cliff dries rapidly after rain in most seasons.
Campsites and Bunkhouses Large campsite at the head of Great Langdale; F.R.C.C., Wayfarers' and Achille Ratti Huts (3 miles).

Note: Ash Tree Slabs was downgraded from HVD to VD in the 1980 guide. Should 'C' Route be occupied, 'D' Route, though not described here, is a pitch of outstanding quality, being singular in line yet varied in detail, exposed, well-protected and on excellent rock. Highly recommended.

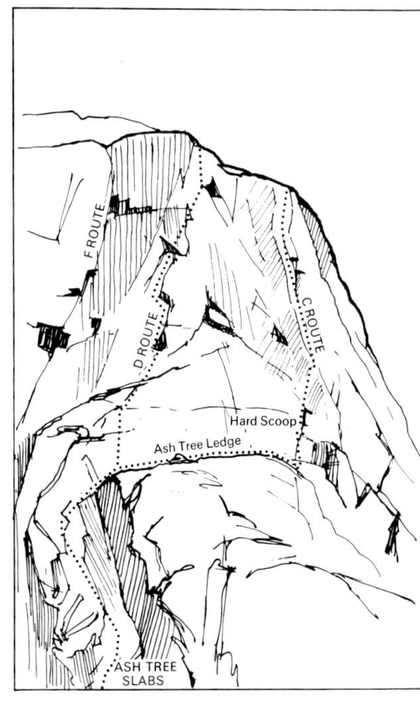

Left: A general view of the South-East (right) and South-West faces of Gimmer Crag. Bracket and Slab takes a line up the centre of the South-East Face. Ash Tree Slabs are situated on the side of the shadowy left-hand gully, and C Route takes the steeper upper face at approximately the line of sunlight and shadow.

Chris Hall

too easy, in favour of a good finishing wall a little to the left, when you reach a ledge. The final 50ft. ends slightly above Ash Tree Ledge, from which the second climb starts. The whole of this slab route can be described as delightful, with enough holds to provide no real effort or anxiety at any point.

The climber is now almost directly beneath 'D' route, which offers a natural sequence. But it is short – only 100ft. – and, with the whole range of choice now available from Ash Tree Ledge, I would go for 'C' every time, despite the break in continuity involved in making a 60ft. walk downwards to the right. In 1936, we were armed with those earlier Fell and Rock guidebooks, dyed red in the Club's colours and allegedly impermeable. The trouble was that in wet conditions the dye ran off on to your hands and stained the inner edges of the book: I have specimens loaned by Alan Hargreaves and Sid Cross to remind me of the fact. But what delightful descriptions they contained! George Bower, one of the 'Barrow Engineers' who pioneered so many classic Lakeland routes in the years immediately after the First World War, wrote of Ash Tree Slabs and 'D' (two of his 'Firsts') that they provide 'a full course of soup, fish, meat and "afters" '. But his friend George Basterfield, another 'Barrow Engineer' and joint author

Left: At the difficult section of Ash Tree Slabs. *Climber: John Harding*

of the old Langdale guidebook, made 'C' an even more appetizing 'after' by calling it 'as full of good things as a Christmas pudding'. Those words have remained in my memory verbatim over all the years between.

You start (in common with 'A' and 'B' Routes) with a diagonal upwards scramble from Ash Tree Ledge, at a point some 15ft. left of a large cairn near its lowest right-hand end (and close to an improbable 'green bay tree', according to Basterfield), which brings you to a belvedere 30ft. above. Here, another cairn at the foot of a scooped-shaped wall marks the start of the serious climbing. In the following 15ft. section, pulling up on awkwardly placed holds and bridging the scoop, you make what are probably the hardest technical moves on 'C'. Last year, repeating the climb with Chris Bonington, I was thankful to note that he, too, found the pitch difficult. You arrive at Thomson's Ledge (named after A. S. Thomson who, with H. B. Lyon, pioneered several Gimmer climbs, including 'B', at the beginning of the century). The ledge is narrow, and has an exiguous belay 10ft. to the right. A much better stance and anchorage lie 30ft. along the ledge to the left, at the base of Forty-Foot Corner, but this takes you well off the climb and calls for quite a lot of rope.

You are now on very steep ground and climbing becomes sensational: up a groove, moving right on to good holds, and up again to Green Chimney in 35ft. At the foot of this chimney is the next stance and belay, both of them satisfying in this airy spot. From here the climber starts on the left and goes left-handed upwards, in considerable exposure but always with a sufficiency of holds, to the sloping ledge of Lyon's Crawl (named after another great Lakeland climber whom I was privileged to meet while on an expedition in Sikkim). Again a stance, and a small one, at 35ft. Above is a groove and, 15ft. above that, a roof. The finale in 'C' Major is about to begin.

So up this groove, finding comforting hand-holds under the overhang. Moving left, find a welcome hold for the left hand which enables you to swing up past the obstacle and reach a ledge; but it is small, like every comfort in these parts. So don't stop here for your second, but climb up the continuing groove. Another ledge is passed and you are on the last lap: a slight depression in the uncompromising steepness, veering rightwards, marks the way – small holds, space beneath your feet, glorious, exhilarating stuff. Both the 1926 and 1938 guidebooks mention a 'doubtful flake' some 25ft. below the top; it was still there, rendering yeoman service, when I 'treated it with kindness' (*à la* Basterfield) in 1975.

We have arrived on the Balcony, and I am looking south to Dow Crag and west to Bowfell Buttress. There, too, lurk many memories and I am well content.

Chris Hall

Above: The upper part of C Route seen from the foot of the South-East Face. *Climber: unknown*

24 Bowfell Buttress

by Walt Unsworth

It had been a rough night in the Wall End barn. One of the Fylde lads had won a piglet in a raffle the night before and had insisted on its sharing the accommodation, which was already overcrowded. Though the piglet fitted in well with the general standards in the barn, it did make a considerable rumpus until the small hours and nobody got much sleep.

So Dave and I were fairly bog-eyed when we tramped up the Band next morning on our way to Bowfell Buttress. I don't know whether you know this track? The Band is a thrusting ridge of fell which points like an arrow into the head of Langdale, splitting the valley in twain. To the left is dark Oxendale, leading up to Crinkle Crags and Hell Gill, where you can have good fun in a hard winter, and to the right is Mickleden leading to the twin highways of Rossett Gill and the Stake Pass. Across Mickleden are the Langdale Pikes, with Gimmer glinting like a pink jewel in the morning sun. I wished we'd gone to Gimmer, or better still, Raven – the Band is heavy going after a hard night, and Dave and I must have made a melancholy pair, for what with the beer, the piglet and the barn, trudging up the Band was sheer masochism.

The Band leads up between Crinkle Crags and Bowfell to a col called Three Tarns, presumably because this is the minimum number of tarns you'll find there, but long before this a good track veers away to the right, below the crest of the ridge. Known as the Climbers' Traverse, it leads with magnificent abandon across the screes and outcrops to Bowfell Buttress.

We fumbled along the Climbers' Traverse, ignoring the splendid series of crags which overlook this superb path, and it wasn't until we came to the spring, issuing from the rock like an echo from Moses, that we shambled to a halt, had a morning wash, and prepared to face the day.

Bowfell Buttress glowed in a warm Easter sun: a big, bold bastion of rock, so impressive that I marvelled at its late discovery. I suppose the main reason is that it is scarcely noticeable from the valley, for even the vast bulk of a crag like this is absorbed and lost in the ragged skyline that forms the head of Langdale. Two novices, Tom Shaw and G. H. Craig, discovered the buttress towards the end of the nineteenth century, but they didn't climb it until 1902, when Shaw led a rope of five to the top. It has remained a firm favourite to the present day.

The first pitch is a scrambly affair up a broken rib, but it soon leads to a short chimney, which, in my condition on that day, I found a bit of a thrutch. I brought up Dave, who doesn't like chimneys anyway. He landed like an out-of-condition porpoise on the ledge beside me, inviting me to continue while he recovered.

Up a steep wall with good holds to another large ledge. As Dave wandered up in slow pursuit, I figured out the theory of the buttress: a series of capacious ledges interrupted by steep walls. Like all theories, it was only partially true, and the next bit of the climb found me crouched in a sentry-box, while Dave came up. He took one look at the stance and went on up the broken chimney, until he reached the third ledge.

If you are one of those people who must eat on a climb, then this is the place to do it on Bowfell Buttress. For one thing the ledge is large enough for a picnic and is conveniently situated about halfway up the route. For another, the climb gets distinctly harder from here on.

I need not dwell on the famous crack pitch which comes next, except to say that it is an awkward little bastard. Even when you pull over the top, muttering 'But I *can't* fall off Bowfell Buttress', like a Buddhist monk chanting his mantra, it is not all over. The belay is reached with relief. I remember thinking how warm the day was, and wondering what I was doing there after such a rough night. I brought up Dave; he doesn't like cracks, either.

The crack pitch is the acknowledged crux of Bowfell Buttress, but the pitch which follows it is not all that simple, though quite different. The route slopes up to the left and the rock slopes out into space. There may be protection on it, but the question was academic at the time since Dave and I didn't have any. Our armoury was a rope and some bendy boots, suitable as we thought for classic rock. I crabbed across inelegantly, reaching the belay with a certain degree of humility and thankfulness. I began to

Route Bowfell Buttress, Difficult (hard), 350ft.
Cliff Bowfell Buttress, Great Langdale.
First Ascent T. Shaw, G. H. Craig, G. R. West, C. Hargreaves and L. J. Oppenheimer, May 1902.
Map Reference O.S. Lake District Tourist Map, 1–50,000 Sheet (ref. 245069).
Guidebooks F.R.C.C. *Great Langdale* by J. A. Austin and R. Valentine; *Rock Climbing in the Lake District* by Geoff Cram, Chris Eilbeck and Ian Roper.
Nearest Road Car park at Old Dungeon Ghyll Hotel at the end of the B5343 Great Langdale road (ref. 285060).
Distance and time from cliff $2\frac{1}{2}$ miles/1,800ft. Allow $1\frac{1}{2}$ hours, follow The Band to 2,000ft. where a track leads across the northern slopes of Bowfell to the foot of the crag.
Good Conditions The crag needs several days of dry weather to come into condition, and the climb is a good deal harder when damp.
Campsites and Bunkhouses Large campsite at the head of Great Langdale; F.R.C.C., Wayfarers' and Achille Ratti Huts (3 miles); L.T.M.C. Hut at Blea Tarn (2 miles).
Bibliography *A Progress in Mountaineering* by J. H. B. Bell (Oliver and Boyd, 1950) contains an interesting account of an ascent of the Direct Route by Bell and H. M. Kelly in 1931; *The Heart of Lakeland* by Lehmann J. Oppenheimer (Sherratt and Hughes, London, 1908) contains a first ascent account.

Note: Regraded to Very Difficult in 1980.

Chris Hall

Bob Allen

Chris Hal

suspect Bowfell Buttress of being one of those Diffs. (like Grey Knotts Face) where the guidebook writers have us on a bit.

But then all became sweet reasonableness once again: straightforward and straight up. It can be split into pitches, if you wish, but there's not much point really, and Dave made it in one long run out to Low Man.

Only when the climb is over do you realize what a magnificent buttress this is, standing proud from the parent fell, to which it is joined by a narrow neck, with plunging gullies on either hand. Scafell Crag itself can scarcely better it for dramatic position.

And what of the climb itself? Here's what the late Jerry Wright, who made two hundred ascents of Bowfell Buttress as a professional guide, wrote about it:

'Once upon a wet and cloudy morning two experts, following the advice that it was a good climb for such a day, began the ascent in improving weather conditions. They were so absorbed by its interest that they took little notice of the rising clouds and the sun breaking through. They were still there under brilliant blue skies in the late evening having gone up and down the route four times; they came away reluctantly, after, as they put it, "two thousand feet of perfect rock-climbing".'

We walked along the ridge to Rossett Gill, wondering how the Fylde lads had got the piglet home on a motor bike.

Opposite page: The third pitch of Bowfell Buttress. *Climber: Andy Cairns*

Above left: The fierce crack that forms the crux of Bowfell Buttress. Although safely situated above a grassy ledge, the crack has to be fought hard if it is to be overcome. *Climber: Unknown*

Above right: The leader has continued past the belay after the difficult crack pitch (this can be seen at the foot of the picture) and is continuing up to the sloping groove on the guidebook pitch 6. *Climber: Andy Cairns*

25 Murray's Route

by Anthony Greenbank

The sight of Murray's 'B' on Dow first struck terror into this novice in 1953, and indeed it still does. If you approach from the front, it zaps you at the end of a considerable walk along a rocky track from where you parked the car high above Coniston. If you are foolish enough to approach from above, having come the long way from Duddon, over the Walna Scar path and along the crest of the Dow skyline, it lies somewhere below, in that horrific, gully-riven drop.

On that first visit, the fright began (as always) on first nearing the crag. According to the physiologists, this is when the heart pounds most. The buttresses were streaming with water, drops were flying in the wind from the overlaps, and the cracks all seemed to slope the wrong way. 'B' Buttress in particular looked desperate, and a sense of utter inadequacy began to make itself felt.

Murray's 'B', now known merely as Murray's Route, was first climbed in April 1918, and in fact began the post-First World War new-climbs boom on Dow. There had been seven lean years of exploration just before, following the veritable gold-rush of classics, like Abraham's Climb, Intermediate Gully and Hopkinson's Crack, which appeared around the turn of the century. Murray's 'B' was *the* route, however, displaying Dow's terrific potential for a more advanced and technical kind of climbing such as we know today. True, such climbing was already known on other crags in Cumbria, in the form of Scafell's Central Buttress and Pillar's North-West Climb, but Murray's 'B', although easier, later received no less than four quality variants, branching to and fro, indicating the 'big country' through which this extraordinary Severe makes its way. And all this is quite apart from the excellence of the rock which must have shouted at the prospects of other fine face climbs yet to come – from Eliminate 'B' to Nimrod.

It was impossible not to be aware of this sense of greatness on that wet morning in 1953, as we gazed up at the route. Our eyes followed the line, from where it takes off near the base of 'B' Buttress, to the ceiling at 150ft., then left across almost the whole of the left-hand side of 'B' Buttress. The only thing that didn't look great was, as Bruce put it, 'Hunt'. That was the tight-lipped, ashen-faced one at his shoulder – me and my middle name.

You could watch ice-floes scudding across Goats Water below and the flanks of Coniston Old Man getting soaked. The swirling vapour which passes as mist here, but which is in reality an evil sea fog that blows in over Walney, had smeared the rock with slime as slick as parted seaweed. Within moments its droplets had seized on my RAF payslip – National Service AC2 rate – on which was penned our route description. At once this was reduced to a blur. From then on our previous epics – the mantelshelf on the Needle, the Collie Step and Bowfell Buttress – were as nothing.

Bruce, who like me is no great shakes (there is even a route named after me now in Buttermere, called Paper Tiger), got the shakes on the first pitch. First his boots, then his legs, his body and finally his head.

'Hard, Hunt, it's hard, Murray's,' he gritted, teeth chattering, looking furtively for a place to jump.

'That's not Murray's, mate,' said a voice from somewhere. 'That's Tiger Traverse.'

The resulting thud – from all of eight feet, true, but psychologically earth-quaking nevertheless – was perhaps an indication not only of our inexperience, but also of the quality of Murray's 'B', in that this harder variation had looked to us even easier than the first pitch of the Severe.

The first V-chimney of Murray's opens out at around 20ft. into two smooth, sloping slabs, both slanting up and out. At this point, each of us was terrified in turn, and with good reason, although we didn't know it. We weren't aware that Siegfried Herford (who put up Scafell's Central Buttress) actually failed here on his first attempt; nor did we know that Murray himself (who had been on the first C.B. ascent with Herford) first tried the right-hand slab, then turned his attention to the left one, when soloing, and fell off – only to pick himself up, brush himself down, and bounce back later to lick this postage-stamp-sized sector which opens up an envelope of rock, 250ft. high by 70ft. wide, with more fabulous climbing yet to come.

The problem – and thousands will know the feeling – is that this left-hand slab is not so much steep as smooth: every little flaw is

Route Murray's Route, Severe, 250ft.
Cliff 'B' Buttress on Dow Crag near Coniston.
First Ascent D. G. Murray, W. J. Borrowman and B. L. Martin, April 1918.
Map Reference O.S. Lake District Tourist Map, 1–50,000 Sheet (ref. 264977).
Guidebooks F.R.C.C. *Dow Crag Area* by D. Millar; *Rock Climbing in the Lake District* by Geoff Cram, Chris Eilbeck and Ian Roper.
Nearest Road The unmetalled Walna Scar road from Coniston at ref. 283968 or at the end of a minor road from Torver (ref. 282957).
Distance and time from cliff 2 miles/1,300ft. Allow 1 hour. An obvious path leads up into the valley below Goat's Water, followed by steep scree slopes to the cliff.
Good Conditions Greasy in the winter months but quick drying for the rest of the year.
Campsites and Bunkhouses Convenient but rather exposed camping by the Walna Scar road. M.A.M. Hut, Low House, in Coniston.
Bibliography F.R.C.C. Journal 1917–18 contains a short first-ascent account.

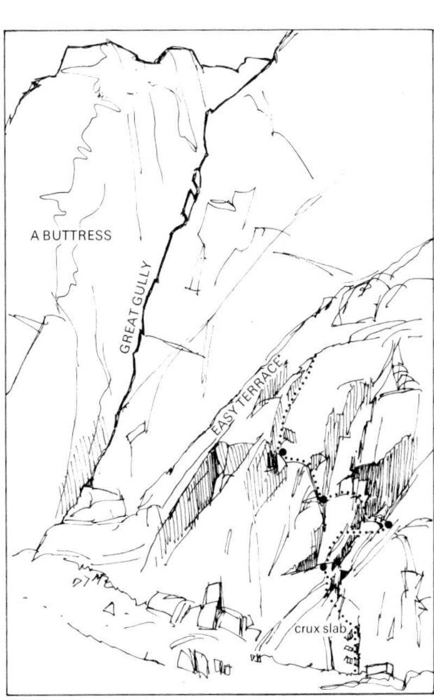

as slick as a cliché. You begin with a good foothold for the right foot, and small holds for the right hand; you must then reach out and up with the left boot to a sloping foothold way over on the slab. But by now your right hand has disappeared into a good crack, and it is with a sense of dismay that you discover that you can only reach that apology for a foothold by making your right hand materialize once more and by keeping it in view on an excuse for a hand-hold some place else. What with having to change feet out on the slab as well, to say nothing of that final lurch left again across to the belay knob, it's enough to blow mild (or bitter, come to that) out into clouds of steam and sweat, or worse.

Frightened climbing leads to lurching. And so it went on – lurch after lurch – even up the rather easier going above: a battle for survival against wet rock, our ineptitude and the wind.

'Bring up both boots,' I yelled, leaving them on a small ledge below Abraham's Cave, which called for a long tricky stride up.

'Yahoo . . . Hunt,' came the return cry, coupled with a cowboy whiplash of the rope which promptly flogged our primitive runners off into space. (This was in response to what had been heard below, the wind having flayed my words into a defiant 'We've burnt the boats.' For that matter, I couldn't always be sure that it was 'Hunt' that was being yelled in support, and not some other word meant as a term of abuse.)

Then came the high-altitude traversing: always leftwards in wind blustery enough to make your eyes watery and your hair impossible to finger-comb. Water fell off the overhangs in big driving blobs. But up here we were in with the gods. All big, sharp, flaky hand-holds, long strides, clumsy foot shuffles, and the most fantastic crag walls below. Huddled over a runner, I desperately sorted out a badly tied bowline. The job done, I straightened up, and the bag tucked inside my anorak slipped out and shot fishpaste sandwiches all the way down the crux of Leopard's Crawl.

It was darkness that finally saved the day. It is said that certain climbers, from Owen

Left and Above: The difficult slab moves on the first pitch of Murray's Route. The corner is climbed until the holds cease. At this point it is necessary to traverse delicately to the left to reach better holds. *Climbers: John Evans and Dave Partridge*

Ken Wilson

Above: Dow Crag, with A, B, C, D and E Buttresses from left to right.

Right: The exposed hand traverse on the modern third pitch (guidebook fifth) of Murray's Route. *Climber: Dave Clarke*

Glynne Jones to Allan Austin, have derived their powerful style from being short-sighted and therefore blissfully unaware of exposed situations. This may or may not be true, but it certainly worked for us. We went up the final crack, with its knobbly yet polished rock, cosseted in gloom as dark as Guinness. Every nerve was keyed up with the knowledge that we had all but done our climb. Our elation was marred only by the nightmarish thought that we might accidentally have strayed on to Murray's Direct instead. But it speaks volumes for the line of Murray's, rather than for our route-finding ability, that we were led to the top automatically, as naturally as if our boots were running on rails. And that's how it's been for hundreds of others with limited ability but plenty of determination, and that's how it should be on all the best climbs.

Twenty-five years later, Murray's 'B' still exerts a powerful effect, but for different reasons. What finished that evening as a painful descent, in socks, down Easy Terrace, and a tin-tack prowl around the screes looking for those boots, actually marked the beginning of an unhealthy respect for the 'golden oldies'. It's unhealthy, because it's vicarious: the more you know of other people's hard times on this route, the more your respect grows. And it's not only a matter of Herford failing or Murray falling; it's also compounded of Fell and Rock members (who knew Dow like the backs of their knuckles) being stopped in their tracks by the little awkward move just *after* the first slab; of Jim Cameron, Lakeland guide and Dow *habitué*, pausing for a considerable time, on a cold February morning, on the steep crack which leaves Abraham's Cave; of Barrow lads (whose fingerprints grace Polaris nuclear submarines beneath the polar ice, and who have spent night after midsummer night on the crag) having a tussle with verglas on the gun-barrel chimney along the top traverse, although they would normally be climbing Hard VS. It's not a climb to be underestimated.

There is protection on all the pitches, with overhangs all around and the crag slanting below into the crater of Goats Water; and you can, as we did, flick sleet off the holds, peer down at your second not quite in sight far below, glance back again at the black-streaked rock under the rim of your crash-hat, and think, 'steady', as you move up under a patter of hail, blow on your fingers and look for another metal chock. But whether this Severe is at the height of your powers, and you wait for perfect weather, or you try Murray's 'B' because Sidewalk is too green, you won't be let down.

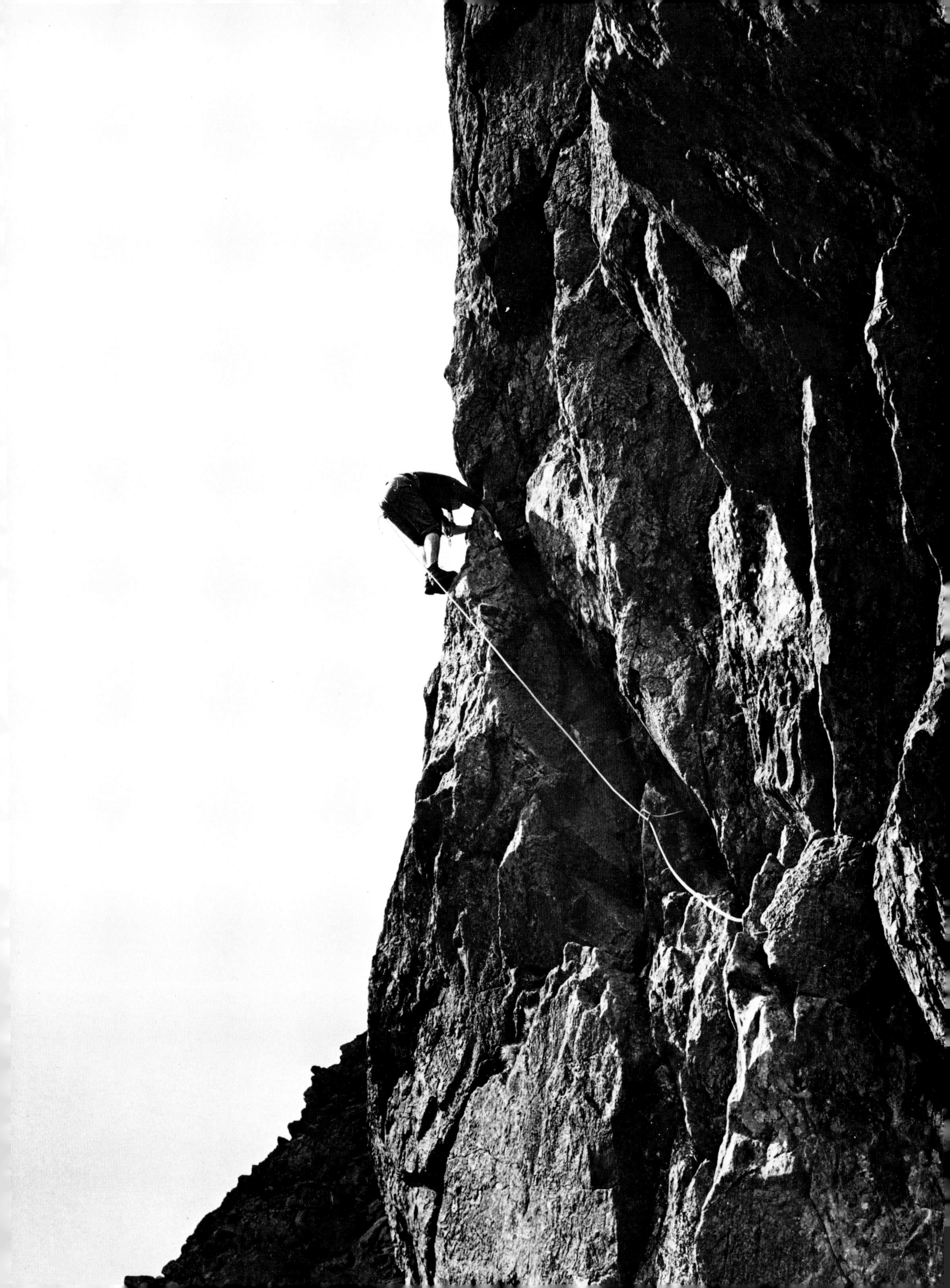

Chris Hall

26 Jones's Route Direct from Lord's Rake

by Tony Toole

Stark remnant of an age when the world was young, and the possibility of Man no more than a formless dream of a distant future, the crag stands in sombre, almost ecclesiastic aloofness. Rooted deep beneath the northern shadows of Scafell, it rises above a morass of boulder and clattering scree which fans down towards Hollow Stones. Bounded on the east by the broad saddle of Mickledore, and on the west by the ugly gash of Deep Ghyll, it guards the secrets of permanence and durability against the yearnings of transient life. Whether the eyes focus on the Central Buttress or on the tapering spires of Pisgah and the Pinnacle, they cannot rest, but are drawn higher and ever higher towards the vision of an unattainable bliss. High on the crag, a flash of sunlight hints of the warmth which soothes the shaking muscles and eases the clammy coldness of the sweating skin. And the brooding walls also issue a glimmer of hope that from some high point, the impossible goal of the spirit, that persistent dream which induces a recurrent and unquenchable melancholy, may yet be glimpsed and held for a fleeting moment before it wanes once more to a memory, and the thirst returns to desiccate the soul.

The Pinnacle Face Direct, O. G. Jones's Route, was the farewell wave to the passing of the earliest era in British rock-climbing; the sudden explosion of *fin de siècle* confidence in the coming generation. It was almost the first step across an evolutionary threshold separating the grovelling safety and shelter of the gully from the open exposure and freedom of the wall: the primordial slime from the dry land. One easily imagines the early adventurers into the new realm of the vertical, as they struggled up the dark, dank confines of the gullies, casting a hesitant eye towards the beckoning challenges of the faces, and perhaps encroaching fearfully on to their peripheral reaches. There, the call and the promise would indeed have been strong, and would have waxed stronger with each doubt-laden glance and each inch-wise step closer to the threshold. And when the threshold was brushed, it had to be crossed, for the call to the spirit is stronger than the weakness and trepidation of the flesh.

A short, slabby scramble brings the muscles from their lethargy, and soon, all too soon, the crux is imminent and a commitment is demanded. A pause for reflection and the abandonment of doubts.

A gentle Zephyr, in random wandering, tiptoes into the shadowed funnel of Deep Ghyll. Trapped, it frets and eddies for a moment, then, finding its escape, dances across the cracks and crannies which split the slabs above Lord's Rake. On its whispering breath, it carries a slight shiver of winter chill, though the year has advanced a month beyond the vernal equinox. And the doubts are cast away, to be scattered by the breeze on its eastward Odyssey, as the decision is made and the irrevocable step taken.

The Gangway: a sloping misnomer of friction-clinging tentativeness, on which there is an increasing awareness that the ground is receding in geometrical ratio to the number of faltering steps taken away from the succour of the belay. One can almost sense the presence, close by, of a tweed-jacketed, stocking-footed ghost, his exhalations a cloud of vesperal incense rising soundlessly into the gathering gloom of a long gone twilight. And ghost and man together, though separated in time by nearly eight decades, pad silently inch by inch towards an ever-growing commitment and an ever-diminishing security and feasibility of retreat, until the seductive come-hither of the belay to the front exerts a stronger pull than that to the rear, and an easing of the technicalities leads to the First Nest.

Here, one can gain a brief respite in the hope that the pitches yet to be climbed are, at worst, no harder than that just completed. For the first time, one is conscious of the other world below, from which these craggy fastnesses have become, for a short while, a solitary retreat. Scattered walkers loll about the sunny hillside, or plod tortuously along the track towards England's highest point. Near the foot of Lord's Rake, a pair of climbers gaze over at the Central Buttress, before proceeding on their way, their muffled murmurs camouflaging their secret fears and aspirations. Beyond the springtime warmth of the valley, an infinity away, the bowl of Mosedale shimmers in the hazy air of noon.

A short, steep ascent ends at a platform, the Second Nest, from which Hopkinson's

Route Jones's Route Direct from Lord's Rake. Severe, 215ft.
Cliff The Pinnacle Face, Scafell Crag.
First Ascent O. G. Jones and G. T. Walker, April 1898.
Map Reference O.S. Tourist Map of the Lake District, 1–50,000 Sheet (ref. 208068).
Guidebooks F.R.C.C. *Scafell Group* by M. Burbage and W. Young; *Rock Climbing in the Lake District* by Geoff Cram, Chris Eilbeck and Ian Roper.
Nearest Road A minor road along Wasdale, at the Wasdale campsite (ref. 181076).
Distance and time from cliff 2 miles/ 2,200ft. Allow 1½ hours.
Good Conditions Four dry summer days are needed as the rock is very greasy when damp.
Campsites and Bunkhouses F.R.C.C. Hut, Brackenclose; Campsite by car park.
Bibliography *Rock Climbing in the English Lake District* by O. G. Jones (Abraham, Keswick, 1900, and republished by E. J. Morten, Manchester, 1972); *Mountaineering in Britain* by R. W. Clark and E. C. Pyatt (Phoenix House Ltd/Dent, 1957); C.C. Journal 1914 has notes and photographs of Scafell Pinnacle by S. W. Herford.

Note: Upgraded to Hard Severe in 1984.

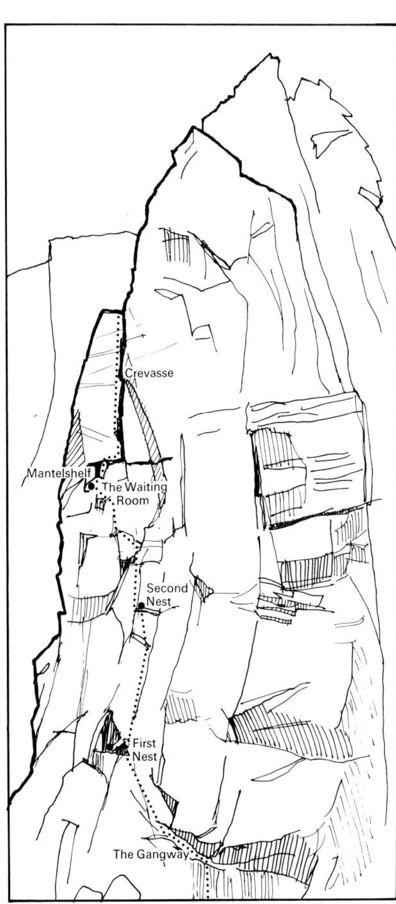

Left: Scafell Pinnacle. The leader has joined the second (Gangway) pitch with the short third pitch and is belayed in the Second Nest. *Climbers: Steve Beavan and Willie Parkes*

Chris Hall

Above left: The Gangway pitch. The climber is at the foot of the The Gangway which leads off the picture above the climber's head. *Climber: Steve Beavan*

Above right: An early ascent of Jones's Route sometime before the First World War. The climber is making the awkward mantelshelf move on the fifth pitch. *Climber: Siegfried Herford*

Opposite page: The leader, having linked the guidebook second and third pitches, is making the final moves to gain the Second Nest. *Climber: Steve Beavan*

Gully, another misnomer, falls away to the left. A few seconds' breather is all that is required before making the step into the shallow depression. Here, the mind can switch off all knowledge of the abyss below the heels, but only for a minute. A delicate traverse, brief echo of what has gone before, recalls the awareness, and the Waiting Room is attained with a little relief.

Here, one could remain for a time in comfort, were it not for a roof above, which casts an ominous shadow over the perception of beauty. The realm begins to feel alien, and the sunlit summit calls.

The Mantelshelf – the scorpion sting. A sharp crack of falling stones, set in motion by a wanderer on the screes far below, ricochets hollowly around the walls of the crags: a sudden reminder of the close proximity of the limit of loneliness. And the limit hovers over the void for a few breathless seconds as the hands press down and the toes reach up for a purchase on the ledge, until the breathing can resume again. A traverse, a crack and a chimney bring the climb to an end, though the Pinnacle still soars above. An easy unwinder up Slingsby's Chimney and the Knife Edge Arête wins the summit.

A picnicking couple wave from across Jordan Gap, and the wave is returned. But this summit is not theirs, nor can they share in the emotions by which it was gained, for these are indivisible.

On the scramble across the gap and down Deep Ghyll, the memories begin to fade. Once more on Lord's Rake, the gaze is again drawn upward. Though it is less poignant than before, the call is renewed and a response demanded.

Another day.

W. B. Brunskill

Chris Hall

27 Moss Ghyll Grooves

by Tom Price

To the extent that risking one's life can ever be so described, Moss Ghyll Grooves is a delightful climb. It is a Severe with the hall-marks of a VS. It takes you right up in the air above Hollow Stones, and the rock is perfect.

My first attempt to climb on Scafell was not a success. It was wet, cold, greasy, and out of the question. Not surprising, since it was January, and on a north-facing crag at 3,000ft. But I was young, and there were fewer books on how to do it in those days. Good conditions, however, completely transform Scafell. On a summer's afternoon or evening, when the sun has worked round west to cast its red-gold warmth on Pinnacle Face, Pisgah and Central Buttress, I know of no more delectable place for a climber to be than Moss Ghyll Grooves.

Moss Ghyll is the narrow cleft that splits the crag down the middle. On the right is Pisgah; on the left, a sweep of slanting grooves forms the flank of Central Buttress. Viewed from across the combe, these grooves are seen to lie in the same plane as Botterill's Slab. On them one can experience the excitement of being on vertical rock without the inconvenience of being out of balance. This is the climb's special charm.

H. M. Kelly had his eye on the Grooves for seven years before he finally accomplished it on 1 July 1926. His earliest assessment was: 'If these grooves are to be climbed, the climber must be prepared to run out at least 100ft. of rope on similar rock to Botterill's Slab, minus its resting-places and probably without the same splendid ledge to finish on.'

The start is reached via the prominent, deep, green chimney on Moss Ghyll itself. It is dark and wet inside, but full of holds. Anyone anxious about his clothes can avoid it on the right. At the top, to the left, rises the first pitch of the Grooves proper. It is possible to cross here on to the Oval, at the foot of the Great Flake on the great Central Buttress route, but our route goes up over a block on the right to a stance in a corner. The next pitch is the crux. Here one must pay the toll, so to speak, that gives access to the Elysian expanses above. From a point about ten feet up the corner, a very delicate traverse is made to a resting-place called the Pedestal. Describing the first ascent, Blanche Eden-Smith wrote that there was 'no hand-hold except a small protuberance the size of a damson stone, on which, moreover, the hands had to be changed somehow. Twice Kelly tried it and came down to the grass from the cramping footholds from which this movement must start. The third time he went straight for it and seemed to flow over those 'holdless' strides to the Pedestal.'

Small but sufficient holds now lead up the arête and the groove to a stance. The climb continues up an exposed, narrowing slab from which one is rescued at the psychological moment by an unexpected traverse into the next groove. Here is a massive belay, the Look-Out. (Scafell abounds as no other crag in these place-names.) There follows a splendid 80ft. pitch up a long slab, with moves on and sometimes over its exposed left edge. We are now in the same area as the upper traverses of C.B., a wonderful position. Two more pitches take us to the top.

Moss Ghyll Grooves is very much a climb of its period. Those were the pre-nylon days, when the leader had to pin his faith on not 'coming off', as the term was. Climbers like Holland advocated Beale's slender hemp line for VS run-outs, as exerting less drag on the leader; since one was not countenancing the possibility of a fall, the lower breaking strain was hardly a consideration. This encouraged a poised and circumspect style of climbing, and Moss Ghyll Grooves is a fine, bold product of this philosophy. It yields to cool and delicate movement, any heavy breathing on the part of the leader being due to emotion, not exertion.

The leader-shall-not-fall approach gave climbing down a certain *cachet* among conscientious cragsmen. My old friend and climbing mentor, George Graham Macphee, told me that after Moss Ghyll Grooves was climbed the expression 'irreversible' was bandied about with regard to the traverse to the Pedestal. So, in 1928, a party comprising L. H. Pollitt, H. G. Knight and G. G. Macphee made the first descent, with Macphee leading from the rear. The chief motivation for this feat was Macphee's desire to make the succinct entry 'MGG ↓ GGM' in the Brackenclose hut book.

Moss Ghyll Grooves by any standards is a fine route. Seen in the context of 1926, it is a great classic.

Route Moss Ghyll Grooves, Hard Severe, 260ft.
Cliff Scafell Crag.
First Ascents H. M. Kelly, Blanche Eden-Smith and J. B. Kilshaw, July 1926; Variation Start – T. G. Peirson and M. H. McFarlane, July 1946.
Map Reference O.S. Tourist Map to the Lake District, 1–50,000 Sheet (ref. 208068).
Guidebooks F.R.C.C. *Scafell Group* by M. Burbage and W. Young; *Rock Climbing in the Lake District* by Geoff Cram, Chris Eilbeck and Ian Roper.
Nearest Road A minor road along Wasdale at the Wasdale campsite (ref.181076).
Distance and time from cliff 2 miles/ 2,200ft. Allow 1½ hours.
Good Conditions Four dry summer days are needed as the rock is very greasy when damp.
Campsites and Bunkhouses F.R.C.C. Hut, Brackenclose; Campsite by car park.
Bibliography *Mountaineering in Britain* by R. W. Clark and E. C. Pyatt (Phoenix House Ltd/Dent, 1957); F.R.C.C. Journal 1926; *M.G.G.* by Blanche Eden-Smith; Rucksack Club Journal 1927; *A History of Moss Ghyll Grooves* by H. M. Kelly.

Note: Upgraded to Very Severe in the 1995 guidebook which also proposed Gill rather than Ghyll as the correct title, and changed all other Ghylls to Gill.

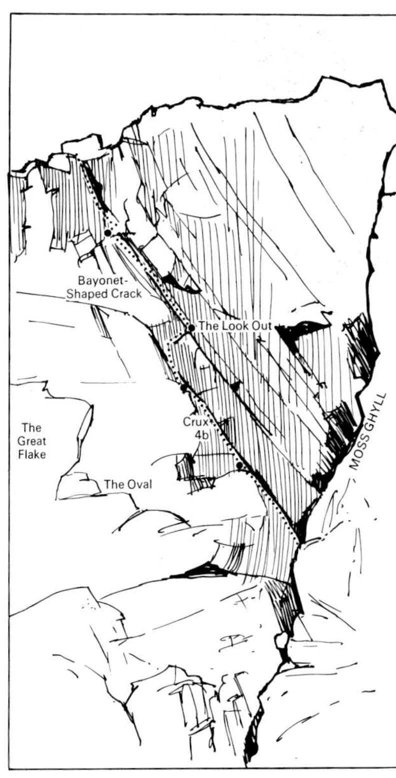

Ian Roper

Chris Hall

Above: Looking down the long initial groove of Moss Ghyll Grooves. The climber is just below the crux where a move has to be made out on to the edge.
Climber: Jill Aldersley

Right: The climb continues up the lower left groove until it is possible to traverse right to gain the grassy ledge below the central groove. The climbers are completing the fourth pitch, which links the climb with the top section of Central Buttress.
Climbers: Ken Jones and Glenn Bennett

28 Napes Needle and Needle Ridge

by Paul Nunn

Routes Napes Needle (Wasdale Crack), Hard Very Difficult, 55ft.; Needle Ridge, Very Difficult, 325ft.
Cliff The Napes, Great Gable.
First Ascents Needle Ridge – W. P. Haskett-Smith, September 1884; Napes Needle – W. P. Haskett-Smith, June 1886.
Map Reference O.S. Tourist Map to the Lake District, 1–50,000 Sheet (ref. 211099).
Guidebooks F.R.C.C. *Great Gable* by P. L. Fearnehough; *Rock Climbing in the Lake District* by Geoff Cram, Chris Eilbeck and Ian Roper.
Nearest Road A minor road at Wasdale Head (ref. 187088). It is also possible to approach from Borrowdale – nearest road at Seathwaite (ref. 235122).
Distance and time from cliff 3 miles/ 2,000ft. Allow 1½ hours. Both the Wasdale and Borrowdale routes converge at Sty Head Pass from where an easy angled track leads round Great Gable to the foot of the Napes.
Good Conditions Generally greasy in winter but both routes dry rapidly after rain in summer.
Campsites and Bunkhouses F.R.C.C. Huts Brackenclose (Wasdale) and Salving House (Borrowdale). Campsites in Wasdale and Borrowdale.
Bibliography *Fell and Rock Journals* of 1914 and 1936 contain accounts of the first ascent of Napes Needle by Haskett-Smith; *Mountaineering in Britain* by R. W. Clark and E. C. Pyatt (Phoenix House Ltd/Dent, 1957) contains a comprehensive summary of the early explorations of the Napes and Haskett-Smith's influence on Lake District climbing; A. J. 1976: *The Napes Pinnacle* by W. P. Haskett-Smith (a reprint of the original first-ascent account published in the *Pall Mall Budget*, 1890)

Note: The Wasdale Crack route up the Needle was upgraded to Hard Severe in the 1990 guidebook. There is no change in difficulty, the action appears to have been taken in order to register greater attention on the problems of descent.

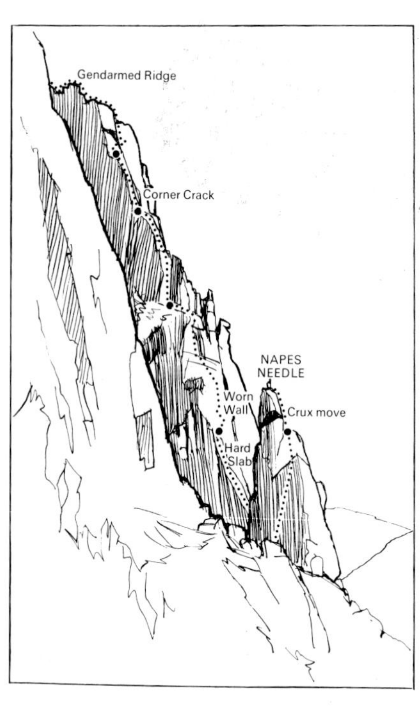

Going away from home at Christmas for the first time created creeping guilt. The cold stars disappeared behind veils of thick, yellow fog, as the train roared past rank upon rank of Manchester 'back-to-backs'. Richard, *agent-provocateur* in this enormity, suitably attired in the black cagoule of the Munich school, waited in the gloom behind Manchester Central Library. After a few cups of tea the saga of the Keswick double-decker began.

The walk along the road to Seathwaite seemed endless, but midnight Christmas cheer stopped none of the wildly driven cars, and there were no lifts. At some ungodly hour the tent went up by Styhead Tarn, after a weary stumbling plod along the ancient packhorse trail.

Rain was the excuse for a long morning doze in which the old tent dripped, but about midday it stopped, the cloud lifted a few feet and the camping gear was stowed under a convenient boulder by Kern Knotts. Thin sleet touched the fell tops and not a person stirred. A raw nor'wester drove ragged clouds in tattered strands by the Napes, and howled wildly in the narrow gully below the Needle. What a Christmas Day!

The Needle was the symbol of our purpose. Probably little else was required of the whole outing to the Lake District. Chapter and verse of selected passages from *Nanga Parbat Pilgrimage* hummed through our brains as the rope came out and the first cracks were attempted. The holds seemed terrifyingly polished, lubricated by slime. The raw cold soon obscured whatever pleasure was to be found in progress, and at the windswept shoulder the pinch of wet-cold hands began to destroy my resolution; but Richard came up quickly and, with a characteristic edge and near-inflexible purpose, he attacked the final obelisk. The mantelshelf seemed impossibly polished and wet, but, after a try or two, he sat astride the summit, wrapping the rope around it as belay. In a few precarious seconds we occupied that famous block together. There are few pinnacles in British rock-climbing, and none combine such a spectacular and testing move to reach a summit with such a grandiose setting. Wasdale was desolate, a far cry from summer evenings when it seemed impossible to breathe, even on the fell tops. We were too young to feel obliged to stand on our heads on the summit, in the Haskett-Smith tradition.

With help from the rope I was soon back to the shoulder, and Richard returned with the rope protecting him in an ingenious loop over the summit. An abseil led to the base of Needle Ridge.

The ridge appeared to offer few major problems, although the early polished slab proved difficult, with sleet in the holds melting down the rock below. As the ridge narrowed to a crest, holds increased in numbers and size, and it was possible to keep off the arête where the gale seemed likely to pluck us away. A couple of little cracks were very slippery but somehow secure, with lots of hitches on which to hang our thick spliced sling. The slack rope billowed into space and, as the last rocks merged into Gable, rain pelted in from the west and cloud curtains seemed to end the day. The summit attempt was abandoned as the main ridge was climbed, and we collected our belongings and scuttled to Wasdale Head and the traditional haven of Wilson Pharaoh's barn.

There lay the glittering prizes. Richard had long been scheduled to out-eat Paul Smoker in a meat-pie competition and, as the fells remained sodden, our remaining efforts were undistinguished. We were forced to settle for cream teas and black velvets made possible by the arrival of the club treasurer, who thereby set the invaluable precedent of the statutory single embezzlement, which was to be of such service in later impecunious years.

Right: The final moves of Napes Needle. The Wasdale Crack Route has been taken, following the obvious shadowy crack facing the camera to gain a stance on the shoulder. A very precarious move follows, to gain the climber's present position. The top is then easily reached. *Climber: Martin Richardson*

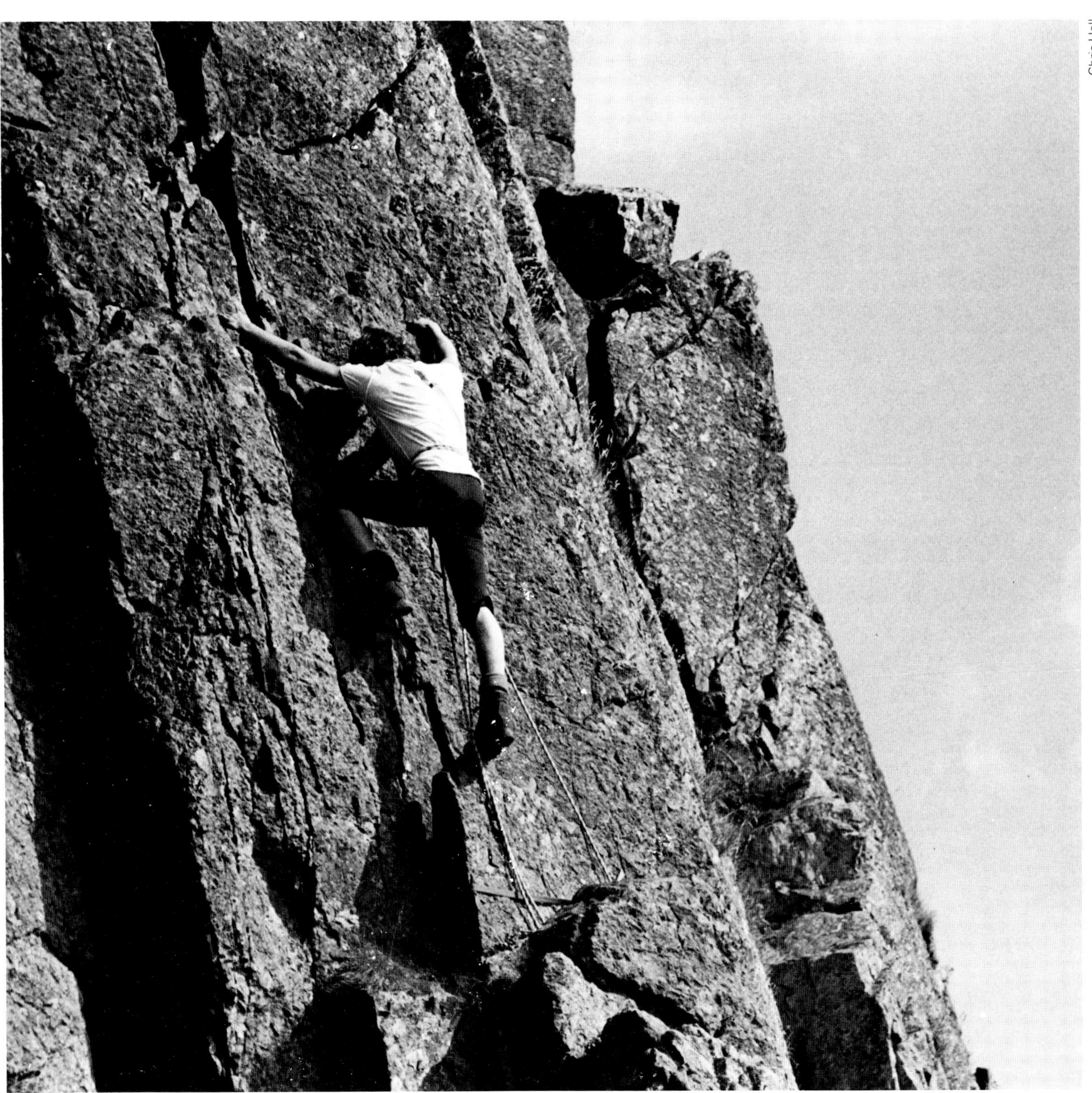

Chris Hall

Left: Negotiating the difficult moves on Napes Needle. This polished mantelshelf move is tricky to reverse. Runners should be left in place and reclipped on descent. Some leaders also fix up backrope systems over the summit block to safeguard an escape. Abseiling is not recommended. *Climbers: Unknown*

Above: The short steep wall on the second pitch of Needle Ridge. *Climber: John Harding*

29 Tophet Wall

by Dennis Gray

Route Tophet Wall, Severe, 245ft.
Cliff The Napes, Great Gable.
First Ascents H. M. Kelly and R. E. W. Pritchard, July 1923; Direct Start – M. de Selincourt, August 1925.
Map Reference O.S. Tourist Map to the Lake District, 1–50,000 Sheet (ref. 211099).
Guidebooks F.R.C.C. *Great Gable* by P. L. Fearnehough; *Rock Climbing in the Lake District* by Geoff Cram, Chris Eilbeck and Ian Roper.
Nearest Road A minor road at Wasdale Head (ref. 187088). It is also possible to approach from Borrowdale – nearest road at Seathwaite (ref. 235122).
Distance and time from cliff 3 miles 2,000ft. Allow 1½ hours. Both the Wasdale and Borrowdale routes converge at Sty Head Pass from where an easy angled track leads round Great Gable to the foot of the Napes.
Good Conditions The wall can remain greasy in the winter months but dries rapidly in summer.
Campsites and Bunkhouses F.R.C.C. Huts Brackenclose (Wasdale) and Salving House (Borrowdale). Campsites in Wasdale and Borrowdale.
Bibliography *A Progress in Mountaineering* by J. H. B. Bell (Oliver and Boyd, 1950) contains a brief account of the climb and an interesting comparison of English and Scottish gradings; F.R.C.C. Journal 1924: *Tophet Wall* by H. M. Kelly.

Note: Tophet Wall was upgraded to Hard Severe in 1990.

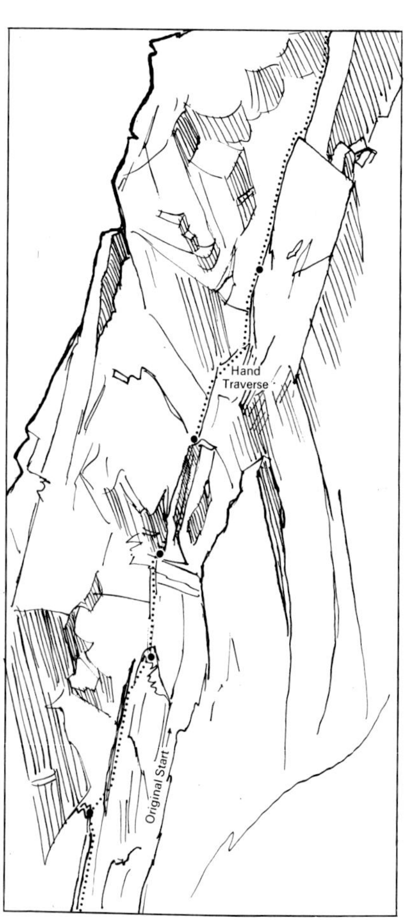

Easter 1950 was early. Snow was much in evidence on the high fells of Lakeland, and a succession of north-easterly blizzards had put down a thick, wet mantle of the stuff, which covered the screes and clung to the ledges and holds of the crags. I was a mere fourteen years of age at the time, but kept awesome company of a kind that planned daring deeds, took on mighty odds and carried the thing out to its bitter end, whatever the cost to flesh, bone or nerve.

Pete Greenwood was a few years older than me. Of medium height, dark and lithe in appearance, he could have been a Latin or even a Mexican. Extremely gymnastic, daring and agile, he meant to be a name in the climbing firmament. And he did indeed go on to make many 'firsts' in the Lake District (Hell's Groove, Pegasus, Angel's Highway, Thirlmere Eliminate, etc.) which mark him out as one of the great but unacknowledged masters of his time on rock. But, funnily enough, once having reached his self-appointed goal, he discarded the rôle of grand master which others so rightfully bask in and enjoy. Like another contemporary, Ron Moseley of the Rock and Ice, he hung up his climbing boots, took on the world of commerce and industry, and is now, I believe, a highly respected (and well heeled!) businessman. In 1951, however, he was feeling his way in the worlds of climbing and adulthood, and this seemed to involve him in attempts to find his limits, his weaknesses and his strengths. Being quick to temper, that often meant getting into fights, and it was nothing for him at seventeen to challenge grown men, giving away many stones in weight. The opposition was sometimes of such strength and power that his own beating was inevitable, but Pete took such drubbings in good heart and never gave best until he lay battered into unconsciousness or had collapsed from sheer physical exhaustion. Within a few days he would recover and he was soon ready for the next flare-up, when he would wade in once more. Sometimes, of course, against all odds, he would knock hell out of the opposition.

He had the same approach to his climbing. He took some mighty falls, and survived some incredible events, but, as already mentioned, he also produced some of the best

Chris Hall

new climbs in Britain for his era. Frankly, such drive, violence and ambition frightened my young heart, and at times rocked my notions of 'decent' living to their foundations; but there was a strong bond between us and I would have followed him wherever he cared to lead.

Having hitch-hiked to the Lakes from West Yorkshire, we bivied the night in Borrowdale. Early next day we walked up through snow to Sty Head, accompanied by Fred Williams. Older than both of us, Fred was the exact opposite to Pete in temperament. Tall and very good looking, calm and reflective, he was quiet and efficient in everything he did. We stopped off at Kern Knotts, and Pete led the famous Crack. Wearing boots the like of which today's young novices would not under any circumstances be seen in, we battled our way to the top, finding the wet and cold rock almost too much. But now for the Tophet Wall.

In 1951, Tophet Wall had a reputation akin to that of, say, Cloggy's White Slab today, and it owed its fame to a rare feature at that time – media exposure! It had been the subject of a major photographic essay and article in one of the popular magazines of the period, a very unusual occurrence then. We had a copy of this, and, as picture after picture unfolded the secrets of the wall, we set our young hearts on climbing it. We had no guidebooks, but we got details about climbs by hearsay, or by copying them out of old manuals in reference libraries. We had talked about the Tophet Wall, or at least I had, until it had acquired an aura that is difficult to imagine in this age of instant knowledge and immediate information.

Just getting from Kern Knotts to the foot of Tophet Wall was no easy task, but Pete kicked manfully up the snow-covered screes of Hell's Gate. Gradually, a bulging rock wall appeared, looming over the left bank of the shoot and looking very impressive. The day was dark and drear, and, without Pete to push us along, we would certainly never have gone near the place in such conditions.

We reached the foot of the prominent overhanging crack which marks the start of the climb, and proceeded to change our footgear. Peter produced his by then famous Bata boots (the PA of 1951 – a kind of brown baseball boot) and we put on our ubiquitous black 'gym' pumps. We then pulled on our socks over the outsides of these, for the whole face was running with water and experience taught us that socks over rubbers held good for such days. Not surprisingly, no other party was anywhere in evidence.

Peter led off up the wall at the side of the crack, climbing on 120ft. of full-weight nylon

Opposite page: The first pitch of Tophet Wall. *Climber: John Vincent*

Above: Completing the second pitch of the climb. It is easy to link the first two guidebook pitches, as these climbers have done. *Climbers: John Vincent and Julian Summers*

Previous page: Tophet Wall's hand traverse pitch, sensationally situated in the centre of the wall. *Climber: John Vincent*

Stephen Reid

Above: Starting the hand traverse on Pitch 4 of Tophet Wall. *Climber: Jilly Reid*

rope (our first ever). Fred belayed him and I stood by, almost quaking at the thought of the struggle to come. Our leader moved left after a bit, then managed to lodge himself in the crack, while water poured about him. A quick succession of lay-back moves and he was up the first pitch and belayed on a sizeable perch. At that time, the first two pitches were known in climbing circles as the 'Direct Start', for it is possible to traverse into the climb after this section along an easy terrace; but the young Greenwood would have greeted any such suggestion with hoots of derision, so we followed his lead as best we could. Fred neatly balanced his way upwards, but I found myself unable to match his air of aplomb. Pete then led on rightwards across a steepening wall, making a rising traverse from left to right, to end up once again on a ledge which, he informed us, lacked good belays. Again Fred followed comfortably, but I was gripped every inch of the way, unsettled by strong wind, wet rock and cold fingers, and conscious that a slip would mean an arching fall. We had no running belays on this pitch, although Pete was one of the first persons in the U.K. to carry large quantities of thin nylon slings for looping over spikes and round chockstones. Greenwood acquired these nylon slings well ahead of any 'gear' dealer in the country, taking advantage of undisclosed sources at his work place; indeed it was he who first introduced Joe Brown to such methods of protection, and he kept the Llanberis idol of later years initially supplied with such goodies.

Gingerly I worked my way up, while Pete encouraged me by saying that if I did fall he might have to let me go, as the belays were none too good. This was, of course, a jest, but it was sufficient to make my final landing feel like dry land after days in an open boat. Thankfully, I pulled up the last little wall and on to the sizeable ledge occupied by the other two. In stepping over, I tore a hole in my right sock: my best socks ruined already! Socks over rubbers or PAs really do work in the wet, but the price is high: a wet week in Wales once cost me thirteen pairs of such hosiery, sacrificed on the altar of climbing ambition.

The next pitch was known as the crux! A short but steep wall had to be climbed on small holds, made harder by the water being sprayed from above. Pete hitched up his pants and set forth. All was well for a few feet but then he stuck, with water running down his jacket sleeves and his fingers obviously frozen. A fall seemed imminent to me, but not to our Bradford Lad: somehow, despite the conditions, he kept control. Indeed, in my experience, Pete never seemed to lose his control, however bad things became. Even if actually about to part company with the rock or drop his infamous 'Red Hunter' bike on a death bend, he would somehow keep calm and spy out the best landing! This time, however, all was well: hanging by his left hand, he warmed the fingers of his right in his mouth, then made a sudden swing leftward followed by a quick series of pulls, and he was up. He landed in a comfortable corner, despite the wet, and, with the rope held by him almost directly above, Fred and I also managed the pitch, although not without some anxious moments.

The next section was a straightforward crack, green and wet with slime. It yielded to gritstone techniques and, after about 25ft., our leader was once again in another corner and well belayed on its right wall. We quickly followed and Pete then built himself up comfortably until a sensational swing right took him out of our range of vision. The howling wind made communication difficult, but a series of tugs on the rope told us that he was belayed. In following, I was happy to find that after the swing right one landed on incredible hand-holds. A sort of semi-hand-traverse, under overhangs of impressive dimensions, led into yet another cosy nook, which was thankfully out of the wet. From here, I climbed up to join the others, who were belayed in an awesome position out on a rib below a pinnacle. Here it was wet again, and by now we must have looked a pretty sorry crew. My cut-down raincoat, tattered trousers and shredded socks must have marked me out as a potential hypothermia case for sure, but, as we had never heard of such matters, we simply kept up our spirits by being unkind to one another in a not-too-serious banter of insults. Fred was obviously getting as worried as me, but Pete was by

Right: The last difficult pitch of Tophet Wall. The leader is climbing the crack above the pinnacle. *Climbers: John Vincent and Julian Summers*

Chris Hall

now bubbling: 'It's all over lads – just a walk from here on.' I remained unconvinced!

Pete swung up the rib almost hand over hand, then, after yet another swing right, the rope began running swiftly. It ran and ran . . . then stopped! 'Must be getting a belay,' suggested Fred, but nothing happened for half an hour, except that it began to snow. We learnt later that hikers were getting themselves lost all over the Lakes, that people were being buried in avalanches, and that sheep were dying like flies. Meanwhile, we were not amused ourselves. 'Oh God, we'll be lucky to get down if a real blizzard sets in!' I moaned, almost whimpering now. The rope became tight between Fred and Pete, and Fred just had to move. Pete was on his way to the top, snow or no snow! Fred had to go, like it or not, and soon the same fate befell me. I was terrified at the thought that we were now all moving together, and I pictured one of us slipping and dragging the other two along with him. But I need not have worried, for Pete was by now well anchored on the ridge and, as I swung off the top of a pinnacle and into an easy jamming crack, the rope twanged at top 'E'. A sensational move and it was all over, except for about 30ft. of steep ground which the other two heaved me up, protesting, kicking steps, sliding and slithering, finally to reach the ridge which marked the end of the climb. We could look down now into the swirling cauldron of Hell's Gate (or, at least, into what we thought was Hell's Gate) and up through a momentary clearing in the spindrift to Westmorland Crags. Somewhere in that direction, a little way along the ridge, we should find an easy descent gully, not to be taken lightly in socks over rubbers, with snow about, but a mere scramble in summer. But what did we care about such things? Tophet Wall was behind us, we were heroes (or so I thought) and, with a man like Pete at the helm, all seemed possible to me then. However, credibility was later stretched to the limit, when darkness caught up with us as we struggled down through the snow. There followed a night out at Sty Head–Kern Knotts, but that is another story! When you are young, no discomfort is too much (nor should it be) to stop you trying to achieve the climbs of your dreams!

30 New West Climb and Rib and Slab Climb

by C. Douglas Milner

Classic rock must, of course, be linked with classic climbing styles, and for some of us the Golden Age of British climbing was between the wars, when such styles reached their zenith. We went to the mountains for pleasure, and had no thought of character-building, adventure-training, competition or publicity.

Equipment was cheap and simple: a pair of clinker-nailed walking boots and sixty or perhaps a hundred feet of full weight manilla. The orthodox used 'Alpine Club' rope (with the red thread), while a few foolhardy fellows diced with death by using Brand X (without the red thread). Clothes were old and patched, not to say scruffy, and cut-down macs served as anoraks. Like the Sikhs, we didn't have crash helmets.

We had to follow the route as laid down, or it didn't count. Sometimes, a tempting jug-handle could not be used, if it belonged to the adjacent climb. Pitons were, of course, unthinkable, and even slings were improper. There was one exception: a sling to stand in was allowed to be fitted on the little spike behind the chockstone of the Great Flake on the Central Buttress of Scafell. We were not quite in the Norfolk jacket and Deerstalker era, with its strenuous gully and chimney climbing. More open work was the thing, calling for some modest skill and style, rather than muscle. Ideal for the dilettante who graduated from strenuous fell-walking with a sigh of relief, as he found rock-climbing a welcome refuge for the lazy man.

The sight of Pillar Rock must have inspired many walkers to take up climbing. It is a magnificent buttress, projecting from the slope of Pillar Fell and separated from it by an 80ft. gap. The north, or valley, face drops in two tiers for a total distance of 500ft., the summit of the buttress and the apex of the lower tier being known as High Man and Low Man respectively. The whole buttress is composed of steep and extensive crags, seamed here and there by impressive gullies and chimneys. Except for the line of weakness of the Old West route, the western flank of the rock is particularly fine and open. At the north-west angle, the Nor'-Nor'-West and North-West climbs give between 400 and 450 ft. of sustained climbing to the Low Man, after which about 200ft. of easier climbing leads to the High Man. The high angle of the western flank proper is sustained as far as the West Jordan gully, which descends from the Jordan gap, where the buttress ends. Our two selected climbs are to be found not far from that gully.

Pillar Rock has a long and interesting history, which is fully related in the Fell and Rock Club Guide to the area. It was first climbed in 1826 by an Ennerdale man, John Atkinson, via the rock and turf slopes between the High Man and the Low Man, now known as the 'Old' West. Few further ascents were made until 1863, when the Slab and Notch approach was discovered on the east side. Thereafter, interest in Pillar increased and George Seatree estimated that, by 1876, over a hundred ascents had been made via these two routes, or other easy variants still used today as descents from the High Man.

Between the wars, Pillar seemed to bear much the same relationship to Lakeland climbing as Lliwedd to that of Wales, in that it was apparently fully explored and provided good climbs of all ranges from Moderate to Very Severe. When post-war climbing moved into higher gear, and equipment became more elaborate, the younger generation rather neglected the older cliffs. But renewed attention to Pillar in the late 'sixties showed that it was by no means exhausted, and many new climbs have been added in the top categories, above the pre-war summit of VS. Yet the essence of this account, and indeed of this book as a whole, is to emphasize the charm and quality of climbs in the middle ranges of difficulty, being neither the oft-trodden elementary climbs nor the seldom repeated pyrotechnic displays by our estimable hard men.

Pillar provides many routes in this middle range, mainly upon sound rock, with a variety of situations in chimneys, cracks, slabs and walls, and of good length by English standards. I say 'English' advisedly, for Lliwedd in Wales, and Sron na Ciche in Skye, are but two cliffs which have climbs that are much longer.

Considerable space was given to Pillar in Haskett Smith's first ever guidebook to climbing in Britain, published in 1894. Later, George Abraham dealt with it in his *British Mountain Climbs* (1907), for by that

Routes New West Climb, Difficult (hard), 290ft.; Rib and Slab Climb, Severe, 300ft.
Cliff West Face of High Man, Pillar Rock, Ennerdale.
First Ascents New West Climb – G. D. Abraham, A. P. Abraham, C. W. Barton and J. H. Wigner, May 1901; Rib and Slab Climb – C. F. Holland, H. M. Kelly and C. G. Crawford, July 1919.
Map Reference O.S. Lake District Tourist Map, 1–50,000 Sheet (ref. 172123).
Guidebooks F.R.C.C. *Pillar Group* by A. G. Cram; *Rock Climbing in the Lake District* by Geoff Cram, Chris Eilbeck and Ian Roper.
Nearest Road A forestry road in Ennerdale, directly below the crag (ref. 171131). It is essential to arrive early as a barrier at Bowness Knott is manned and enforced during the summer.
Distance and time from cliff ½ mile/1,200ft. Allow 30 minutes. Park cars off the road (it is important not to block it), and take a forestry track directly up the hill to the cliff. A longer (2-hour) approach can be made from Wasdale by the Black Sail Pass.
Good Conditions Allow three dry days in all but the summer months. The rock can be very greasy when wet, and the climbs then become considerably harder.
Campsites and Bunkhouses Camping in Ennerdale and Wasdale. Youth Hostels at Ennerdale (Gillerthwaite) and Black Sail. F.R.C.C. Hut Brackenclose in Wasdale.
Bibliography *C.C. Journal*, 1901, contains an account of the first ascent of New West Climb; *Mountaineering in Britain* by R. W. Clark and E. C. Pyatt (Phoenix House Ltd/Dent, 1957); F.R.C.C. Journal 1919: *New Climbs in the Wasdale District* by C. F. Holland has a first-ascent description of Rib and Slab Climb.

Chris Hall

Right: The third pitch of New West (small photo) – the slabby traverse leading to the foot of the crux chimney. The chimney (large photo) gives awkward climbing to gain the exposed upper section of the crag. *Climber: Alistair Hopkins*

Left: The final slabs of New West Climb. Jordan Gap is on the right and final pitch of Rib and Slab takes the cleaner rock to the left of the climber. *Climbers: Charlie Weller and Pete Grant*

time it had emerged from the Victorian period of university reading parties who did early ascents by the short routes, and had acquired a few good 'mountaineering' routes, such as Walker's Gully, led by Owen Glynne Jones, and Haskett Smith's own North Climb.

Almost the first of the new, more open, routes was the New West – so called to distinguish it from Atkinson's 1826 original. It was brilliantly devised by the Abrahams, up the only line of weakness on the West Face of the High Man.

New West is graded as Difficult – a low level in these days of HVS and XS routes – but it has great quality for its class. Like almost all the climbs on the west side, from Appian Way to the South-West, it is of respectable length, some 300ft. It is continuously really steep, so that from the first steps you experience agreeable exposure, and its standard is maintained pitch by pitch. It has continuity: you can't walk off at any point. Once committed, you must either go up or go back. The traffic on it has ensured that all loose turf and rock have long since gone, but the holds and belays are all there. Pitches are short, averaging only 25ft., and provide examples of most standard problems: ribs, grooves, slabs and one chimney, perhaps the most difficult bit. The chimney, which provides orthodox back-and-foot work for a few feet, eventually became quite tricky in nails, due to the rock wearing smooth. The adoption of the vibram sole has made this, and indeed most climbs, easier *in dry conditions*. This must be emphasized, for many popular Lakeland climbs have worn smooth, mainly due to the volume of traffic, but also the fine-grained character of the volcanic ash in the Lakes, so different from the rough gritstone of the Pennines, the gabbro of Skye or even the felstone of North Wales. The greatest danger with any rubber sole is on damp or mossy holds, rather than on really wet ones. Indeed it is surprising that no one today seems to use the Eastern Alpine *Kletterschuhen* with soles of felted fabric. Support for this idea comes from the fact, or maybe the legend, that Pendlebury made the first ascent of his traverse in carpet slippers! While Lakeland climbing is a sport in

Stephen Reid

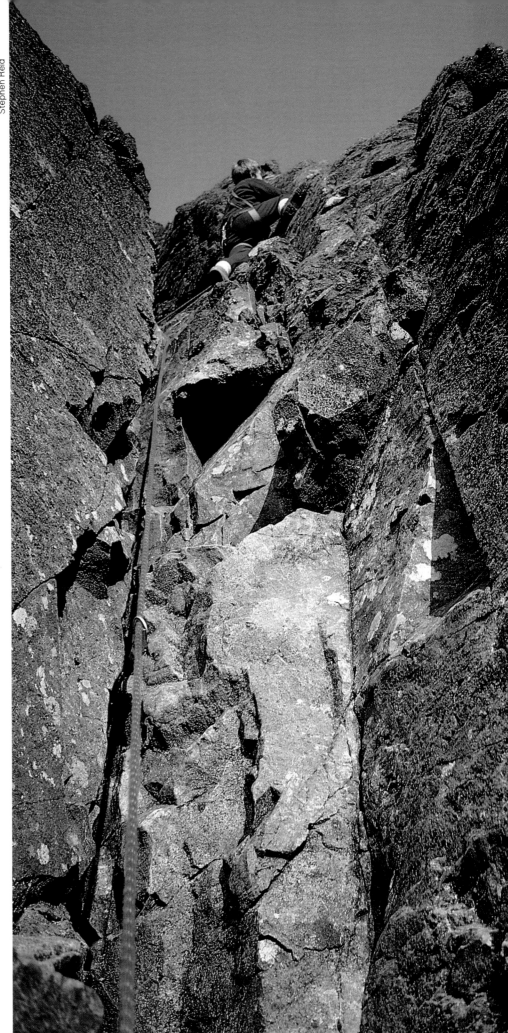

itself, the younger climber with his eyes on the Alps or Dolomites will rightly think of a climbing descent as essential training: the New West is one eminently suitable place to do it.

Obviously if, having read thus far, anyone is disposed to look closely at Pillar, the latest Fell and Rock Club guidebook should be consulted. It is pointless to take up space here with detailed instructions, nor can I enliven my account with any hairbreadth escapes. My parties have stuck to the maxim ascribed to Jack Longland, that 'British climbing is organized cowardice'. Or, as John Hirst puts it in one of his songs:

We're mountaineers most disingenuous
And of ourselves we take great care.
We never conquer courses strenuous,
When danger lurks we're never there.

I still remember with what trepidation Eric Byrom and I stood at the foot of the climb, forty-five years ago, before making our first ascent. Of course we were in nails, for to some extent that was part of the rules.

Gordon Gadsby

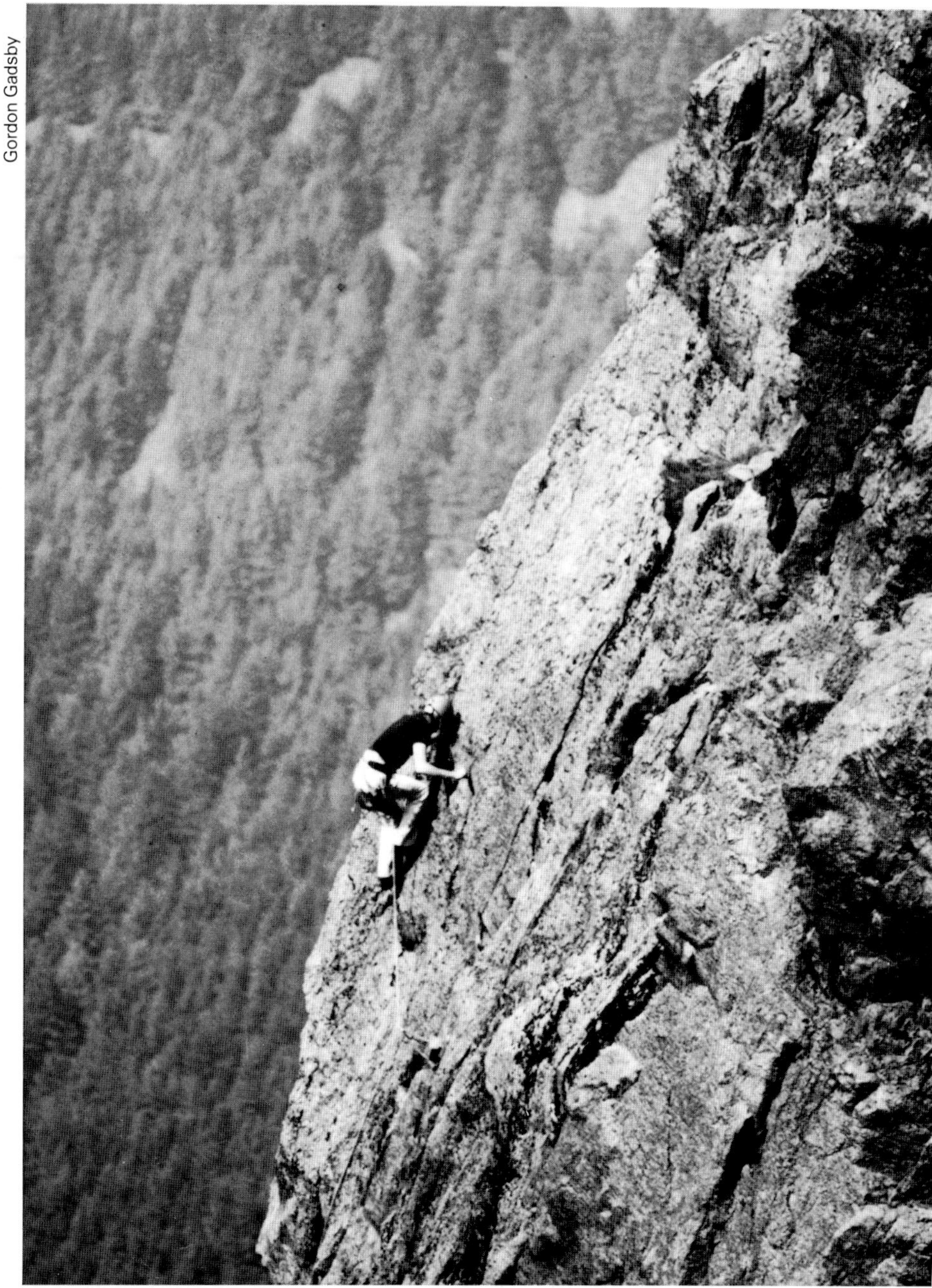

Above: Looking across the final 'blistered' slab of Rib and Slab from the adjoining final pitch of New West Climb. *Climber: Unknown*

The formidable R. S. T. Chorley (now Lord Chorley) once laid it down that climbing in rubbers was improper because 'it didn't give the rocks a chance'.

In those days you loyally worked your way through the list of Diffs. and V.Diffs., before sliding quietly into the tail end of the 'experts'. At this point you craftily switched from rope to line – half-weight manilla. In short, you climbed on 'string', which was useless for holding a falling leader and merely served, it was said, 'to maintain the illusion that man is a gregarious animal'. But you also slid into rubbers – the best were six old pence a pair at Woolworths. Thus equipped, you could head for the delights of the delicate Severes, and even the occasional VS, 'on a warm, windless day'.

Which brings me to Rib and Slab. This is quite a contrast to the New West, which follows, as I have said, a natural line up the cliff. Rib and Slab is a deliberate selection of steep, open pitches, starting left of the New West, and crossing over at mid-height by a beautiful little traverse of a wall with small square-cut holds to reach the Slab. This is ascended to a belay common to both climbs, and then directly to the top of the Low Man. The climb was invented by my old friend, the late C. F. Holland, in 1919, when the post-war surge of exploration began the modern manner. Either by himself or with Harry Kelly, he devised many routes fairly described as 'elegant', a word often seen in Italian guidebooks to their own regions. Holland derived much of his flair for high exposure from his Dolomite climbing, and he had been on the original ascent of C.B. in 1914.

Rib and Slab is rightly graded as Severe and has the same basic qualities as the New West: a sustained standard with continuous exposure. Admittedly, it is unlike the New West in that you can escape – in fact to the older climb – but of course the discipline and charm of these 'stylized' routes lies in doing nothing of the kind.

Few expeditions have stayed longer in my memory than ascents of Rib and Slab, in rubbers, on a warm, dry afternoon, with the sun on the West Face. The climb is well suited to vibrams or PAs, firmer soles being better than the old flexible ones in dealing with the square-cut holds found at many points.

Having tried to give you the good news, now for the bad. Pillar is tucked away above the remote and seldom visited Ennerdale valley. Approaches from Wasdale, Buttermere or Borrowdale involve some walking, and weekend parties with little time to spare can be excused a preference for the crags around Mickledore, or the Napes on Gable.

But you should make the effort. To spur you on, I will mention that once (and once only!) Gilbert Peaker and I set out from Eskdale, over Burnmoor and the Black Sail, did a couple of routes on Pillar, and walked back. It made quite a mountain day. Try that some time.

Note: Rib and Slab (to HS) and New West Climb (to VD) were both upgraded in 1990.

31 Great Gully

by Tony Moulam

Large and rambling, Craig yr Ysfa simulates solitude at the head of Cwm Eigiau. It was neglected by climbers until 1900, perhaps because it could not be seen from their nineteenth-century haunt at Ogwen. Cox and Kretschmer (in the 1943 guidebook) report its legendary discovery through a telescope from Scafell and go on to say that, as a precipice, it 'relies too much on mere bulk and not enough on steepness.' This is a fair assessment and I do not think that anyone would regard it as 'great' in the sense that Cloggy and Scafell are, but Great Gully certainly lives up to its name. An immense cut, as if made by a giant's sword, slices straight through North Crag, providing what is generally recognized as the best gully climb in North Wales.

The first authority for this opinion was George Abraham who wrote, in *British Mountain Climbs* (1909): 'Except for the Cuillin, this is the finest climb of its kind in Britain; there is no gully or other course in Wales to compare with it for sustained interest.' After nearly seventy years of exploration, the 'other course' bit has become somewhat out of date, but Great Gully is still a classic and taxing climb. *Climbing in the Ogwen District*, the second of the Climbers' Club guides, describes it as 'exceedingly difficult and delectable . . . for strong parties only', and goes on, 'the unpretentious opening at the head of a grassy slope, and the apparent height, of which 400ft. might seem to be a liberal estimate, offer no indication of the lofty pitches which occur at convenient intervals on the course of not less than 700ft.'

I first climbed Great Gully on Boxing Day 1945. Four of us took four hours and finished in the dark. Our leader set off walking in a circle that would have lost us in the middle of the Carneddau, but two of us were too wise for that and we stumbled down to Helyg still bound with frozen knots to the recalcitrant hemp!

Thirty years on, and with two twenty-year-olds, I did it again and took six hours! My companions agreed with Archer Thomson's grading (XD!) but their epithets were certainly not 'delectable'! The climber's appreciation of entertainment has changed: even though such wet routes are more comfortable in modern waterproofs than in the tweed and woollen costumes of the first performers!

Craig yr Ysfa is not a roadside crag, although the C.E.G.B. has done its best: the track from the A5 up to Llyn Llugwy has been metalled, marring the scenery but at least speeding the climber on his way. We hardly noticed the desecration, or the rain, as we sweated up to the Saddle and squelched down below the cliff and round to the right place. Initially it was easy to scramble up and avoid the stream but soon a chockstone blocked the gully bed. A plunge into the icy water flushing the groove to its left marked real commitment to the climb and, somewhere in the next hundred feet or so, we roped.

The famous 'Door Jamb' pitch is really misnamed, as it has not yet been climbed direct except with the aid of piles of snow or pyramids of people. The smooth left wall, decorated tastefully with multi-coloured moss, is no more amenable than the smooth one on the right. An ugly, leering boulder surmounts them, and any ambition is finally quenched by the water gouting over its top. This obstacle, and the true gully line above, full of chockstones and assorted dripping vegetation, were avoided on the right. We huddled in the gully bed gazing up at the Great Chimney – scene of many mighty struggles.

The walls are set apart at the maximum for back and foot technique. Progress can be made by a sort of buttock rotation on the smooth left wall, but only slowly and with considerable effort. Luckily it is possible to decorate the crack, between various chockstones, with nuts and slings; so much easier than having to untie, thread the rope behind a conveniently jammed stone and then tie on again! Eventually an enticing ledge appears where the right wall stops. It is still a stretch to reach a convenient and not *very* loose spike to aid a transfer to the belvedere and a well-earned rest beside a handsome belay.

The leader's pleasure is here enhanced by the outward view of Gleddr Ffordd as a backdrop to Great Gully Pinnacle – seemingly yearning to return to the void – and by the grunts and groans of those who follow, which waft up satisfyingly from below. Looking inward, a big black 'V' defines the Great

Route Great Gully, Very Difficult, 725ft.
Cliff Craig yr Ysfa, Carnedd Llywelyn.
First Ascent J. M. Archer Thomson, R. I. Simey, W. G. Clay, April 1900.
Map Reference O.S. Tourist Map to Snowdonia, 1–50,000 Sheet (ref. 694637).
Guidebooks C.C. *Carneddau* by Les Holliwell; *Rock Climbing in Wales* by Ron James.
Nearest Road A5, three miles west of Capel Curig (ref. 688602), where a metalled service road leads up the hillside to Ffynnon Llugwy. The climb can also be approached up Cwm Eigiau from Tal-y-Bont, to a parking place at Hafod-y-rhiw (ref. 724649), or easier driving to the road head in the centre of the valley (ref. 732663).
Distance and time from cliff From A5 3 miles/1,600ft. Allow 2 hours. From Hafod-y-rhiw – 2 miles/1,300ft. Allow 1½ hours.
Good Conditions The climb goes in any conditions and is usually damp or wet. In winter heavy snow makes the climb easier, except for the top pitch.
Campsites and Bunkhouses Camping near the A5 at Gwern-gof-Isaf or in Cwm Eigiau. C.C. Hut, Helyg, on the A5, and Leicester Mountaineering Club hut in Cwm Eigiau (ref. 714638).
Bibliography *Rock Climbing in North Wales* by G. D. and A. P. Abraham (Abraham, Keswick, 1906); *Climbing in the Ogwen District* by J. M. Archer Thomson (Edward Arnold, 1910).

Tony Moulam

Above left: The start of the Great Chimney pitch, which involves wide bridging and backing and footing moves. *Climbers: Anona Timberlake and Dave Nicholson*

Above right: The leader, triumphant, on gaining the outer bridge on the Great Cave Pitch. *Climber: Anona Timberlake*

Opposite page: Craig yr Ysfa's Great Buttress. Great Gully is the shadowy cleft in the centre of the picture and the Amphitheatre is on the left.

Cave and the eye leaps to it, ignoring two more pitches that intervene. These proved to be more annoying than difficult, so that we eventually crept up the scree slope to the back of the imposing cave. The smooth left wall (true right) of the gully and the broken leaning crags opposite crowded in claustrophobically. Over our heads the inner chockstone seemed about to crush us, and dazzling light from the now snowy landscape confused our anxious glances to the outer bridge, and safety beyond difficulty. Vapour rose from our breath, making the humid depths of the cave resemble Euston in the steam age.

Having wrapped a tape round a chockstone trapped by the inner bridge, Dave cavorted briefly on the small holds on the wall. Quite suddenly he seemed to have had enough and subsided, ululating, to the ground, suspended from his sling. This excitement discouraged the rest of us but I soon persuaded Anona that she should lead, for I was much older and wanted to take some photographs. So we emerged, satisfied, to the anticlimactic runnel at the top.

All in all, Great Gully is a challenging and satisfying climb. For its type it is first class, with lots of pitches of an even standard. The interest is continuous, for there is not enough scrambling to make the climb boring; rather, it provides an interlude in which the eye can appreciate bold rock scenery, while the body relaxes and recovers for the next effort of getting up. The two main pitches are unique, with the most difficult reserved for the end. Even then, the solution to the final problem is complicated and demanding, making a fitting climax to the climb.

32 Gashed Crag, First Pinnacle Rib and Grooved Arête

by Showell Styles

Routes Gashed Crag, Difficult (hard), 565ft.; First Pinnacle Rib (also known as Overlapping Rib Route), Difficult (hard), 580ft.; Grooved Arête, Hard Very Difficult, 700ft.
Cliff The East Face of Tryfan.
First Ascents Gashed Crag – H. B. Buckle and G. Barlow, September 1902; First Pinnacle Rib – E. W. Steeple, G. Barlow and A. H. Doughty, September 1914 (though sections in the upper part of the route had been climbed as early as 1894 by J. M. A. Thomson and H. Hughes); Grooved Arête – E. W. Steeple, A. G. Woodhead, G. Barlow, H. E. Bowren and A. H. Doughty, April 1911.
Map Reference O.S. Tourist Map to Snowdonia, 1–50,000 Sheet (ref. 665596).
Guidebooks C.C. *Tryfan and Glyder Fach* by A. J. J. Moulam; *Rock Climbing in Wales* by Ron James.
Nearest Road The A5 below the Milestone Buttress (ref. 664603).
Distance and time from cliff 1 mile/1,400ft. Allow 1¼ hours. It is best to approach by the Milestone Buttress, either starting up a route there, or climbing the steep scree path to the left to gain the North Ridge of Tryfan at a prominent shoulder. It is then possible to climb up and round to gain the Heather Terrace which leads to the foot of the climbs. Alternatively a slightly longer route leads from Gwern-y-Gof Uchaf.
Good Conditions Clean rock and good holds enable these climbs to be done in virtually any conditions, without an undue increase in standard. In summer they dry quickly but in winter they can be verglassed in places. On sunny winter days the face often provides very pleasant conditions.
Campsites and Bunkhouses Both can be found at Gwern-y-Gof Uchaf and Gwern-y-Gof Isaf (ref. 673663 and 685661).
Bibliography *Rock Climbing in North Wales* by G. D. and A. P. Abraham (Abraham, Keswick, 1906); *Climbing in the Ogwen District* by J. M. Archer Thomson (Edward Arnold, 1910); *Let's Go Climbing* by C. F. Kirkus (Nelson, 1941); *A Climber in Wales* by Showell Styles (Cornish, Birmingham, *c.* 1955); *On Climbing* by Charles Evans (Museum Press, 1956); C.C. Journal 1912 contains a first-ascent account of Grooved Arête by E. W. Steeple.

For a century and a half, travellers going westward along Telford's Holyhead Road have seen the piece-by-piece revelation as Tryfan's East Face slides into view from behind Gallt-yr-Ogof. To the outside passengers on the roof of the Holyhead Mail it was a horrid crag, dreadful in its bare and rugged steepness. George Borrow, tramping from Capel Curig to Bangor in 1854, didn't think it worth a mention in *Wild Wales*, though it was a clear day when he passed the 'wretched hovel' of Helyg. A few connoisseurs of *avant-garde* taste had perceived the charms of this most attractive of Welsh peaks, however, and the Reverend William Bingley had climbed it from the west side in 1797; it was his companion who first made the long stride from top to top of the two summit rocks, Adam and Eve, a feat that caused Bingley's blood to 'chill with horror'. But it took the newly educated eyes of rock-climbers at the end of the nineteenth century to recognize the splendid symmetry of the East Face: the three peaks with the highest in the centre, the three buttresses soaring with satisfying directness to each peak, and the straight dark gullies between the buttresses. The Gully Epoch was ending, and the delights of the buttresses were soon discovered. On each of them emerged a definitive route, the best of several, to be for fifty years and more the most popular climbs in Snowdonia for the proletariat of the climbing world.

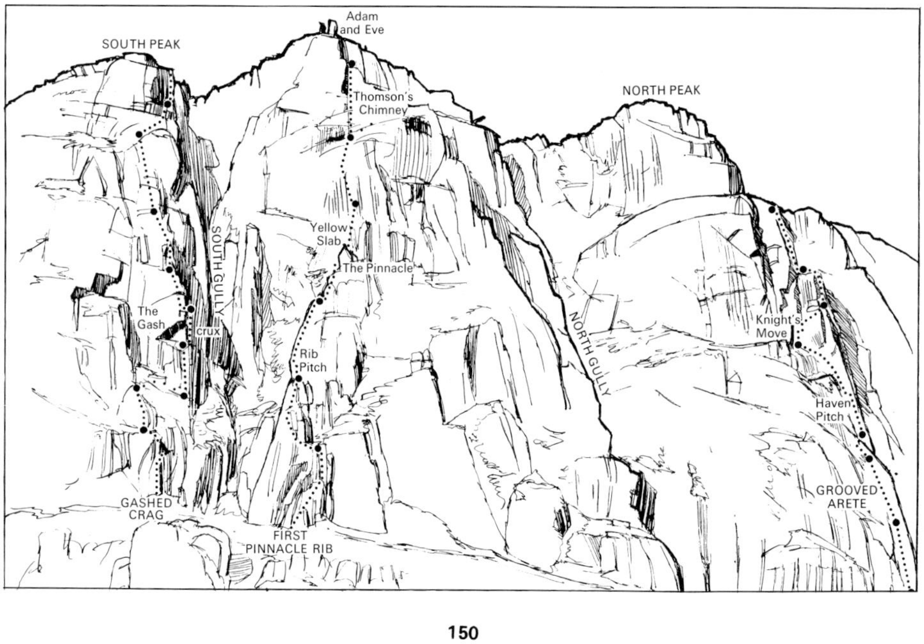

Gashed Crag Route up South Buttress, the left-hand buttress as you look up at the East Face, is my personal favourite; a route for all seasons, but decidedly an expedition in a white winter. Graded VD by Ron James, its 525ft. include a variety of position and scenery that makes the climb seem longer than it is, though all too short when it's over. The rather scrappy start is some distance left of South Gully, where the gash itself interposes gaping shark-jaws between the climber and any prospect of upward progress. Tiptoeing across the slant of the lower jaw, you sidle round the corner to the foot of a chimney so good and old-fashioned that it must have gladdened the hearts of Buckle and Barlow when they came upon it during the first ascent in 1902. Its depths are of course tenacious, contrasting with the airiness of the more stylish outside route; Tryfan everywhere induces the adjectives of those irrepressibly jovial pioneers. At the chimney-top you find yourself well down on the side-wall of the gully, in a pleasing position which is left by an equally pleasing zigzag move: a step or two rightward and then up to the left on the wall via a mantelshelf to the edge above the Gash.

Now the ridge tries to put away childish things and hold a straight and serious line, with a tricky move or two on the lower pitches of the three or four that ensue. But Tryfan rock is too good-natured to show a really hard face for long, and the difficulties ease up above. As you deal with them you can peer over the edge at Münich Climb, down on the right, where sacred Welsh rock was riven by a dastardly German piton; thereby hangs a tale. But the last pitch of Gashed Crag is a place where a little extra protection will only be disdained by the vainglorious. The nose of the final wall looms above and, by way of a hollow just round on the right of it, and an easy little groove beyond that, you come to a respectable rock platform at the foot of a vertical chimney; an inescapable pitch unless you go back and traverse left to finish up Bubbly Wall, a Severe. The chimney has some degree of exposure and an undercut bottom, and a runner goes on for most leaders before starting it. The mood of retrospect and Auld Lang Syne could well result in the leader being 'given a shoulder' here, but for proper observance of this rite he should be wearing nailed boots. Once fairly lodged in the chimney, you find enough holds to avoid any thrutching and pull out easily on to the top of South Peak. This chimney provided an icicle-draped crux when I led H. W. Tilman up the route one winter's day and heard with gratification the veteran's encomium: 'Very nice. Just not too hard to be enjoyable.'

Tilman's comment showed he was tuned-in to Tryfan. The rule here is enjoyment of the not-too-hard and, though there are a few exceptions (Belle Vue Bastion is one of them), the charm of Tryfan lies not in its challenge but in its welcome. For all its wealth of steep rock, it is for those who feel, with Wilfrid Noyce, 'there is a mountain presence behind, which has no regard for the type of activity you indulge in upon the slopes'. The routes, as Edwards plaintively commented, hardly feel serious; and pernickety folk whose indulgence is too limited to match the mountain's will always grumble at the soft options and the frequent opportunities to potter off on explorations to left or right of the chosen route. The Pinnacle Rib keeps near the rim of South Gully (opposite Gashed Crag) and allows no pottering off on that side.

The Rib has a pretty start from the Heather Terrace, which runs along the bottom of all these buttresses. By means of a rib thirty feet right of South Gully, you bypass some overhanging rock and step less strenuously on slabs leftward, gaining the back of a purposeful ridge aimed straight at Tryfan summit. Looking back over ascents of forty years, this 500ft. rib seems always afternoon, like the land of the lotus-eaters; only it was pipe-smoking, not lotus-eating, that tempted to indolence on one or more of the sunny platforms between the pitches. Not that the pitches are all that easy. One of them, the third of the climb, is a little square-cut rib that calls for care as well as skill; and on the stance at the top of it a pipe tastes doubly sweet. These are days when it doesn't do to praise tobacco too loudly, but for the leisurely climber-smoker the Tryfan buttresses are unequalled, and in the 'thirties I used to wonder whether the lack of midges in their

Ken Wilson

heathery nooks could be due to persistent impregnation with the fumes of the purifying weed.

Halfway up comes a break and an incident. Compared with the artfulness of Gashed Crag, Pinnacle Rib appears almost naïve in its openness, and the advent of the Pinnacle itself – a big flake jutting from a ledge – is a welcome change. Ashley Abraham 'amused himself by struggling up to its pointed summit' in 1905, while brother George climbed the Yellow Slab behind it. The guidebook grade of the Slab is D+, but it can be much harder; indeed, it has been said that if it was at the top of a pitch on Dinas Mot it would be considered VS. In

Above: The strenuous chimney that forms the crux of Gashed Crag. The climber has to 'make progress' by wedging techniques until it is possible to make a determined pull out on to the right wall. *Climber: John Fitzgerald*

Note: Both Gashed Crag and Pinnacle Rib were graded Very Difficult in the 1982 guidebook but the 1993 guidebook downgraded Pinnacle Rib to Difficult – this despite the fact that the Yellow Slab (4b) offers, technically, the hardest moves to be found on all three climbs. With Grooved Arête remaining as Very Difficult the relative difficulty of the climbs still remains disguised – the original *Classic Rock* grades are still the best indicators of relative difficulty.

John Fitzgerald

Ken Wilson

verglas conditions, or on an off-form day, one can move round the corner to the right and find a slightly easier route. But when form and conditions are perfect it's a pity to miss it. Winthrop Young's recipe of balance-climbing combined with continuous movement gets you up, toe-creeping from left to right for a grope to a slanting handhold, and then the customary jug-handles to a niche 40ft. above.

Then it's the ridge again for the last 150ft. – quite steep and not do indubitably sound as most of the rock hereabouts. A curving formation of parallel flakes, not unlike what you get by cutting a Chelsea bun in half, ends at a more diffuse final section. James's guidebook (*Rock Climbing in Wales*) assigns the first ascent of Pinnacle Rib to Steeple, Barlow and Doughty in 1916, but Archer Thomson had done most of it twenty years earlier, reaching the Pinnacle from the Second Pinnacle Rib farther north, and the brothers Abraham certainly climbed it all in 1905. Both of these parties evidently felt the lack of a chimney on this route, for on the easy ground above they made over to the left and finished up the vertical 60ft. cleft now called Thomson's Chimney (VD +). This was meritorious but uncalled-for. Nowadays most climbers finish at the top of the rib and walk round the summit, where they may or may not crown the ascent with the 180-year-old ritual of striding from Adam to Eve, which traditionally accords them the Freedom of Tryfan.

Tradition and association are interwoven

Opposite page: Approaching the Gash on Gashed Crag. The Pinnacle of Pinnacle Rib is in the background with the Yellow Slab to its left. *Climber: Ken Wilson*

Above left: After climbing Gashed Crag's crux chimney (see page 151) the crest of the buttress (above the Gash) is regained by a traverse across this steep wall. *Climber: Ken Wilson*

Above right: The Yellow Slab on Pinnacle Rib which offers a short section of unprotected 4b climbing above a large ledge. The climber has just completed the hard moves and has reached good holds. The upper rib continues with exposed and delightful climbing on excellent rock. *Climber: John Kingston*

Left: The magnificent 600ft East Face of Tryfan with South Buttress (Gashed Crag) on the left with the shadowy South Gully (Munich Climb taking the sunlit rib in the centre of the main shadow) separating it from Central Buttress (Pinnacle Ribs). North Buttress (Grooved Arête) is on the right, its upper headwall (the Terrace Wall) being breached by Scars Climb and Belle Vue Bastion.

John Woodhouse

with the web of routes on Tryfan. You stand or cling where the fathers of the sport stood or clung; where, after them, the great men of the Golden Age – Mallory and Herford, Finch and Holland and the rest – took their first steps on rock. Kirkus was here in the late 'twenties, soloing Central Route and straightening out a V.Diff. or two, and about the same time Ivan Waller, with gramophone music from Belle Vue Terrace to encourage him, led the first VS, Belle Vue Bastion. The Bastion is the right-hand edge of Terrace Wall, in the centre of North Buttress and halfway up it. Round the corner on the right of it are the upper pitches of Grooved Arête (VD+), said by Moulam to be 'as good as anything of the kind in Wales'.

E. W. Steeple led Grooved Arête in 1911, with one of those five-man ropes beloved of the old-timers; an unusual crowd for this leader, for Steeple normally climbed with one partner, Guy Barlow, and was retiring to the point of unsociability. I have a shamefaced memory of E.W.S. when I was at the beginning of my climbing days and he was near the end of his. It was on a large and heterogeneous club meet that included some elderly non-climbers. I found myself walking across moorland with a small insignificant stranger, large of nose and drooping of moustache, who could hardly have been more unlike my idea of a great climber and was probably (I thought) a very moderate hillwalker. Having just made my first lead on a rock, I was at some pains to explain to him the delights of Milestone Buttress and assure him that even now, with a steady leader, he might experience those delights himself. He listened with quiet courtesy and, when I'd finished, remarked that he did in fact regard rock-climbing as a very fine sport. But it was not until next day that I learned his name, and that E. W. Steeple had thirty first ascents in Skye to his credit besides the Welsh climbs that included Grooved Arête.

The one defect of Grooved Arête as a line up North Buttress is the definite break at a little below half its height, where a 100ft. walk to the right has to be taken to get into position for the good things higher up. But the break indicates a change of character

Left: The upper part of Pinnacle Rib with Gashed Crag in the background. *Climber: John Kingston*

Right: The Knight's Move (large photo) on Grooved Arête followed by a rising traverse to the ledge at the top right corner of the slab. The smaller photo shows the same exposed situation looking down the Knight's Slab. *Climbers: Ron and Barbara James*

and so doesn't spoil the artistry of the route. The ribs and grooves sprouting upwards for 350ft. from Heather Terrace level produce their considerable difficulties from a typical Tryfan slope – goat-browsing, pipe-smoking territory – which ends under the steeper barrier running across the mountain northward from Terrace Wall. Here is the rightward walk across to a long curving rib on a gully edge. And, once on the rib – the arête proper – you see that seriousness has crept in. Not that the rib is steep or difficult, but it leads up and up into what looks like a dead-end of rock, a great block of wall rising to overhangs with more and darker steepness still above. Pipes are tapped out and put in pockets here, not to be relit for 300ft.

The rib hoists you gently enough for 100ft. and then becomes too steep for comfort, pushing you left and up, left and up, until at last you end on the fine grass ledge of the Haven, along which you walk to the left at the base of the verticalities. This snug stance is comfort for the needy. For what comes next is the crux, and sixty years have made it no easier than it was for Steeple and his quartet of followers. The steep wall against which you rub a shoulder is topped by a slab scarcely less steep, and both are hard if conditions are at all greasy. A second who is both confident and competent can go some way towards making up for the lack of the usual Tryfan jug-handles here.

A wide crack on the left of the wall gives access to the bottom corner of the slab above. The square bollard at the top of the crack is a good place for a runner as you cross the chessboard squares of thin cracks up to the right-hand corner, the Knight's Move, and ooze round it on the edge of all things into a sloping niche out of sight of your second. This is a superb position, beyond anything on the other two routes of my trilogy, and would be a ticklish one were it not for the excellent belay just where you want it; of course you expect nothing less from Tryfan. Seated and secure, you look down past your boots to the far-sunken valley and the ribbon of road winding eastward into the haze of distance, and praise the gods that you are where you are.

But the end is not yet. Sixty feet of dark groove behind the niche are alternative to he arête on its right which Edwards thought pleasanter' and Moulam 'sensational', and)y either way you arrive under the rough)lack rock which is the backside of Terrace Wall. There is a platform here by which you :an walk off to the right and up the easy slopes beneath North Tower, but the direct ine up the black buttress is furnished with eal Tryfan holds and is the proper finish. But what am I saying? The proper finish, ıaturally, is on the summit by Adam and Eve, a ten-minute scramble away. You :limb the peak, and it doesn't much matter vhich route you came up by so long as 'ou enjoyed it. Tryfan is that sort of moun-:ain.

Ken Wilson

33 Milestone Direct Route

by Barbara James

Eric, my leader, was 100ft. up, a head without a body but with a voice. The hemp waistline was cutting me in half, the footholds were impossibly small and the handholds (which were being described by regular yells from above and below) did not exist. Eventually Eric's patience disappeared, and another gibbering novice was lowered unceremoniously to the ground.

The place was the Milestone Buttress and the climb was the Direct Route. An obvious central ridge, facing the tenth milestone on the A5, divides the steeper, greasy back of the buttress from the slabby, polished front side. The ridge is climbable by three lines. The Ordinary Route (Moderate) wanders up easier alternatives, mainly on the left of the ridge; the Super Direct, a series of VS boulder problems, takes a direct line up the ridge itself; while the Direct Route is usually started on the right of the ridge, which it then joins and follows by a series of interlinking cracks and chimneys. All three routes are very close together and often share stances.

It was some years and even more climbs before I found myself earning a living by taking pupils up the very route on which I had had such ignominious beginnings. However, the years had not dulled the painful memories, and I vowed that for *my* beginners it would be different. The starting slab, the diagonal traverse left, the move up and left on to a smaller slab and the further moves into a corner would never be rushed so that a second would be left unaware. The delightful swing left out on to the main crest of the ridge would be savoured, not suffered. The variations, too: the more direct start leading up a groove to a wild move round an overhang and then round to the right to join the slab. Whatever the way taken, this fine pitch should be enjoyed, for it is one of the most varied and interesting for its grade in Wales.

As one stands on the lip of the large ledge at the top of the first pitch, belayed to superb anchor points, there is time between tugs at your second to watch the flow of traffic on the road below and to look across to the valley Pen yr Ole Wen. That mountain can have changed little since those on the first ascent of Direct Route viewed it from this position in 1910. However, the fascination of watching a car overtaking another on a blind bend, and being able to see a third approaching fast at the same time has gone with the recent road 'improvements'. But the excitement of the climb continues. At one time, guidebooks described the rock on the front of the Milestone as 'rough'. This is not strictly true today. The rock is sound, but the small holds have become rounded and polished by a decade of novices fighting their way up the main trade-routes: Direct, Rowan and Pulpit. The Milestone is the classic beginners' crag. Correct climbing calls cascade through the air and even an occasional, 'Your left hand. No. The *other* left hand,' can be heard as yet another weary instructor reaches exasperation point.

Milestone Direct continues behind the large pinnacle and up an awkward corner to a truly leg-gripping crack. Eventually a comfortable niche is reached and a possible stance and rest. A pessimistic leader can stop here, at best to encourage a nervous second, at worst to facilitate the extraction of the jammed knee! The crack continues steeply to the base of the Bivalve, a large jutting pinnacle whose junction with the slab below provides the handholds for the little Bastard Hand Traverse, described by Edwards and Noyce in an early guide. This is distinctly exposed and quite delicate. Often, the toehold opportunities offered by the rippling rugosities on the slab are overlooked by the novice, who is panicked into partial blindness by the dramatic situation. The traverse left, the teetering balance move up ('interesting' on a windy day) and the rounding of the corner of the Bivalve are further admirable features of this surprising route; but the excitement is soon eased, as an expanse of easy ground comes into view, contrasting sharply with the recent exposure. The easy ground leads up to an impressive corner chimney, with steep walls of fine rock on either side.

With the Bastard Layback (an alternative Severe start to the first pitch) avoided, and the Bastard Hand Traverse enjoyably subdued, only this chimney remains to be vanquished. Significantly, guidebook writers use no daring adjectives to describe the series of grotesque moves required to climb it, moves which are often found to be the crux of the climb. A struggle (body in, right leg

Route Milestone Direct Route, Difficult, 200ft.
Cliff Milestone Buttress, Nant Ffrancon Pass.
First Ascent G. Barlow and H. Priestley Smith, August 1910. Various sections of the climb had been done in 1899 by O. G. Jones and party.
Map Reference O.S. Tourist Map to Snowdonia, 1–50,000 Sheet (ref. 664600).
Guidebooks C.C. *Tryfan and Glyder Fach* by A. J. J. Moulam; *Rock Climbing in Wales* by Ron James.
Nearest Road The A5 one mile east of Ogwen Cottage (ref. 664603).
Distance and time from cliff 300 yards/200ft. Allow 5 minutes.
Good Conditions The rock is very clean and the climb is possible in virtually any weather conditions.
Campsites and Bunkhouses Camping by the lake at the foot of the crag and at other campsites in the Nant Ffrancon. Various club huts and a Youth Hostel near Ogwen Cottage.
Bibliography *Rock Climbing in North Wales* by G. D. and A. P. Abraham (Abraham, Keswick, 1906) includes a description of the Ordinary Route; *Climbing in the Ogwen District* by J. M. Archer Thomson (Edward Arnold, 1910).

Note: Upgraded to Very Difficult in the 1993 guidebook. As a 'yardstick' classic this action will inevitably disrupt the relationship of all the climbs in the lower grades. This grade places it alongside such climbs as Grooved Arête, Sub Cneifon Rib, the Chasm and Angular Chimney, all of which are harder.

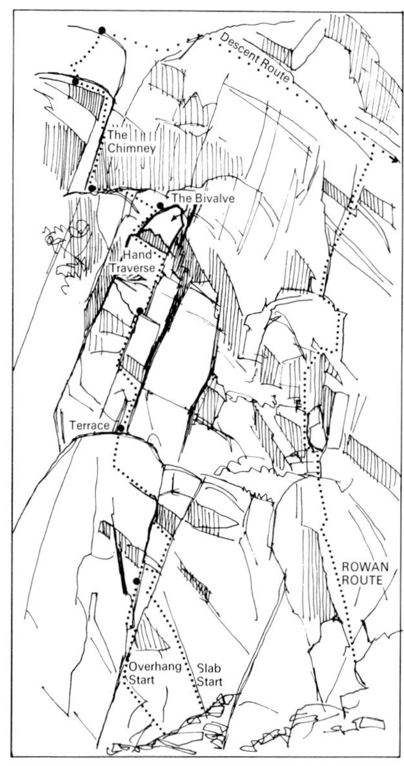

out, facing right) will, with any luck, overcome the initial chockstone and defy gravity long enough for the climber to reach a ledge on the left. At this point, a pirouette and a series of airy moves up the left arête of the chimney lead up to a spacious, rocky platform set in a fine situation near the top of the buttress. A glance up reveals the short but delicate final wall. This provides a few more feet of exhilarating climbing to complete a varied and satisfying route.

John Cleare

Ken Wilson

Top left: The initial slab moves on Milestone Direct. *Climber: Sean Williams*

Bottom left: Starting the third pitch of Milestone Direct, a steep groove that leads up to the Hand Traverse under the Bivalve. *Climbers: Chris Bonington and John Sandilands*

Top right: Just below the Bivalve. At this point one can mount the rib and place a runner before embarking on the Hand Traverse, which moves off to the left. An awkward and not particularly pleasant alternative takes a line to the right at this point. *Climber: Ken Wilson*

Bottom right: Moving up on to the ledge at the end of the Hand Traverse, an exposed and precarious move that requires good technique if it is to be accomplished in style. *Climber: Dave Alcock*

Far right: The chimney pitch. An awkward fight is required to gain access to the chimney, which maintains its interest until a ledge high on the left rib is reached. *Climber: John Fitzgerald*

Ken Wilson collection

John Cleare

Ken Wilson

34 Direct Route

by David Cox

Route Direct Route, Hard Severe, 300ft.
Cliff Glyder Fach, Main Cliff, Cwm Bochlwyd.
First Ascent K. M. Ward and H. B. Gibson, April 1907.
Map Reference O.S. Tourist Map to Snowdonia, 1–50,000 Sheet (ref. 656588).
Guidebooks C.C. *Tryfan and Glyder Fach* by A. J. J. Moulam; *Rock Climbing in Wales* by Ron James.
Nearest Road The A5 at Ogwen Cottage Outdoor Pursuits Centre (ref. 650603).
Distance and time from cliff 1½ miles/1,500ft. Allow 1¼ hours.
Good Conditions Dries quickly in the summer but is usually greasy and inhospitable in the winter months.
Campsites and Bunkhouses Numerous campsites and club huts in the Nant Ffrancon valley. Youth Hostel near Ogwen Cottage.
Bibliography C.C. Journal 1908: *Some Climbs on the North Buttress of Glyder Fach* by K. M. Ward; *Climbing Days* by Dorothy Pilley (Secker and Warburg, 1965); *Climbing in the Ogwen District* by J. M. Archer Thomson (Edward Arnold, 1910).

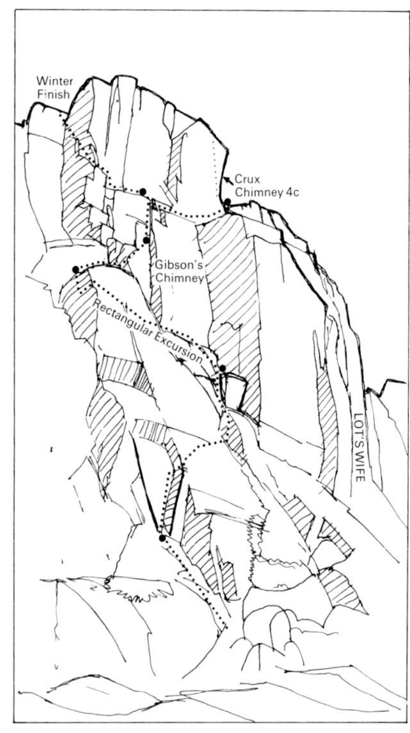

In the early 1930s, particularly in Wales, most people's standards were modest and the routes they did were pretty conventional. Hardly any of my own friends in the O.U.M.C. possessed a guidebook more modern than Abraham's *British Mountain Climbs*, which covered Scotland, the Lakes and Wales in a single fat volume. This indicated clearly which 'courses' (as they were called) were worth while, and also graded them very generously; and in consequence it seldom occurred to us to try anything harder or more original than routes like the Tryfan Buttresses, Faith, Hope and Charity, Route II or Great Gully. Glyder Fach Direct was not a route which Abraham recommended, and we regarded it as right out of our class. Admittedly, it was not one of the horrific Kirkus VSs, of which we read in the Helyg book; but C. F. Holland, who had been on the first ascent of C.B., had described it as recently as 1925 as 'probably the hardest climb in North Wales'.

Then, on the second day of an O.U.M.C. meet in March 1934, a recently joined member of the Club, John Hoyland, whom nobody knew and who was on his first visit to Wales, went off with two other new members and took them up the Direct. Snow was lying down to 1,200ft., and there was a lot of it higher up. Hoyland said nothing special about the Direct, except that it was 'a marvellous climb'; we discovered later that he had walked the whole way back to Helyg in the snow with one stockinged foot, having taken off his left boot on the top pitch and accidentally dropped it. This ascent of Hoyland's stands out in my mind more vividly than the details of the two or three occasions on which I subsequently did the Direct myself, because it suddenly made us wonder whether, given somebody prepared to lead them, we might not safely try some of these harder climbs ourselves. The next day, in fact, Hoyland took us up a Severe on Dinas Mot without anything too awful happening; and only two days later we were getting into terrible trouble on Cloggy.

The Direct, of course, is not a desperate climb at all, especially if the easiest combination of alternatives (the Rectangular Excursion, which bypasses Gibson's Chimney on the left, and the Winter Finish) is taken. The rock is somewhere near perfect, pitches are short, and most of the stances and belays are large – some of them enormous. The route has the old-fashioned qualities of the traditional routes on Tryfan, except that the Direct is about 20° steeper. There is far less heather and vegetation than on Tryfan – indeed, hardly any; there is a far greater sense of exposure; and the technical difficulty is high for a route made as long ago as 1908. The shallow, near-vertical groove of Gibson's Chimney, which is rarely used, remained for twenty years one of the hardest pitches in Wales, and is still just VS; and the Final Crack would not be out of place on one of the Chamonix Aiguilles. The crag itself is perhaps the nearest thing that Wales has to offer in the way of Chamonix-type climbing: clean cracks, sharp edges, firm holds, good situations, and a feeling of security despite the steepness of individual pitches.

The easiest line involves nothing harder than varied and enjoyable V.Diff. climbing, except for about a dozen feet of Hard Severe, two-thirds of the way up the route. This is the last part of the alternative which avoids Gibson's Chimney, and it is a notorious place – an almost pure hand-traverse rising quite steeply from left to right across a more or less blank wall. Once embarked on it, you have to keep moving, for it is difficult to get back and, if your arms start to give out, you feel you are a very long way above the scree. It was here that on a memorable occasion in about 1935 a brand new manilla rope broke when the last man of an O.U.M.C. party came off; luckily, he just managed to save himself on the outer lip of the narrow terrace 25ft. below. An equally fine pitch is Gibson's Chimney itself, which is not much harder than the Hand-Traverse but, being 40ft. high and very open, gives a slightly greater feeling of exposure. I seem to remember Jack Longland taking me up it in 1936 or 1937; he had a delicate pair of tricouni-nailed shoes, and also carried a sling and karabiner – the first time I witnessed the use of one of these modern protection devices. Many people will think, though, that the classic pitch is the Final Crack. Curiously, the Winter Finish, a much easier V.Diff. line round to the left, was only discovered in 1930 – perhaps an indication of how seldom

Ken Wilson

Above left: Looking down Gibson's Chimney at climbers involved in the Rectangular Excursion. The wide crack in the centre of the picture was first climbed by Joe Brown; the thin crack to its right is still unclimbed.

Above right: The East Buttress of Glyder Fach.

Left: The Hand Traverse on Glyder Fach's Direct Route, a strenuous but well-protected pitch demanding a bold approach. *Climber: Ron James*

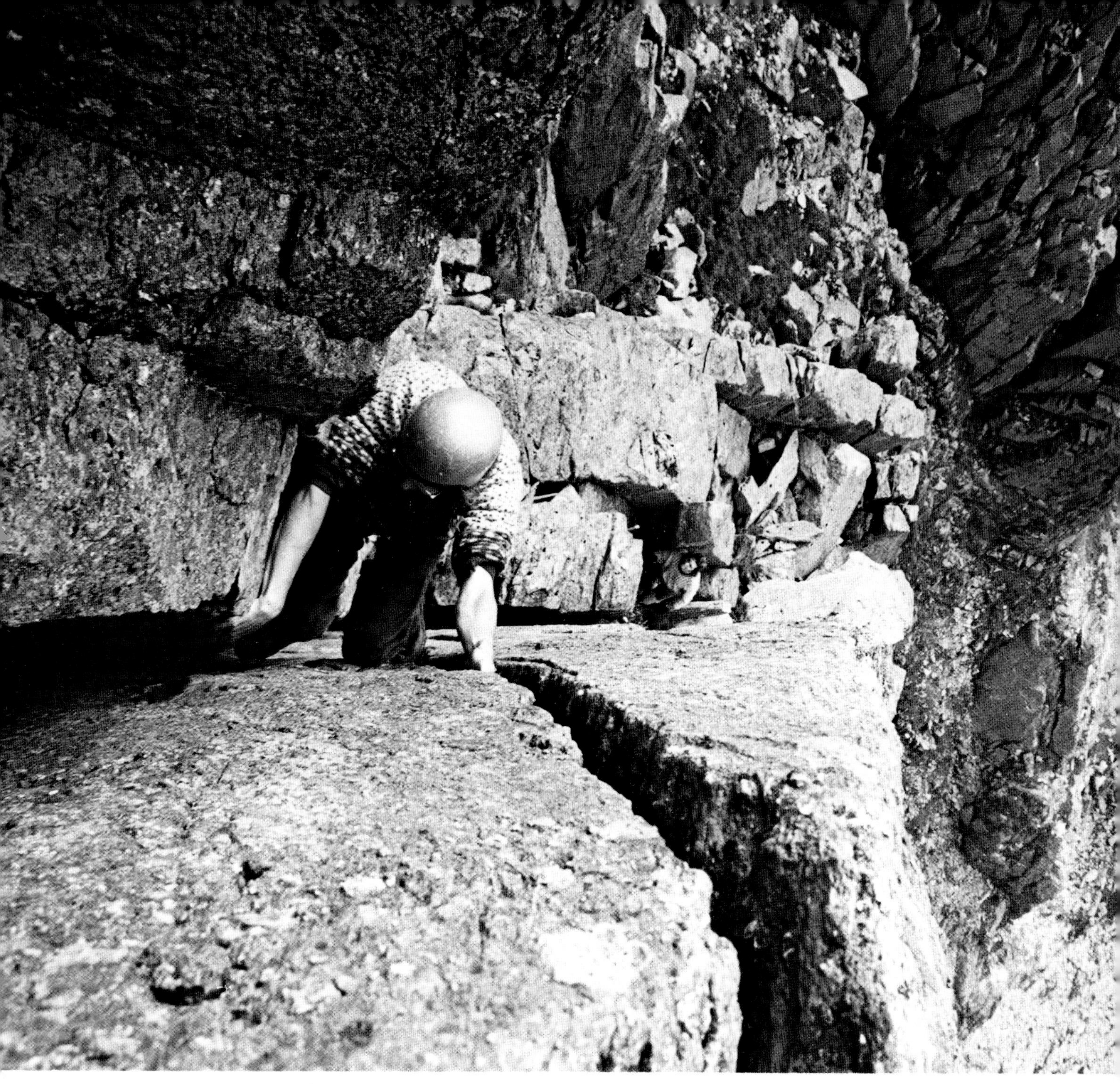

Above: Looking down the final (crux) pitch of the Direct Route. The crack on the left can be wedged, and further assistance is gained by jamming the right-hand crack. The climber has just overcome the main difficulties and has reached more secure jams where the right-hand crack has widened.

Right: The same climbers, with the second man tackling the crux. This is the view from the descent path down East Gully. *Climbers: Unknown*

the climb was visited before then. It is nice that this escape is there; but the Final Crack, part of the original route, should not be missed – if you can get up it! Again, no more than Hard Severe, it is a teasing and very strenuous problem of about 30ft., though the difficult part is shorter than that. The crack is boot-width and runs up a vertical right-angled corner; there are few positive holds; and it would be very hard indeed, but for a narrow subsidiary crack in the wall out on the left. Anyone who has been on this pitch will realize why John Hoyland, climbing in nails, wanted to take off his left boot.

The whole climb is only 300ft., but you can spend a lot of energy on it. You feel, too, that you are on a mountain, not on a little facet of one, for you are high up on Glyder Fach and there is some of the best scenery in Wales below you while you are climbing. And if you are a traditionalist, as you should be to get the real flavour of the Direct, you can round off the climb by walking the remaining short distance up to the summit.

Just as a postscript, it is worth recalling that Ward and Gibson climbed both the Rectangular Excursion *and* Gibson's Chimney, not to mention the Final Crack, in the course of the first ascent. Ward, who led the

Ken Wilson

‐est of the climb, was defeated halfway ıp the Chimney, so they took the Rectangular Excursion (Ward described the Hand Traverse simply as 'comfortable'). From the top of the Chimney, Gibson then lescended and did it on a rope, after which hey both descended again and Gibson led it. It is unquestionably the best route to take,' vrote Ward. Incidentally, his short account nentions that they had walked up to Llyn Bochlwyd 'in a seething snowstorm', and hat they had to wait at the foot of the rocks vhile the snow melted, so conditions cannot ıave been ideal. They must have been a airly hard pair.

35 Hope, Lazarus, The Arête and Grey Slab (Lost Boot Climb)

by Ron James

Two gates, a well-made path and a gentle walk lead to the threshold of one of the most attractive cwms in Wales. High on the right, Y Garn's horseshoe of ridges beckon the walker; round the lake the nature trail channels the environmentalists and innumerable school groups; while the predominantly rocky hillside at the head of the lake leads the climber's eye from moraines to the summit of Glyder Fawr: 2,000ft. of rock with possibilities of inter-linked routes at most standards. In winter, the climber may be attracted to other parts of the corrie – the ice on the Devil's Kitchen or the snows of the Nameless Cwm – but on a warm summer noon the prospect of four or five hours of smooth, continuous movement on good rock must set any self-respecting mountaineer's pulse racing.

Historically, it was the higher cliff that was climbed first, and in fact Central Gully on Glyder Fawr Upper Cliff, climbed in 1894, was the first rock-climb in this area. The adjacent Central Arête fell in 1909 to Guy Barlow, while the then grassy furrow up the side of Idwal Slabs – the Ordinary Route – was climbed in 1897. Eighteen years passed before Hope was conceived and led by Mrs Daniell, while her second on that day, I. A. Richards, returned next year to share in the discovery of the other virtues and in 1918 to lead up the first break in the Holly Tree Wall above. His Original Route, still quite a respectable VS today, was followed in 1922 by the hard part of Lazarus, which at Severe standard provides the easiest link between the Slabs and the walls above. In 1929 two routes appeared on the Continuation Wall, making possible a continuous climb from the foot of the Slabs to the summit of the mountain. Central Arête does not provide a real climax to so fine a climb, but it was not until 1932 that Menlove Edwards, seconded by a young boy, virtually soloed Grey Slab, thus offering a fitting crescendo to this combination of routes.

I first climbed Hope at the age of seventeen. It was my second day of roped climbing and I led in clinkers. We had one sling and karabiner (ex-W.D.), a hundred feet of hemp rope, a pencilled copy of Edwards's route description which we hoped would show us the way, and a first edition of Barford's *Climbing in Britain* which we hoped would show us how to belay. The route notes dissolved in the rain after two pitches, while the book, which had cost a shilling new, fell apart above the twin cracks. I found no belay but a good stance after 30ft. and again after the third pitch, wandered all over the slab on the second pitch and had both feet shoot off as I lunged for the jug at the top of the twin cracks. My memory of the rest of the route includes six or seven pitches, at least two more belay-less stances and a sudden awareness that the angle had changed, that the way off was below me and that I was halfway up Javelin Gully. I had climbed the first pitch of Lazarus.

Lazarus thus started as an exciting failure involving me in my first abseil, and it has continued to give regular thrills. During my years at Ogwen Cottage I climbed it frequently, usually doing the second pitch – an exposed traverse leftwards away from the secure chockstone stance in the gully – without runners, so as to belay on nuts directly above the crux groove. By moving over a little, I could then keep the rope above my pupils on the traverse. However, one slippery day, the low right jug-hold, which I used to start the groove, snapped off and I swung outwards like an opening door, supported by a finger-jam and a toe-hold. It seemed as though I was fixed in place, while my worried second's face, then the Kitchen and

Routes Hope, Very Difficult, 450ft; Lazarus, Severe, 140ft.; The Arête, Very Difficult, 80ft.; Grey Slab, Hard Severe, 270ft.
Cliffs The Idwal Slabs. Holly Tree and Continuation Walls and the Upper Cliff of Glyder Fawr, Cwm Idwal.
First Ascents Hope – Mrs Daniell and party, August 1915; Lazarus – I. A. Richards and party, 1922; The Arête – F. E. Hicks and party, June 1929; Grey Slab – climbed as Lost Boot Climb by A. S. Bullough, J. Cooper and J. Marchington, July 1932 and rediscovered and named Grey Slab in August 1932 by J. M. Edwards and A. M. D'Aerth.
Map Reference O.S. Tourist Map of Snowdonia, 1–50,000 Sheet (ref. 6458).
Guidebooks C.C. *Cwm Idwal* by Ken Wilson and Zdzislaw Leppert; *Rock Climbing in Wales* by Ron James.
Nearest Road The A5 at Ogwen Cottage Outdoor Pursuits Centre (ref. 650603).
Distance and time from cliff 1 mile/500ft. Allow 25 minutes.
Good Conditions The lower routes dry quickly in the summer, and Hope goes easily in the wet as the rock is clean. The Upper Cliff takes longer to dry, and Grey Slab often retains wet streaks for some time.
Campsites and Bunkhouses Camping and huts at various points in the Nant Ffrancon Valley. Youth Hostel near Ogwen Cottage.
Bibliography *Samson* by Geoffrey Sutton and Wilfrid Noyce (private publication *c.* 1960) contains a brief reference to the first ascent of Grey Slab; *Climbing Days* by Dorothy Pilley (Secker and Warburg, 1965) refers to explorations on the Holly Tree Wall.

Note: Grey Slab was upgraded to Very Severe in the 1993 guidebook because of its poor protection and the likelihood of meeting damp sections on the critical part of the second pitch. When dry Hard Severe is more applicable.

Left: The Twin Cracks on Hope. Some difficult moves are required to gain the top of the cracks. 70 ft. of magnificent slab climbing then leads up to the left, to a small stance by the overlap above. *Climbers: Unknown*

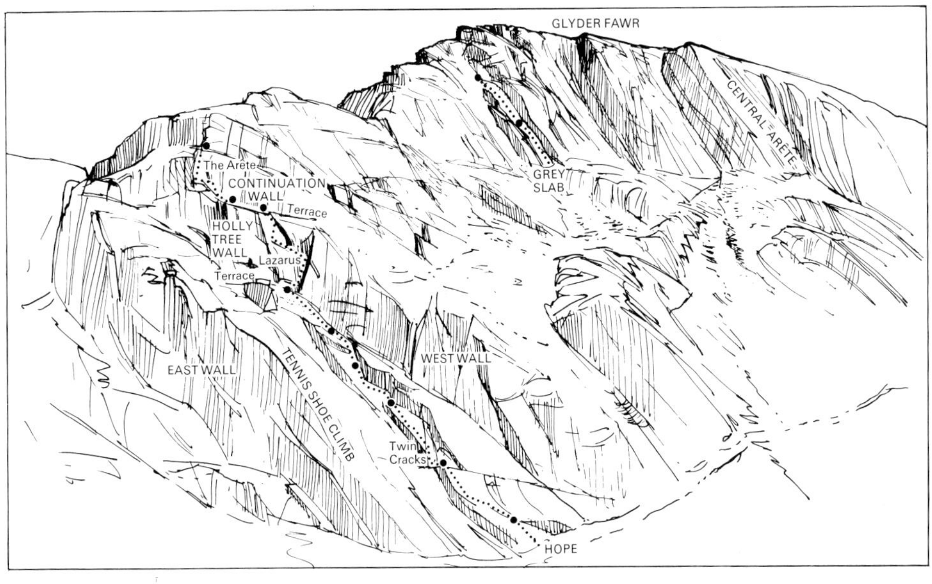

Above: Completing the third pitch of Hope. *Climbers: Unknown*

Left: The Idwal Slabs. Climbers can be seen on the Direct Start to Tennis Shoe Climb and on the second pitch of Hope. The East Wall of the Slabs is on the left and the West Wall is on the right, above the main sweep of the Slabs.

Below: The corner on Hope's fifth pitch. The Holly Tree Wall is seen above, with climbers on Piton Route and in the upper groove of Lazarus. *Climbers: Unknown*

Ken Wilson

Above: The Holly Tree Wall, with a party on Piton Route. The Leader is just starting up the crux wall of Lazarus; he is using it as a finish to Piton Route, instead of taking that climb's harder and more devious finish, which moves off to the left at this point. Lazarus itself reaches this point by a traverse coming in from the right.
Climbers: Unknown

Y Garn, and finally the sweep of the Slabs and the Nant Ffrancon, slowly passed before me. A pause and the procession of images reversed and I was back in position, the hold still firmly clutched in my sweaty palm. I pocketed it and finished the route in pensive mood. I recalled two nasty rescues of leaders who had lobbed off that move during the previous month, and the image of me bouncing down the top pitches of Hope gave a final warning: I needed to protect the move in future. On the left of the groove is a rounded spike, and the finger crack will take a nut, but both give problems: the rope to the spike gets in your way and quickly lifts off, while the nut increases rope drag and removes your second's protection. Both anyway assume your novice second can hold you, so I devised an alternative which avoids these hazards. A full-weight sling or tape, clipped into one's waist-tie, can be slipped over the spike as you start the moves up; it stays on until you reach the pocket jugs above and then lifts off as you step on to the stance.

Continuation Wall is more like an outcrop, rising 80ft. above a wide terrace. It has outcrop standards: Groove Above is VS to start and a real knee-knocker if you slip, and the Arête Climb on the left, at V.Diff., gives exposed, awkward and poorly protected climbing.

Above this, walls and slabs lead up towards Senior Ridge with the delightful, pocketed Lava Slab ending on the quartzy traverse which leads across to the foot of the upper cliff. Here, the steep Grey Group of rocks catches the eye, although it is possible to continue across below Central Gully and High Pasture to Central Arête: 600ft. of Difficult climbing, which starts well and continues over various pinnacles, but finally peters out into the main hillside.

However, if you have climbed Hope, Lazarus and the Arête Climb in boots, with sacks and in fine style, Grey Slab could be the only logical continuation. It is poorly protected and often wet, and involves long run-outs, plenty of commitment and a poor stance at half-height. It certainly merits its Hard Severe grade.

My most memorable ascent of this route was made one typical March day with a P.E. organizer from Birmingham. We had already climbed Angular Chimney on the Gribin, and Tennis Shoe and Original Route on the Slabs. Each route had been, for me as the leader, more greasy, colder and more awkward than the previous one, while even my athletic second had had his moments. But we had got up them and the motto of the day had become: 'If we are going to struggle,

Right: An early ascent of Grey Slab. The leader is correctly equipped for the period with tweed jacket, nailed boots and hemp rope and, of course, has no runners. *Climber Gilbert Peaker*

C. Douglas Milner

let's do it somewhere worthwhile.' We arrived at the foot of Grey Slab in late afternoon; the sun was trying to break through and the promise of a sunset from the summit of the Glyders encouraged us to continue in boots and to carry our sacks. Soon I was padding up the first pitch; runners were not much in evidence, but, unlike the earlier routes, neither was the moisture. So, despite cold hands, I enjoyed the movement and finally grovelled up the little groove to the awkward stance below a bulge. The panting intimacy of the changeover seemed all too short, and soon I was ejected over the bulge and up to the good runner on the next pitch. I moved left on to apparently dry rock, my feet slipped a little and my ostrich brain suggested, and rejected, 'dirty boots' and 'careless footwork', before finally accepting the inevitable dread word – 'verglas'! The adrenalin flow reached maximum as a series of long breath-holding moves led up towards the overlap. Still the optimist's brain abstracted itself from the real seriousness of the situation, until one peep over the bulge and the alarm bells rang. Above, the little wet streak which usually stipples the upper slab had frozen solid, creating a pathetically thin, but very well attached ice-rink, set at 60°, for the next 40ft. The ensuing ten minutes were spent balanced on two small footholds, removing my sack, searching in it for pegs, hammer and more slings and finding only the hammer. Half an hour of delicate chipping, usually where I remembered holds to be or where a protective nut would slot, a delicate tiptoe up odd protrusions of dry rock, a quick mantelshelf on to a hammer jammed into a frozen sod, and I was up. We reached the summit at ten; no sunset, but a full moon and no hurry, for no one would come out from Og to look for me before closing time. As usual, Cwm Idwal had given a good day!

Note: In 1988 it transpired that the Grey Slab (claimed by Menlove Edwards in August 1932) had actually been climbed six weeks earlier by the Rucksack Club men Bullough, Cooper and Marchington and contemporaneously recorded as Lost Boot Climb in the club logbook. Edwards, the guidebook writer, was unaware of this ascent and the guide was published in 1936 with Grey Slab described. No counter-claim was made, so this remained the record for fifty-six years until the error was discovered.

36 Nea

by Nea Morin

A chance meeting in North Wales in the summer of 1939 led to my climbing with John Barford and subsequently with Menlove Edwards. Having lived in France for the previous ten years, my experience of Welsh rock was limited, and John set out to introduce me to a selection of classic routes. On our first climb – the Girdle Traverse of the East Wall of the Idwal Slabs, in nails, in the wet – I literally only just scraped by, while my Alpine-style belaying techniques met with very definite disapproval. Great Gully on Craig yr Ysfa, the Direct on Dinas Mot combined with Reade's Route on Crib Goch, and Longland's on Clogwyn du'r Arddu, all impressed me with their style and variety.

It was two years before we again had the opportunity to climb together. By then, my husband had escaped from France after the French capitulation and was with the *Forces Françaises Libres* in London. John intended camping in the then deserted and ruined cottages of Ynys Ettws, but, since my camping equipment was rather sketchy and the cottage roofs far from rainproof, I decided to book a room at a small café in Llanberis, where I could return from time to time for a change of clothing and a dry bed. I explained that I would be camping and climbing further up the valley. No comment was made at the time, but I thought I detected disapproval: climbers were then almost unknown in the valley and the locals were not at all familiar with their ways, as I was to discover later.

Next morning I took the bus to Gwastadnant and humped my gear up to Ynys Ettws. After a day or two in the Pass, we went off to Clogwyn du'r Arddu. Near the top of the initial pitch of Curving Crack, John who was laybacking, fell off and damaged a knee. However, he did not wish to abandon the climb, and this gave me an opportunity to try out the jamming technique in which I had been well trained on the sandstone rocks of Fontainebleau; the method worked excellently.

Next day, Menlove joined us; he had finally secured his status as a conscientious objector and was now living alone at Hafod Owen, an isolated farm cottage above Llyn Dinas in the Gwynant valley. He was absorbed in his work on psychology, and would allow himself only limited periods of climbing. I already knew him by reputation and had heard much about him from John. Nevertheless, I was quite unprepared for the impact made by his powerful personality, exceptional physical strength and unyielding determination. We wandered across to the Three Cliffs, at that time Menlove's territory *par excellence*: here, with the exception of Sabre Cut, he had made the first ascent of every climb done; some twenty in all. On the Grochan, he had already recorded seven routes, including Slape and Brant. We skirted round the base of the cliff, looking for new routes, and Menlove was at once drawn towards a horrid noisome cleft, the great overhang of Goats' Gully, a place after his own heart. Here, he battled away for upwards of an hour, giving an incredible display of strength. John's knee had stiffened up and he was not intending to climb; suddenly I realized that if Menlove were to succeed I should have to attempt to follow. To my great relief, he finally gave up and we moved along to the foot of Hazel Groove. Here he stopped and, pointing up, remarked that there was a good line just to the right and why didn't I have a look at it? I did, and it 'went'. Thus my climbing Nea was entirely fortuitous. I hadn't spied out the land or planned the route, and I knew nothing of the cliff. In fact, it was not until some years later that I first saw the climb from Cwm Glas across the valley: I was amazed to find how attractive it looked from there and that it was indeed a 'good line'.

After a lapse of thirty-five years, it is not possible to recapture either the original excitement of the climb, or the impression made by it; still less is it possible to conjure this up realistically for others. Those first impressions become blurred, not only by the passage of time, but also by subsequent ascents. The most recent of these, made only a few months ago with a considerable physical disability quite apart from that of age, temporarily scrubbed out all my previous impressions. The occasion was a rather splendid three-generation party, with my daughter Denise and eldest grandson Chuck Evans, together with Barbara James without whose enthusiastic encouragement and

Route Nea, Severe, 230ft.
Cliff Clogwyn y Grochan, Llanberis Pass.
First Ascent Nea Morin and J. M. Edwards, September 1941.
Map Reference O.S. Tourist Map to Snowdonia 1–50,000 Sheet (ref. 622573).
Guidebooks C.C. *The Llanberis Pass* by Geoff Milburn; *Rock Climbing in Wales* by Ron James.
Nearest Road The A4086 at a layby 1½ miles south-east of Nant Peris.
Distance and time from cliff 100 yards/ 300 ft.
Good Conditions The cliff dries quickly after rain in most seasons, but the first pitch of Nea can remain greasy for some time, making the crux moves a little harder.
Campsites and Bunkhouses Camping below the crag and bunkhouse accommodation at Humphries Barn halfway to Nant Peris.
Bibliography *A Woman's Reach* by Nea Morin (Eyre and Spottiswoode, 1968).

Note: Regraded to Very Severe in the 1987 guidebook. A rockfall destroyed the final pitch and the climb now finishes up the last pitch of Spectre (4b) which is slightly harder than anything else on the route. The photograph of the old final pitch is retained for historical interest.

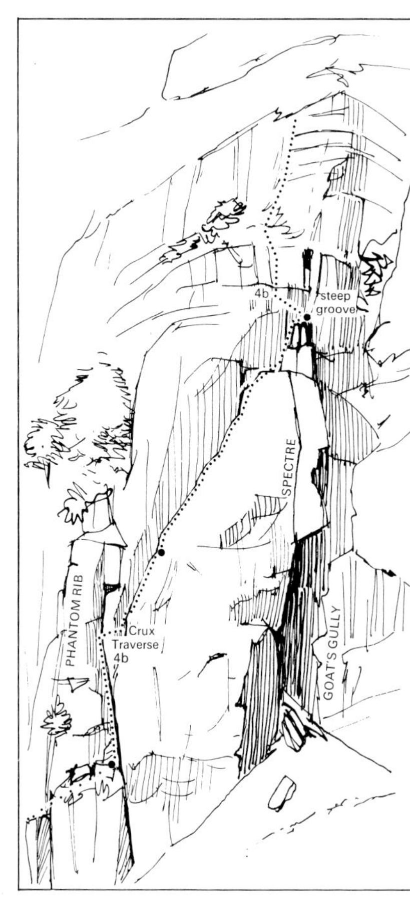

John Cleare

Left: The first pitch of Nea. The climber, with socks pulled over her P.A.s to combat the greasy conditions, has to make some balance moves round the rib (defined by her hand) to gain a groove on the right. *Climber: Lady Denise Evans*

Near right: The steep groove that was the start of Nea's final pitch until it collapsed in the late eighties. The photograph is retained because of the historic links with the climbers. *Climbers: Lady Denise Evans (née Morin) and Nea Morin*

Far right: The middle section of Nea. *Climbers: Unknown*

leadership I would never have got off the ground.

The first sixty-five feet of the climb immediately establish its steepness, and also include the crux. The route starts up a corner groove which, for twenty-five feet, is common to Nea and to the ordinary start of Hazel Groove. The groove then divides, and the left-hand branch is followed for another twenty-five feet up towards an overhang. Here, a delicate step, the crux, is made round to the right and across an intervening rib back into the line of the main vertical fault, at the top of which there was originally a solid holly tree. On the first ascent I had no particular difficulty with the crux, but immediately following it is a steep crack, which at that time harboured some exceedingly spiky gorse bushes, taking up essential climbing space, and pushing one painfully off balance. I found this the hardest move on the climb and was thankful to reach the holly tree, where Menlove joined me.

I took it for granted that Menlove would lead through, but he insisted I should continue in the lead throughout: no doubt he had guessed how much I was longing to do so. His burly presence gave one complete confidence and I felt I could have tackled anything. On the following pitch I think I kept further out to the right than is now usual: the rock was then rough and unused and the situation one of fine exposure. Next came the rising corner crack (likened by John Barford to the Rateau de Chèvre on the Grépon, only harder), leading up to the perched blocks of Goats' Buttress, at the top of what are now the first five pitches of Spectre, and from which one has a splendid plunging view of the valley. The steep cracks and shattered blocks above are of smooth, hard, yellow-brown rock, quite different from that below, and they give excellent climbing: not difficult, but strenuous and immensely satisfying. All too soon the good rock runs out and the climb finishes on ground that is steep, but loose and broken.

After the climb, Menlove and John ran me down to Llanberis in a small open car, deposited me on the doorstep of my café and, waving a cheerful goodbye, drove back up the valley. This time, my arrival was greeted with stony looks and the information that my

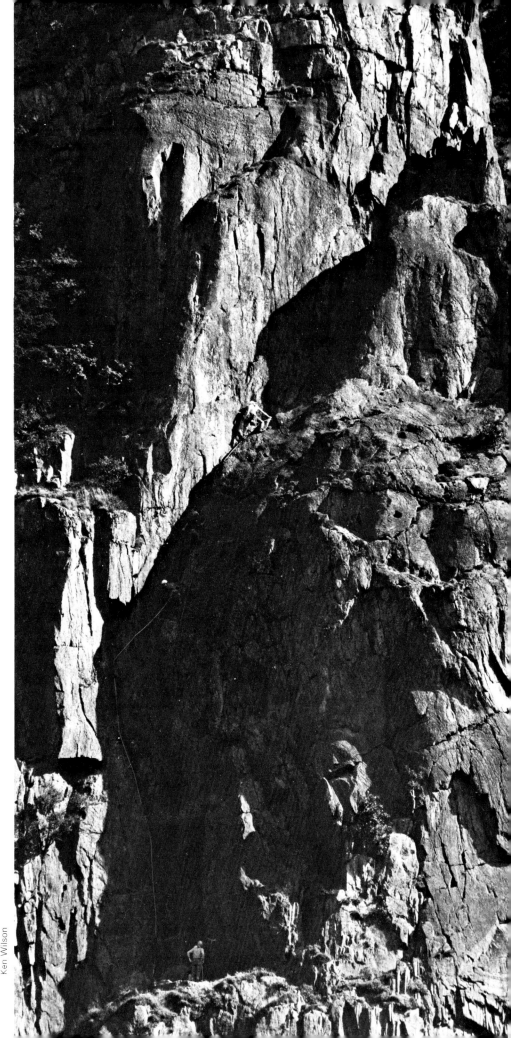

room was no longer available: it was let! I stalked out miserably, found a small hotel nearby, and in the morning returned to the camp at Ynys Ettws.

Happily, all unpleasant memories were rapidly swept away by an exciting attempt on Bow-Shaped Slab on Clogwyn du'r Arddu. Nothing much was achieved other than a dramatic new entry to the West Buttress, employing lengthy lassoing operations and involving some 200ft. of hard climbing. It was now my turn to be horrified by a technique I had never seen before: Menlove's jammed-pebble method of belaying. By the time we had crossed the foot of Narrow Slab and reached the top of the first section of Great Slab, with Bow-Shaped directly above, it was already late with only an hour of daylight left. A bivouac was considered, but finally vetoed; we retreated back along the ledges, and by way of Linnell's Leap in reverse, to the foot of the slab on Longland's. John wrote a few years later: 'A day of great climbing and a good introduction to what were then the wilder parts of the West Buttress.'

A week after our attempt, Menlove made the first ascent of Bow-Shaped.

Ken Wilson

37 Crackstone Rib and Wrinkle

by Dave Cook

For a week, tight ropes had pulled her, not only as his second on the hard routes they had climbed, but just as surely in the crowded bar. Even in the chilled speed of their love-making, she felt the unequal imposition of their days on rock.

His protestations of concern were formal. 'Any particular climb you fancy?' didn't offer much choice on cliffs where the only routes she could consider leading were slimy sideshows. As the escalator of his sports-plan mounted the grades, she began to feel as helpless in their relationship as she did on the harsh ways they climbed.

It was determination on her part, as much as the morning's gloomy sky, that led them finally to Carreg Wastad. For days she had panted up his routes high on the south side, looking across at the inviting little lump of tilted ribs and kindly yew trees, so cleanly separate from the Cromlech hillside. She realized very clearly that his disdain for the cliff expressed not only his ambitions elsewhere, but also the subordination to which this world of hard climbs and 'hard' men condemned her.

Now, traversing leftwards towards Crackstone Rib, she felt a thrust of excitement she had not experienced before. At last it was her route, her ambition, in her own time.

'Get a move on,' he shouted, 'and we can do Erosion Groove before it rains.'

Anger flared within her, and crackled back towards him along the rope. 'Get knotted,' she yelled, 'we do Wrinkle next.'

On the beautiful, exposed rib that gives the climb its name, she dawdled, savouring for the first time those fluttering moments of commitment of which she had heard him speak. How much more rewarding than the feeling of strain and apprehension with which she had seconded. She thought: 'No wonder he's so selfish on this rich food.'

She led on, past a dying tree, and then along a sloping ramp, stringing two pitches together into one. It was like roaring out an ecstatic 'yeah' at a rock concert; something she had never before dared to do. 'No, you can't lead the next pitch,' she said, 'it's mine, too.'

He grimaced with surprise as she stripped the slings from his harness and tied him like a novice to the big block belay. He usually did that to her, and with a squeeze as well.

At the top of the final groove the climb grew hard again. A spiky canopy pushed her back to the crest, a thin leftwards move, stretching. But the sideways flake was good when it came. When later she recalled that day, it was the few feet of climbing actually astride the rib that stuck in her mind. Crackstone Rib was like a hinge. Its pivot was the important part.

The rain drove away his thoughts of Erosion Groove, but not hers of Wrinkle.

Every day from their tent she had watched the zigzag skein of ropes on the first two pitches, and then the long straight lead up the beautiful final wall. Now, exulting in the equality of a grade at which she could stay in control, it would need more than rain, or a slowly comprehending man, to stop her reaching it.

A fat and senile tree was the first objective: the damp holds were like polished tea trays, and then the line right-angled along a steep downwards traverse to get there. The second pitch, although technically no harder than Crackstone, was very tricky in the heavy rain. She was pleased at his grunts in the fluted groove, as his feet slid on the streaming rock.

Routes Crackstone Rib, Severe, 175ft.; Wrinkle, Very Difficult, 235ft.
Cliff Carreg Wastad, Llanberis Pass.
First Ascents Crackstone Rib – J. M. Edwards and J. B. Joyce, July 1935; Wrinkle – M. P. Ward, J. E. Q. Barford and B. Pierre, 1947.
Map Reference O.S. Tourist Map to Snowdonia, 1–50,000 Sheet (ref. 625571).
Guidebooks C.C. *The Llanberis Pass* by Geoff Milburn; *Rock Climbing in Wales* by Ron James.
Nearest Road The A4086 directly below the crag and 1 miles south-east of Nant Peris. It is best to park in the layby below Clogwyn-y-Grochan.
Distance and time from cliff 200 yards/400ft.
Good Conditions Both routes dry quickly after rain, though the rock on Wrinkle is rather more greasy than on Crackstone Rib. After prolonged bad weather the top pitch of Wrinkle can stay wet for a few days.
Campsites and Bunkhouses Campsite at Blaen-y-nant. Bivouac boulders at Pont-y-Gromlech. C.C. Huts at Cwm Glas Mawr and Ynnes Ettws.

.eft and below: Views of Wrinkle – soloists on the second ınd third pitches, and a detailed view of the fluted slab of ıe second pitch. *Climbers: Unknown and Martin Evans*

Right: Approaching the crux of Crackstone Rib. The tree ·elay no longer exists and this section is best done in one ong pitch. *Climbers: Meg Evans and Margaret Tebbutt*

Her addiction to the sport began on that ast pitch. On its seventy feet of wet and ›oorly protected overlapping slabs, she ought to answer questions which had never ›een posed on the hard routes she had econded. She had to confront both her own, ınd his, expectations of the rôle she was ex›ected to play in climbing with a man. In he lead she had to judge, to protect, and ıot to fail. But as the responsibilities were ;reater, so too were the rewards. The reality :limbing offered was a simple one, she was to earn, but by Christ it was real.

Her trajectory was high that night. Rain ell again on the Wastad, and he was washed ıway by her body.

38 Flying Buttress and Spiral Stairs

by Roger Grimshaw

Routes Flying Buttress, Difficult (hard), 300ft., Spiral Stairs, Difficult (hard), 180ft.
Cliff Dinas Cromlech (Dinas-y-Gromlech), Llanberis Pass.
First Ascents Spiral Stairs – J. M. Edwards and S. B. Derbyshire, 6 December 1931; Flying Buttress – J. M. Edwards, 18 December 1931.
Map Reference O.S. Tourist Map to Snowdonia, 1–50,000 Sheet (ref. 630570).
Guidebooks C.C. *The Llanberis Pass* by Geoff Milburn; *Rock Climbing in Wales* by Ron James.
Nearest Road At Pont y Gromlech, 2 miles south-east of Nant Peris, on the A4086.
Distance and time from cliff ¼ mile/700ft. Allow 20 minutes.
Good Conditions The routes are steep and exposed but quite well sheltered. Even in the wet they are quite reasonable as the rock, though polished in places, is very clean. There are few friction moves and the holds are mainly big and incut.
Campsites and Bunkhouses Camping and bivouac boulders below the cliff, and several club huts in the Llanberis Pass.
Bibliography *Samson* by G. Sutton and W. Noyce (private publication, *c.* 1960) contains several references to Edwards's Llanberis Pass explorations; *In This Short Span* by Michael Ward (Gollancz, 1972) contains references to the naming of Spiral Stairs: It seems that it was originally called *Sodom* by Edwards 'but the guidebook editor objected' and the name was changed.

Note: Both climbs regraded to Very Difficult in the 1987 guidebook but this distorts their relationship with Wrinkle which is harder. Consult the graded list on page 253.

Right: Dinas Cromlech from the Llanberis Pass above Pont y Gromlech. Craig Nant Peris is seen in the background.

Cymru in the 'thirties! Picture, if you will, the Three Cliffs of Llanberis standing, virgin and verdant, in the shadow of the great men of Pen-y-Pass. The times, as they say, are a-changing and new innovators are appearing to press forward the challenge. Just as Brown came to Cloggy in the 'fifties, so here again the right man was at the right cliff, with little in the way of competition. Although no harder than anywhere else, the rock perhaps held an essence of intimidation: steeper than much that had gone before, loose and vegetated and, above all, untouched. The right man was John Menlove Edwards.

Much has already been written about this strange and troubled character. Suffice to say that he had the strength and the will, in the new climate of climbing opinion, to set foot upon these cliffs and make them his own. High above the narrow stone bridge that carries the road down to Llanberis, the Fortress of Cromlech stands astride the screes. The vivid gash of the central corner must have drawn the eye, but we are more than twenty years before the ascent of Cenotaph. The first climb came late in 1931; J.M.E. was the leader, and within two months he had produced two of the finest routes in the valley.

There's a galaxy of jugs on these climbs, perhaps the more regular on Spiral Stairs. But listen to Dave Moore, *in extremis* on the final thrutch of Flying Buttress: '. . . I feel like I'm about to give birth.' On another occasion, a would-be Extreme leader was seen to retreat from the Corner and embark on the Buttress with full paraphernalia – he was subsequently driven to request a top rope on the notorious chimney. But the holds on the Stairs can seem small, and the premier pitch, traversing 70ft. around corners and across little ribs, presents its own peculiar problems, particularly on a wet and windy day, when even leather lungs will not keep you in contact with your partner.

Flying Buttress has something of an Alpine character. Join the queue at the foot of the rib and climb huge polished holds, passing the occasional large ledge, to reach the gendarmes that decorate the apex. Descend to the gully bed and prepare for an assault on the final tower. A keen party, including a demure young lass, came on to the route one chill winter's day. We struggled over screes and up to pinnacles, as the murk swirled around us and the first flakes of snow began to drift down.

'Does it get harder?' enquired the lass, politely.

I nodded.

'Well st . . . it,' she exclaimed viciously, and shot off, solo, down the gully and back to the van without once turning her head.

An awkward pull up, a move left and the void appears: you're committed. The belay ledge at the end of the traverse is narrow, but you can wedge in behind a giant flake and savour the view. A steep little wall lies above, the start a lurch from the point of the flake, then pockets appear when needed most to take you up. A superb thread materializes, and easy moves lead right to the base of the chimney. After the ribs and walls and traverses this is totally unexpected. No doubt there is an elegant solution, but I found it hard on first acquaintance, and it is still a thrutch. It looks intimidating, but you pull up easily on to a big flake and find a jug. You're now lying in a constricting haven, hard to fall out of, hard to pull out of, but the drop disconcertingly close on the right. The jug is too low for most, so you sort of

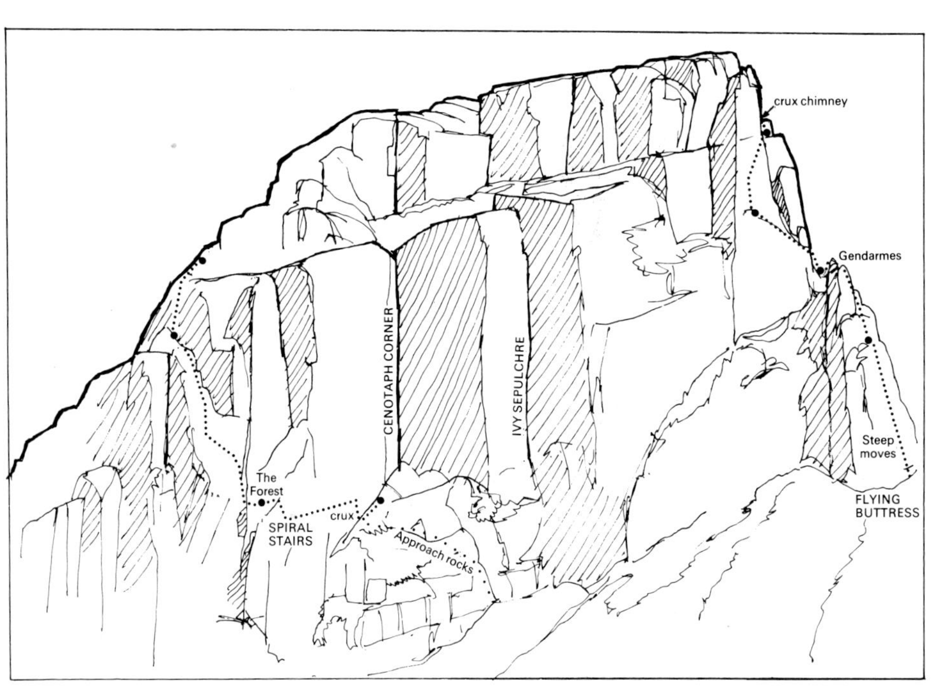

Above left: The very exposed first pitch of Spiral Stairs. A good runner is essential here to protect the second on the hard moves that start the pitch. *Climber: Ken Wilson*

Above right: The steep moves on the fifth pitch of Flying Buttress. *Climbers: Rusty Baillie and Sean Williams*

Opposite page: At the crux of Flying Buttress, where a hard move gives access to the final chimney *Climbers: Sean Williams and Rusty Baillie*

wriggle and push, finding the rock suddenly and sadistically bare, until you can get your foot on to a hold on the edge. It's as well to note this hold before you start – it is easily mislaid in the struggle for altitude. A few moves on comforting jugs to a rock platform and it is over. Think of Edwards's achievement – solo, into the unknown on an unexplored cliff – as you heave your carcass up the big holds.

Now move across to the central cliff, to Spiral Stairs, which was for many years considered the harder of the two. It is probably easier, albeit exposed and more serious for the second man. Scramble up into Cenotaph and gaze in awe at the huge corner. Set it aside for the future and aim yourself at a traverse line a few feet up the left wall. Pull up – it's as hard as anything on the climb – leave a runner for your second and move out of sight and sound; a lonely route, this. Move down, with the exposure snapping at your heels, growing greater with every step. Beware the loose holds: there are not as many jugs as you think. Consider your second as the pitch unwinds, and leave him a runner or two.

Round the last bulge and the angle eases. There are plenty of ledges, but the forest that occupied this site is long gone, represented by one lone tree. There are plenty of cracks. Pull the second on and look down into the void, to the road so far below. Bigger routes come through here: look up to the slash of Sabre Cut, a step on the way to the steeper slash of Cenotaph. Glance down into steepness where the easiest way up is Severe. But our way lies further left, up a crack and past the tree growing out of the cliff, to be pulled on, hung on, trampled on. The crack is steep and overhanging, but, as if to give comfort, the big holds are visible from below. Swing up and it's almost over as you spiral left up and across a staircase, complete with handrail, that gives out on to the easy slabs above. Put your hands in your pockets if you like.

Come in the sunshine, up Flying Buttress and off across the hillside to Craig Nant Peris. Reverse the jugs of Spiral Stairs as evening casts shadows across the corners of the cliff. Or savour the surprises in wind and rain. You won't be disappointed: they are great little climbs, with tradition and position to commend them.

39 The Cracks

by Anne Wheatcroft

I first became aware of the existence of Dinas Mot one cold November day, sitting among the crowds in Cromlech forest. We at least had the inadequate winter sun, which for months had been withheld from the crag opposite, by the bulk of Snowdon itself. However, even as a novice, I longed to get away from the knitted ropes and queueing that climbs on the Three Cliffs often entails, and I envied the two small figures crawling up the face opposite: they seemed completely isolated, in a different world.

Climbing on Dinas Mot is not always such a stern affair, and occasionally, in the heat of summer, its northerly aspect is a positive advantage. It *is* usually serious, as the main face has few natural crack lines and protection is hard to come by. This was irrelevant to the early explorers who were attracted to the stark smoothness of the face at a time when long run-outs were the rule rather than the exception. Before the more ambitious routes were tackled, the Bathurst brothers investigated an obvious line of weakness up the left wall. The route, now called The Cracks, breaks left from the apex of the slabs, trending towards a corner and crack system which leads to the edge of East Gully. From there, a short rightward traverse regains the fault and a final series of terraces leads to the top of the slabs.

Today, while its northerly aspect means that Dinas Mot is not the most welcoming of places after rain, as it is very slow to dry, the full horrors of the pristine crag have long disappeared. The epic first ascent was executed in stockinged feet, because removal of heather from the lower crack had covered the surrounding rock with debris which, mixed with the greasy surface, made a lethal combination. The base of the twin cracks was only gained with the aid of two 'improvised' pitons, left for posterity, and a safety rope engineered from above. One wonders what the climbing establishment of the time thought of these tactics.

The upper half of the climb did not present the same difficulties, although subsequent parties were advised that the leader would almost certainly require 'the help of the second's shoulder to arrive on the second terrace'. I wish I had read that description before attempting The Cracks. It would have saved a deal of heart searching on the top pitch, although whether my second would have co-operated is quite another matter.

I had progressed somewhat from being a raw recruit on Spiral Stairs, to being a competent second and then a rather nervous leader of climbs in the lower end of the Severe range. Now, sights were going higher, spurred on by an element of competition not always acknowledged in classic climbing circles. Whether it was pure coincidence that the friendly prod was coming from another girl of about my own climbing standard, I don't know; nor have I considered the implications for Women's Lib. Anyway, we had set our sights on The Cracks of Dinas Mot.

I got the first pitch. This looks an innocuous patter over the lower slabs to the belay below a small overhang. The guidebook splits the pitch in two, but I could hardly find anything significant for protection, let alone a belay. After 80ft. I was quite relieved to reach the safety of the overhang.

The next pitch was the one that caused the trouble in 1930. As Bathurst predicted, it has become both safer and pleasanter now that it is fully gardened, although it is still very greasy in the wet. Barbara managed to lodge a runner higher under the overhang before committing herself to the delicate rising traverse, using undercuts for handholds. I watched her disappear round the corner, and, from the speed the rope ran out, I gathered things were easier there. It is now a well-worn chimney, a little awkward in places with an imposing drop beneath one's feet.

I was soon confronted by the twin cracks. Not only did I find excellent jams for both hands and feet, but I also managed a rather too secure runner before the final tricky swing round left on to the ledge. Barbara followed up, but after a short time came to a halt, and so we remained for the next ten minutes. Just as she was trying in desperation to extricate the rope from my large nut, the nut itself decided to come free and progress was resumed. I still have that nut and it has never since been so near abandonment.

Route The Cracks, Severe (top pitch Mild Very Severe), 280ft.
Cliff The Nose of Dinas Mot, Llanberis Pass.
First Ascents B. L. and H. C. H. Bathurst (employing much aid and taking a different line), 1930; First free ascent by proper route – C. F. Kirkus, 1930.
Map Reference O.S. Tourist Map to Snowdonia, 1–50,000 Sheet (ref. 627564).
Guidebooks C.C. *The Llanberis Pass* by Geoff Milburn; *Rock Climbs in Wales* by Ron James.
Nearest Road The A4086 at Pont y Gromlech, 2 miles south-east of Nant Peris.
Distance and time from cliff ¼ mile/400ft. Allow 10 minutes.
Good Conditions Greasy and damp in winter months but still climbable at VS. In the summer it dries quite slowly after rain. The route is east-facing and delightful in the early morning sun.
Campsites and Bunkhouses Camping and bivouac boulders below the cliff, and several club huts in the Llanberis Pass.
Bibliography C.C. Journal 1930 has photos of the Bathursts exploring the route.

Note: The main part of the route was upgraded to Hard Severe in the 1994 guidebook. The finishing pitch remains at VS.

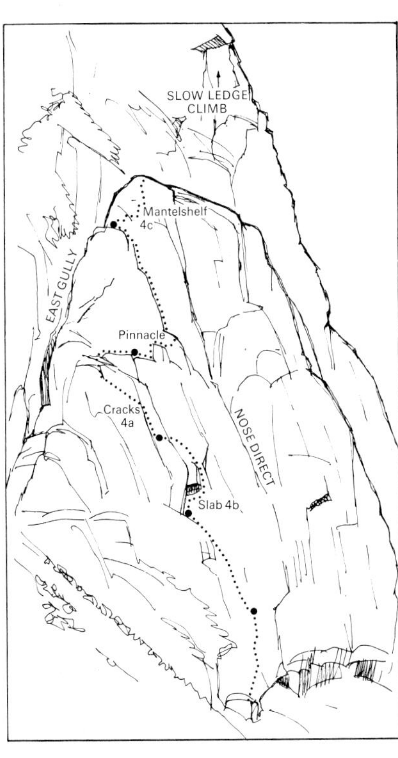

Ken Wilson

Left: The crux move of The Cracks. A fierce pull on indifferent holds is required to gain a ledge near the top of the climb. *Climbers: Unknown*

Near right: The move off the pinnacle on Pitch 5 of The Cracks. *Climber: Unknown*

Bottom right: After the pinnacle move the climb continues up an entertaining crack with a gymnastic exit. The harder corner crack is taken by Lorraine. *Climber: John Hoskins*

The next section started with a half-step/half-mantelshelf from a large pinnacle on to another ledge. Barbara decided to continue without a belay, as the crack above looked relatively straightforward. I think she rather regretted the decision by the time the next stance was reached, for the crack became increasingly more interesting, and a runner placed low down after the change of direction generated a fair amount of rope drag. That runner was reassuring when I made the awkward first move, and as a second I found the crack above delightful.

I was then confronted by the final pitch. This has been described fairly accurately as a boulder problem above a sheer 250ft. drop. I gingerly mounted the parallel ledges until I stood below the final terrace, which bulged out awkwardly. The runner I fixed felt most inadequate and the drop below uncompromising. Time and again I managed to get my fingers at full stretch into the only semblance of a hold, but the move was more a pull-up than a mantelshelf and somehow I could not commit myself. Finally, I retreated. Barbara, too, had been unnerved by my exhibition and we took the easier alternative of the arête above. Whether we could between us have engineered the move (perhaps by means of a second's shoulder!) if there had been no alternative, I do not know. Its very avoidability makes the top pitch rather artificial.

When climbing on the Mot, one cannot relax on finishing any of the main face routes. There remains the alternative of continuing up one of the climbs on the next level (possibly Slow Ledge) or descending down West Gully. Most people choose the latter and the gully can get quite congested, with the associated danger of stone-fall. The initial steep section, which looks rather intimidating, does not present any great difficulty, although care is necessary. It is the final 20ft. down a very greasy slab that I find unpleasant. This is best tackled by traversing leftward (facing out) to meet the rising ground.

The Cracks provide a very worthwhile introduction to climbing on Dinas Mot. Each pitch presents a challenge and the climb has more atmosphere than most routes of a similar standard so near civilization. Its only flaw is the artificial nature of the top

Ken Wilson

pitch, where one could argue that the logical, if less interesting, line is up the arête of East Gully.

Above right: A full frontal view of The Nose of Dinas Mot. The Cracks take a devious line up the steps on the left. The descent from the top of the Nose requires care. Either the East Gully (left) or the West Gully (in shadow on the right) can be taken. Both are quite difficult and great care should be taken to avoid dislodging stones. West Gully is slightly easier, but, if the final pitch of The Cracks is left out, a descent down East Gully is preferable, with a start on the right side to descend the final difficult step. Both descents can be avoided by continuing up Slow Ledge Climb.

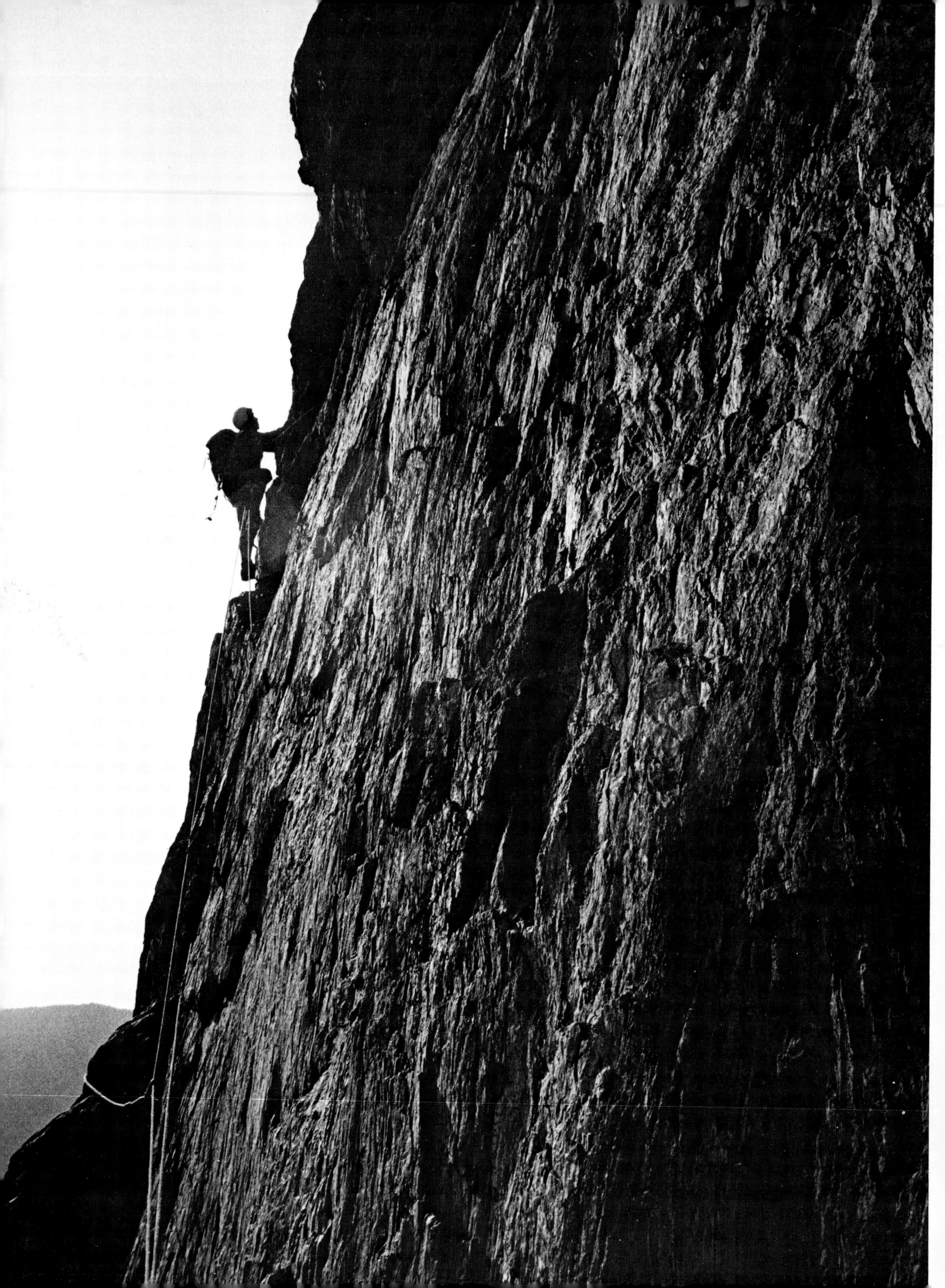

40 Main Wall

by Sir Charles Evans

'One of the finest expeditions in the Snowdon massif . . . technically not of a high standard . . . serious enough to warrant a high Severe classification . . . exposure such as is seldom experienced on Welsh crags, including Clogwyn du'r Arddu.'

The standard of difficulty, and of what is commonly tolerated in the way of exposure, has changed beyond belief since Peter Harding wrote that about Main Wall, but for succeeding generations this extraordinary climb will always retain something of its power to intimidate as well as to delight. It is forbiddingly steep, has no easy options, and yet is nowhere too difficult for the average climber. Such a route can become an obsession: you get to feel that it has something to give you personally and, until you have climbed it, you cannot leave it alone. That's how it was for me with Main Wall.

The route lies on the Great Buttress of Cyrn Las, the crag more properly called Diffwys Ddu ('Black Steep'), a massive, solitary bastion which dominates the lower slopes of Cwm Glas as seen from Ynys Ettws. The steepness is beyond question; the colour is a matter of atmosphere, of weather and of the climber's mood: most people on their way to the cliff for the first time would not quarrel with the word 'black'.

P. L. Roberts and J. K. ('Jake') Cooke, who lost his life at Dunkirk, made the first ascent of Main Wall in 1935, after which it seems to have been unaccountably neglected for about a decade. They used more stances and found more rock belays than the climbers of today, and of course used no pegs or runners. In their original account the grading was 'Severe', unqualified; the phrase 'exhilaratingly steep', which they used about what is now pitch 5, was the only hint at the exposure described by Peter Crew thirty years later as 'tremendous'.

I first went to Cyrn Las with George Band. We were recently back from the Himalayas and were climbing badly: even Great Gully, immediately to the left of Main Wall and largely overlooked by it, seemed desperately steep and difficult. Main Wall, I felt, was for another breed of men.

Wind and rain can give the dark slabs and dripping overhangs of Cyrn Las a grim, sinister look and for me their sombre gloom was reinforced about that time by a particularly distressing double fatality on Main Wall itself.

Then everything changed. After a July day on Dinas Mot, in 1956, I suddenly found Cyrn Las's Great Gully easy; after doing it we ran down to the foot again so that, late evening though it was, I could climb up and down the first pitches of Main Wall to see what they were like. Care was needed, but in three pitches there seemed to be hardly an awkward step: I wondered if the whole intimidating aspect of the climb was after all only a mask.

6 January 1957: at last the mood was as right as it would ever be, the company undoubtedly right, and with the winter's day tolerable after a week of rain. With Dennis Davis, Denise Morin and Gordon Mansell behind me, all far more voluble talkers and better rock-climbers than me, I felt that if ever we got to the foot of the climb I could hardly avoid being persuaded up it. First, however, there was a slight problem: we had only one rope – enough for Dennis and me. Enquiries among friends brought a kind offer from a seafaring inhabitant of Ynys Ettws: 'I've got a hundred feet of flax you can have; it does for all I want.' He added: 'I'm afraid it doesn't quite come up to B.M.C. specification for flax.' I thought that, whatever we used, it had better be up to B.M.C. specification for flax, so I declined the offer and Denise went to see what she could borrow from some girls at Cwm Glas Mawr. Two hundred feet of nylon was forthcoming and we walked up to the crag.

The first 350ft. of steep, loose and dirty ground gave me a discouraging feeling of being high up, even before the climbing started. The rocks were wet, slimy and chill, and to boost my morale I pulled a pair of old socks over some PAs. The slabby first pitch reminded me of Lliwedd; the clean second pitch led on good holds to a sort of rocky bracket, the 'pulpit', where Dennis and Denise joined me. From the pulpit, a sloping gangway with steep rock above and below led in a rising curve to the right for 45ft. That day, the sloping holds were thoroughly wet and I was very glad to be wearing socks. After the traverse to the right was a short

Route Main Wall Climb, Hard Severe, 400ft.
Cliff Cyrn Las; Cwm Glas, Llanberis Pass.
First Ascent P. L. Roberts and J. K. Cooke, July 1935. The first pitch was added by Roberts, Cooke and E. Holliday in March 1937.
Map Reference O.S. Tourist Map to Snowdonia, 1–50,000 Sheet (ref. 614560).
Guidebooks C.C. *The Llanberis Pass* by Geoff Milburn; *Rock Climbing in Wales* by Ron James.
Nearest Road The A4086 at Blaen-y-Nant, a farmhouse 1 miles south-east of Nant Peris.
Distance and time from cliff 1 mile/1,800ft. Allow 1¼ hours.
Good Conditions Dries quickly in the summer months, but is considerably harder in cold wintry weather.
Campsites and Bunkhouses Camping at Blaen-y-Nant. Various club huts in the Llanberis Pass including the Climbers' Club huts, Cwm Glas Mawr and Ynys Ettws.
Bibliography *Snowdon Biography* by Geoffrey Winthrop Young, Geoff Sutton and Wilfrid Noyce (Dent, 1957).

Opposite page: The splendid wall pitch of Main Wall, where the climber moves round a tremendously exposed corner on good holds. *Climber: Ken Wilson*

Ken Wilson

Left: The second pitch of Main Wall – rounding the corner to reach the pulpit. *Climber: John Fitzgerald*

Near right: The crux of Main Wall. The climber has to traverse a delicate slab and then make a series of steep moves to gain this position. The route continues up the open chimney above, which trends round to the left. *Climber: Dave Briggs*

Far right: Climbers completing the wall pitch. *Climbers: Unknown*

chimney, from which I sidestepped left for about 30ft. along a broken fault a few inches wide. Here and there were bits of sodden turf: they added to the precarious feel of a pitch on which protection is not simple to arrange.

So I reached a small turf-covered ledge, the ledge from which I had climbed down on my last visit. In a few moments Dennis was beside me and I went on up to a grassy recess where there was room for the four of us.

Our eyrie was spectacular: very steep ground below and overhangs above. It was almost midway up the climb; nearly 200ft. of climbing lay behind us and there was about 200ft. yet to go. It was too cold to linger long, and I had an urge to see for myself what lay about our heads: soon I was traversing out of the grassy corner to a pinnacle some yards up and to the left. Dennis called out: 'Hey, that step you've just done is meant to be hard: you can't just walk across like that!' Knowing Dennis well, I thought to myself: 'He knows I'm frightened.' Indeed I was, so I put a runner over the top of the pinnacle and felt better. The belay in the grassy recess where the others were sitting had not looked too good to me, so I was glad of the runner, but all the same to put it as I did over the pinnacle was a mistake, because when I had climbed higher it caused the rope to jam.

'Now,' I wrote in some notes at the time, 'a difficult move to stand on the pinnacle and another move, rather less hard, into a niche above. Here I put a second runner – rope now tending to drag on a rocky corner. Saw a good spike to my left and went round to the open wall beyond. Here the exposure is so great you don't really notice it: you see the holds and your hands on them – you see your feet – and then there is nothing – so nothing takes your mind off the rock. Holds good and incut but sometimes awkwardly placed and not quite firm; and in the wind my fingers getting definitely cold. Up a bit, right, across a groove to a very exposed slab – not hard – then left under overhangs to a big block. 90ft.'

Somewhere near the top of that pitch the rope finally jammed; Dennis was now out of sight and we couldn't hear each other because of the wind, but, unasked, he

L. W. P. Garland

climbed up to take off the first runner: the rope then came in easily enough and soon he was beside me.

Only the last pitch and a few bits of scrambling remained. The last pitch begins with 20ft. of climbing straight up on good holds and sound rock; then you traverse left to the very edge of a long slab set at a high angle. Here the rock is firm and rough, the holds are excellent, and you linger over each move, enjoying your emergence from the darker (it must now be admitted) scene below, enjoying the glorious position and the perfect security, and trying to make your enjoyment last as long as possible.

Since that day, twenty years ago, pegs have taken the place of the small rock belay at the grass ledge above the pulpit, the turf has gone from the grassy recess above, and the rock pinnacle on which we stood is said to be less firm than it was; otherwise the climb is not much changed except perhaps in the amount of traffic it carries. For an experienced party, Main Wall is straightforward enough. It is nevertheless a serious expedition: there are places where it would be difficult to extricate a party that had got itself into trouble, the general setting is that of the 'big cliff' climb, and no escape from the line of the route is possible except to climbs which are very much harder.

Ken Wilson

eft: The final slab of Main Wall, superbly situated over-ooking Great Gully. *Climber: John Fitzgerald*

41 Avalanche, Red Wall and Longland's Continuation

by Harold Drasdo

Nobody knows what Lliwedd means. Students of academic Welsh modestly propose two or three tentative readings. Local hill farmers think hard for a minute or two, then give a studied answer, often interesting but never the same thing twice.

The cliff itself has held many meanings for climbers and its image has changed steadily through a hundred years. Nobody knows what to make of it today. The biggest precipice in Wales, set in the finest cwm on Snowdon, it draws any climber's eye as he drives towards the mountain. It stands 1,000ft. in height, with a frontage of more than half a mile. It is encrusted with legend: King Arthur's knights are reported to be sleeping out a long bivouac in a so-far-undiscovered niche in Slanting Gully. It is clad in a tapestry of a hundred routes, woven to cover nearly the whole rock surface. But it is a guide-writer's nightmare. The beautiful simplicity of its two great buttresses, each flanked by a smaller attendant, is lost at closer quarters. The form of the cliff shatters into a maze of ribs, corners, slabs and minor gullies. Vegetated ledges and scree-strewn terraces interrupt and generalize all its features. And it's all history now. Two or three desperate recesses remain unattempted, but the modern climber has made little mark on the place. It belongs to groups of long-gone heroes: Archer Thomson at the turn of the century, Menlove Edwards in the 'thirties, and their shadowy acolytes. It looks as if we'll never take it away from them.

There is a point on the Avalanche/Red Wall/Longland's outing at which the modern climber sometimes meets his moment of truth. It's one of maybe four or five possible situations, depending on his age, experience and scepticism. He is led neatly into this trap by a half-century of myth-making. He knows that the old men who climbed here seventy years ago went out in any conditions. He knows they were encumbered by thick Norfolk tweeds and clumsy clinker-nailed boots. He knows they carried rucksacks stuffed with all kinds of goodies and a lot of unnecessary junk such as half-plate cameras and aneroid barometers. He knows they fooled around, building cairns on every big ledge in a Kilroy-was-here act, and sitting down for long breaks to exchange opinions about the finer points of the view.

Knowing all this he is forced into setting up a demonstration of modern capability. He has to hold the route for a wet day. So he has to climb in waterproofs, rucksack and boots. (The waterproofs still don't work in bad conditions; the rucksack is pretty well the same; the vibrams are really unnerving when Lliwedd's slanting holds are greasy.) To demonstrate his alliance with his contemporaries, he carries a perlon rope and drapes himself with chock tapes and wires. (The nuts and slings are curiously hard to place at the awkward bits of this excursion; a full shoulder rack is an irritating handicap on less than vertical rock.)

In 1907, Avalanche represented an audacious undertaking. Nobody had dared adventure himself on such an open face before. As Lliwedd goes, the climb is easy to locate. It starts from, or just below, a big comfortable ledge, the Heather Shelf, just right of the foot of the East Gully. One can walk on to the left end of the shelf, or take a steep groove, smooth and tricky when wet, leading directly to the right-hand end. Here the climb begins. The leader moves around a rib into a big grassy weakness and then around another rib to find himself on the front of the East Buttress. The last two or three steps take him into a position of surprising exposure. He has lost sight of his second and the route becomes less certain. After a half-century of traffic, climbers still take different lines across the steep slab to ledges in or near the next big corner. When the party regroups, the next pitch looks more straightforward: a pleasant, grooved slab leading to ledges below steeper rock. Then comes the traditional crux. A few feet to the right, a broken quartzy wall offers an exit towards easier ground. From the stance, the angle looks reasonable and the opening fault seems to promise excellent holds. But, with the first step up from the end of the ledge, this impression is corrected. The wall is vertical, the holds are spaced, the quartz feels slippery. A moment of adjustment follows as it dawns on modern man that he is going to have to use himself more fully than he planned. A bit of control is needed, a bit of realism, and a bit more muscle than seems

Routes Avalanche, Very Difficult, 400ft.; Red Wall and Longland's Continuation, Hard Very Difficult, 450ft.
Cliff East Buttress, Lliwedd.
First Ascents Avalanche and Red Wall – J. M. A. Thomson and E. S. Reynolds, 1907; Longland's Continuation – J. L. Longland and party, 1929.
Map Reference O.S. Tourist Map to Snowdonia, 1–50,000 Sheet 115 (ref.625534).
Guidebooks C.C. *Lliwedd* by Harold Drasdo; *Rock Climbing in Wales* by Ron James.
Nearest Road The A4086 at Pen-y-Pass. Parking is difficult in the tourist season so it is best to start early.
Distance and time from cliff 2 miles/900ft. Allow 1 hour.
Good Conditions Allow at least two dry summer days after bad weather. The rock is very greasy and the standard of these climbs increases considerably in all but perfect conditions.
Campsites and Bunkhouses Camping at various points on the approach. Youth Hostel at Pen-y-Pass. Club huts in the Llanberis Pass and the Gwynant Valley.
Bibliography *The Climbs on Lliwedd* by J. M. A. Thomson and A. W. Andrews (Edward Arnold, 1909); *Mountaineering in Britain* by R. W. Clark and E. C. Pyatt (Dent/Phoenix House, 1957). Snowdon Biography by Geoffrey Winthrop Young, Geoff Sutton and Wilfrid Noyce (Dent, 1957); *The Mountains of Snowdonia* by H. R. C. Carr and G. A. Lister (Bodley Head, 1925); C. C. Journal, March 1909: *The East Peak of Lliwedd* by J. M. Archer Thomson, is a very interesting first-ascent account.

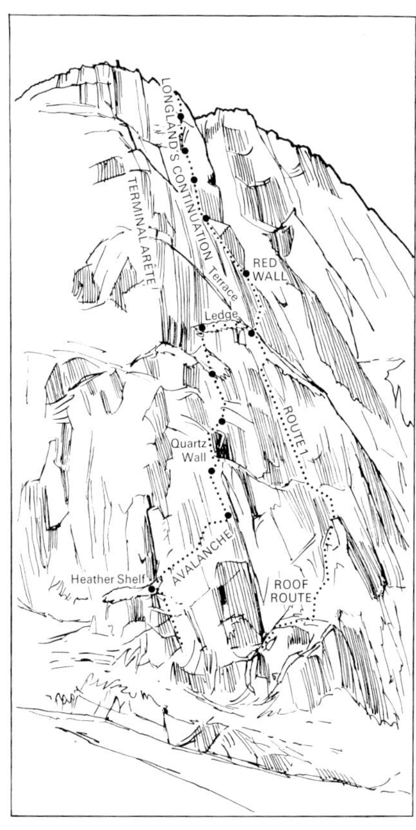

Top left: At the crux of Red Wall, where difficult moves lead across to and up a rib. A piton sometimes appears on this pitch, a criminal travesty on one of the classical test-pieces of the Welsh lower grades. Nevertheless the pitch has seen its full quota of accidents, so carefull nut-placements are advisable. *Climber: Mike Papworth*

Bottom left: The final hard moves of Red Wall, with the climber pulling up on a typical Lliwedd hold, a pinch grip on a tiny rib. The lower part of the Lliwedd cliffs is not noted for its profusion of incut holds. *Climber: John Fitzgerald*

Ken Wilson

right for a route of this vintage. So he pulls it out and reaches better holds, finding a good belay point up and out to the right on the very crest of the buttress. In passing or changing over, the party can savour the situation: it seems almost alpine. The accuracy of Archer Thomson's original note on Avalanche comes to mind: 'Steepness. Absence of grass and gravel. Excellence of rock. Exiguity of holds. Long distance between belays. A succession of breezy situations.'

And then the route declines into scrambling, and a walk out to the right gives on to the wide slopes of the Great Terrace at the very heart of the East Buttress. Any tension is dissipated on this gigantic balcony, with the easy escape of Terminal Arête not far away to the left.

To find Red Wall, the guidebook must be read attentively. The rock here is clean and attractive. A rising traverse to the right gets steadily more entertaining until a severe problem presents itself. The climber has to step up and across into a shallow corner. There is a superb letterbox foothold inserted at precisely the wrong angle. There is a tiny slot, very finicky in its choice of nuts. And here the modern expert has to halt on a move that may not be Severe in dry conditions, but which, given rain, vibrams, waterproofs, sack and a chain armour of unusable protection, is unmistakably very much harder. And, to tell the truth, Archer Thomson had his boots off here. In his guide he remembers the move: 'One fancy foot-hold of limited utility.'

Never underestimate the pioneers. The old climbers weren't all that old when they put these routes up. Most of them were very energetic, very intelligent, very cool young men. They were in excellent training. They knew their cliffs like the backs of their hands. They saved the hard possibilities for the right day. They had all the time in the world. And they were fakers, just like the modern climber. They used a lot of skill to keep the pursuing generation in its proper place. They promoted their own achievements obsessively, sometimes as subtly as the masters of the 'fifties, sometimes as loudly as the superstars of today. (In the Pen-y-Pass book, about the turn of the century, there is a note by some visiting experts on the difficulties of

Above: The final slab pitch of Longland's Continuation. *Climber: Sir Charles Evans*

a new route. Underneath, there is a curt and scathing comment initialled by one of the local giants of those years – Oscar Eckenstein, if I remember rightly. And underneath that an anonymous commentator has written: 'The Welsh forwards are pressing!' It reads very like the exchanges in hut logbooks today.)

So we fight a way up this move somehow or other. After that it gets easier. Then it gets harder again. It throws up, in a perfectly safe situation, a ridiculously grasping move at the top of the next pitch. We can easily walk round it and know in our minds that we haven't really done the climb. So we warm our fingers and wrench a way up. We get on to the engaging opening pitch of Longland's and then come on to easy splintered rocks. It's all over now. Except for the last 40ft. slab to the summit of the East Peak, which calls for delicacy as well as fingers. Then the screaming wind and driving rain on top. It has seemed a long way.

I spent more years than I like to recall in working up the present edition of the Lliwedd guide. It left me wiped out and I couldn't imagine how many more years might elapse before I'd want to go there again. In the event it was in response to a request on behalf of a young American who wished to climb Mallory's Slab. The visitor turned out to be none other than Mallory's grandson. We made our way up the route, soloed by Mallory, the legend says, to recover a pipe left on the Bowling Green. Then we moved on to the Great Terrace and finished up Red Wall and Longland's. It was a perfect summer day and it went like a dream. 'As good a mountain day as I've ever had,' he said, as we relaxed on the summit. And hearing this testimony, and seeing the old cliff through fresh eyes, I saw it in a new light. The first big face climbs remain standards of excellence, undiminished by any later achievements.

Every guidebook-writer worries a little about the first subsequent accident on his cliff. I was at an all-night party a few months after my guide appeared, when I heard that a very large and very heavy man had broken his thigh in the most inaccessible situation on the whole face. I was in no condition to offer my services. Next day I heard the tale. In the early hours the rescue team reached the screes beneath the mighty wall. The leader produced a loud hailer and addressed the mountainside: 'Where are you?' To the astonishment of the team, out of the blackness, voices responded from all over Lliwedd: 'Here!' It seems to have become the favoured place for unplanned autumn bivouacs. Never underestimate the pioneers.

42 Creagh Dhu Wall

by Jim Perrin

Route Creagh Dhu Wall, Hard Severe, 200ft.
Cliff Craig y Castell, Tremadog.
First Ascent J. Cunningham, W. Smith, P. Vaughan, July 1951.
Map Reference O.S. Tourist Map of Snowdonia, 1–50,000 Sheet (ref. 558407).
Guidebooks C.C. *Tremadog and the Moelwyns* by Mike Mortimer; West Col *Tremadog Area* by P. Crew and A. Harris; *Rock Climbing in North Wales* by Ron James.
Nearest Road The A498 at Tremadog. A side road by the school is the best parking spot.
Distance and time from cliff 300 yds/200ft. Allow 5 minutes.
Good Conditions The route enjoys very good weather and is climbable through most of the year. It faces west and is exposed to any rain, but it dries very quickly.
Campsites and Bunkhouses Camping at Cwm Mawr above Craig Pant Ifan. Redditch and Bromsgrove M.C. Hut at Bwlch y Moch Farm (ref. 576406).

In the Alps it would be called a *chandelle*: a narrow pillar of red rock, flame-like almost in its leap from dark surroundings. But this ruddy pillar gains no sterile delineation from snow and ice; around it is the fecund greenery of a British hill-slope. Mottled foliage and a tracery of boughs soften its features, shade them down into a landscape suffused with low western light. The cliff is called Craig y Castell, though for no reason which I can explain. It bears not the slightest resemblance to a castle; indeed, it's almost a domestic crag. It rises above green fields, back gardens, and a school playground, to dome gently over into woodland above. In extent it's a small cliff, perhaps 180ft. high and its breadth not great. In features, too, it is simple: left and right flanks are slabby, the right seamed with overhangs through which fine, hard climbs force their way. A discontinuous corner line, shared in varying degrees by The Wasp and Pellagra, fronts the nose of the buttress, finest feature of the cliff, and here Creagh Dhu Wall frolics along its course.

Despite knowing that it was numbered among the handful of great Severes in Wales, it was a long time before I got round to doing the route. Perhaps I took too literally the Glaswegian understatement of Cunningham's dismissive comment on his own routes at Tremadog: 'boring, trivial little climbs'. However it was, I remember the occasion of my own ascent perfectly. It was a June evening of warm sunlight. I had been living in London and early on this day had packed my car, quit the place for good, and, surfeited of society, had driven up through the lonely centre of Wales to arrive towards evening in Tremadog. The sun was gleaming on this red *chandelle*. I could almost feel the rough warm rock beneath my fingers. Every so often a man needs to recoup his simplicities, and mine was a case in point. There were no ties of companion or equipment upon me, no restraint beyond the sinking sun; I was uncluttered and free to the uttermost. There is no bad wine in youth or new-found freedom, and in just such a mood should a man sometimes taste his rock; from the bridge of a Dreadnought, whose blood is not stirred by a clipper before the wind? So I laced my PAs and walked to the foot of this sunlit evening cliff by a path which led me directly to our present route. There, scrawled on the rock in all the loutish blatancy of modern climbing, was that Scottish name. All the ballyhoo about Sassenach, yet what's that compared to this Scottish bludgeon? At least 'Sassenach' is a Scottish word, and even so it's not scrawled across the foot of Carn Dearg. I edged past the Pictish scribble and applied myself to the romance of the west.

Which began, oddly and awkwardly, behind a tree, with a slanting, quartzy crack, rather painful and wide, in the wall of a groove, and eked out by a hold or two therein; all very steep, a little muscular, and warming. I can't think why you should ever have to leave that lovely, rough, steep little groove, but you do. Above, there are holds, jams, perfection of line; but instead out right you go, round the arête, the one indirection in the life of a climb and all for a couple of brief thrills. It's not responsible and it tempts you along its path, and to this day I've not been up that lovely groove. The traverse has foot-holds, large as long as they last; where they end, a restrained collapse across into an easy groove. All this would be simple but for the fact that hand-holds there are none. Above is a large, sunny ledge with succulent plants and a sturdy oak. But be wary of leaders on harder climbs above, lest they should fall on your innocent head.

Perhaps you've noticed the advantages which accrue from boldness and confidence: the timid create worlds of difficulty which the brave hardly know to exist. The return half of our rectangular excursion is a case in point; leading out on to the nose is an odd line of blocks. The situation of below is neatly reversed, for here foot-holds there are none. So you swing across on your hands and, thus done, it is strenuously straightforward. If you tire, put your right knee in behind the flake; round the corner is a ledge, but oh! the struggle for some. Up the nose now, all air and playing on cat's-tongue slabs, with holds, sometimes good, often less so, and runners much the same, to an area of ledges and blocks where the guidebook tells you to belay. In all honesty I don't think this is advisable, for all these blocks are fundamentally unsound: a bad place for a

second to hold a long fall. To place a runner or two and continue seems the best policy.

Which brings me back to this point on a June evening a few years ago. No guidebook and the propensity to follow one's nose are the best aids to climbing, and thus it was that I climbed on up a slim, delicate, charming groove. It struck me then that there would have been few runners about, but the point was academic at the time. What I didn't know was that the route proper finishes up a groove over to the left – a little, awkward, polished, nasty, hard groove justified only by the runner at your belly. If you don't mind a scarcity of protection then I'd wholeheartedly recommend the straighter way, or even the finishing groove of Sisyphus, round to the right and easier still – anything but the entry to that horrid groove, where once I was stuck for half an hour, standing on my laces, unable to move. Thank God there were no such traumas on that first occasion; just rough, warm rock, small holds, and sweet repose on top. And an evening view almost magical: little, humpy, gnarled Criccieth castle against its crescent of sea; the Lleyn stretching and curving out on its old Pilgrim's Way to Bardsey, beyond that Avalon perhaps; and the perfect mood of sunset. What better place to gaze from than this little, perfect, happy candle of rock?

Top left: The first pitch of Creagh Dhu Wall – moving up into a steep groove. *Climber: John Fitzgerald*

Near left: The foot traverse that completes the first pitch. *Climber: Mike Papworth*

Bottom left: Delightful climbing leads up the crest of the buttress to the second stance. The obvious belays here are large loose blocks, and a more careful search will be required to find a really secure anchorage. *Climbers: John Fitzgerald and Mike Papworth*

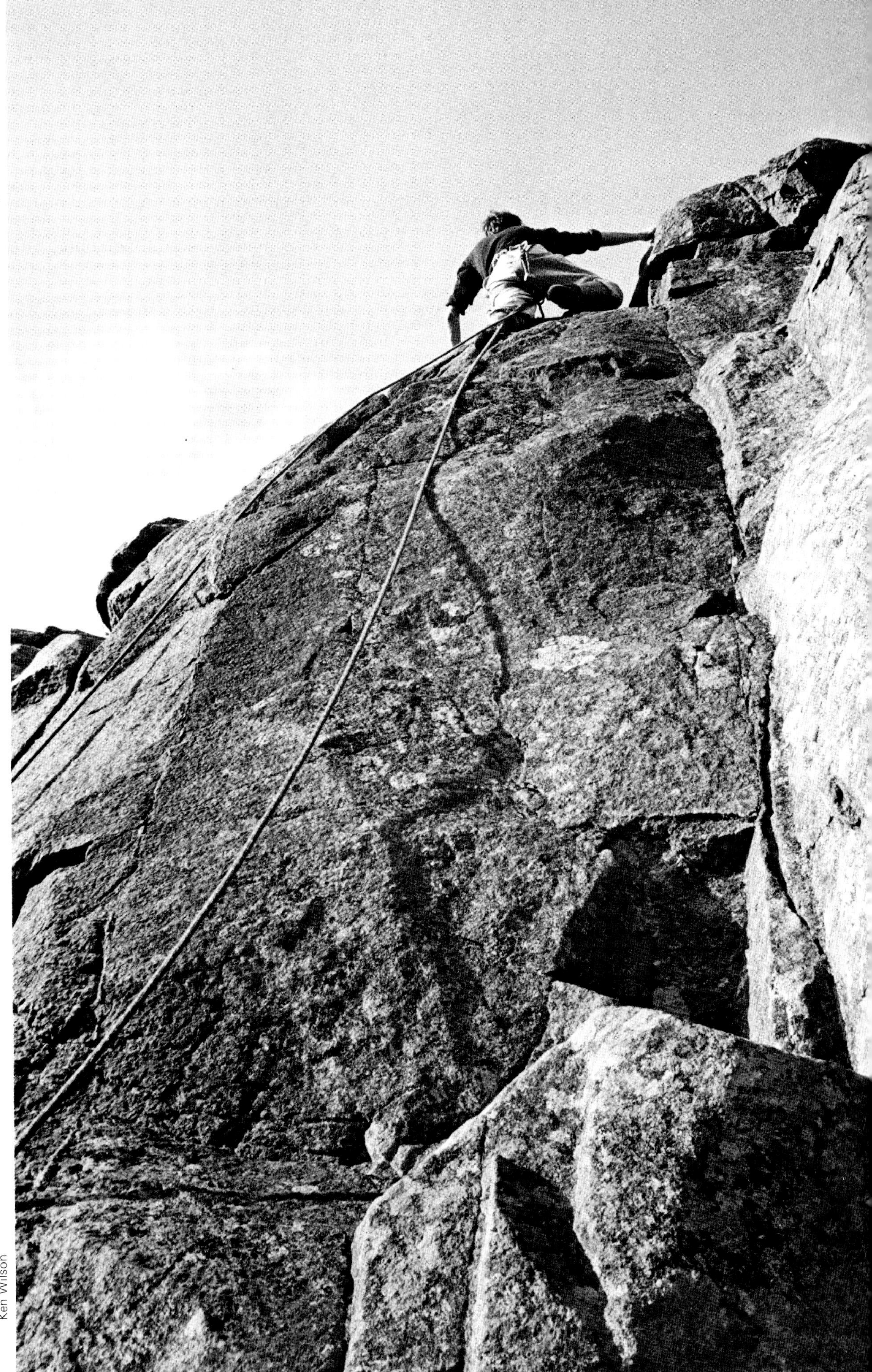

Right: Looking up the hard groove that forms the direct finish to the route. The crack on the left leads up to the polished groove of the normal finish. *Climber: Mike Papworth*

Ken Wilson

43 Will-o'-the-Wisp

by John Sumner

Route Will-o'-the-Wisp, Hard Very Difficult, 310ft.
Cliff South Buttress on Craig Cowarch, Cwm Cowarch, Arans.
First Ascent J. A. Sumner and Miss J. P. Henrickson, April 1972.
Map Reference O.S. 1–50,000 Sheet 124 (ref. 848193).
Guidebook West Col *Central Wales* by John Sumner.
Nearest Road A minor road up Cwm Cowarch. Sensitive parking problems at present and diplomacy and courtesy is essential.
Distance and time from cliff ½ mile/850ft. Allow 30 minutes. Walk up the valley towards Bryn Hafod, climb the hillside and move back to the left at the level of the top of the plantations.
Good Conditions Dries quickly after rain.
Campsites and Bunkhouses Camping in the field beyond Blaencywarch Farm (ask permission). Mountain Club Hut – Bryn Hafod – below the cliff.

As you travel westwards from Welshpool along the A458, through the rolling green hills to Dinas Mawddwy in central Wales, there is no indication of a crag anywhere in the vicinity. Yet you only have to go a mile up the Cowarch valley and the huge, humpy mass of Craig Cowarch comes into view, comprising in fact twenty-three different crags. On the skyline is the prominent nose of North-East Buttress. Out of view round the corner is the north end, with the longer, harder routes. From the common near the head of Cwm Cowarch, Tap-y-Gigfran is seen, with its big overhang, high up in the Cwm on the left. Then, as you walk up the road towards the valley-head, Far South Buttress comes into sight. South Buttress is the next along, with a fairly clean triangular section of rock on its left-hand side, roughly lying above the gap between the two pine tree plantations. Will-o'-the-Wisp traverses across this triangular section, then up its left arête.

Most of the easier grade climbs at Cowarch need a fair amount of hard gardening. With today's climber turning his nose up and writing off routes that have more than a handful of grass on them, it's no wonder that Cowarch is left to the connoisseur. Routes in 'the Pass' used to be heavily vegetated! And I remember when there was a forest on Spiral Stairs: only by thousands of ascents have they been reduced to their present state. Anyway, there was, and still is, a great lack of easy routes at Cowarch. But they are there, sleeping under three feet of earth, heather, bilberry, blood, sweat and tears, etc.

So it was that one cold, sleety, winter's day an easy line was spotted running between VS climbs on a south-facing crag. An intensive cleaning programme began, mainly on cold, rainy, winter days. The blood and sweat came from me and the tears from Jill, as she went numb with cold holding my rope (a hazard from which all my seconds suffer). As the warm sunshine fell on the crag, help was offered on the lower section, and rain and sunshine finished off the job. From the end of the valley, a huge zigzag scar could be seen, eerily gleaming white even in the moonlight. That's how it got its name, you see: it took a lot of catching.

The final product is on good, sound granite, less bleached as the years go by, but with good friction, which one appreciates after climbing some of the North Wales classics. It is a route that can be and has been climbed in all conditions, an ideal warm-up for VS climbs which it crosses, or an easy and exciting route for a beginner. It even has sunbathing ledges on the way up, weather permitting. (End of advertisement.)

When the first pitch was gardened, a stream sprang out of the rock, so the slab is nearly always wet – refreshing on a hot day and not noticed in rain. On the first stance there's a good chockstone thread belay to reassure many a beginner. The next pitch goes up and right to avoid the steep wall, and you're on the first of the 'Tea Ledges'. These were aptly named by Sandy, who once remarked that the next time he deemed to climb Will-o'-the-Wisp he expected to find tables and chairs laid out for tea and cream buns. There is a perfect Moac slot belay at about waist height (depending on your size), and a chance to look out at the beautiful U-shaped glacier valley, before the traverse.

By following the white scar on good holds left and up to a delicate step, protected by a nut runner, the next Tea Ledge is gained. The peg belay is an old sawn-off ice-peg, the only peg remaining incidentally, the peg-baggers having collected the other two. These airy 'promenade-able' ledges finish in a long stride over a gaping gap, which often brings the little orange dots to a halt for a while. I remember once sitting by the roaring fire in the hut, looking out of the window at the sheeting rain, watching the progress of the little orange dots just visible on the white scar. One rope of four spent all day slowly inching their way across and up the route. We were getting slightly anxious as darkness fell, but then their twinkling lights could be seen coming down the hill. All four were soaked to the skin when they arrived at the hut, but all declared that they'd had a great day.

After the gap comes a more technical section, keeping slightly down and more to the horizontal, with a long stride in the middle. People have been known to stray on to VSs here, with leaders thinking 'That's a bit hard for V.Diff.', and with seconds gripped out of their minds! This pitch brings the traverse to

Ken Wilson

an end, on a little ledge on the edge of the arête. Inevitably, one takes note of the big drop all round and the steep wall above, thinking: 'Where do we go from here?'

Then comes the *pièce de résistance* and, surprise, surprise, you pop left round the corner, with a steep drop below, and up the wall on good holds to gain a superb position on the arête above. This is probably the crux, both psychologically and technically. The last pitch is the natural line to the top. A brave move off a square-shaped block is followed by a final little crack, with a small tree which is still intact. With that you have conquered Will-o'-the-Wisp, and gained all the other emotions we climbers never cease to desire. Now you have a chance to look down the valley and absorb its unspoilt tranquillity. We value our solitude at Cowarch, where, if we see half-a-dozen climbers, we declare: 'The crag was crowded today.'

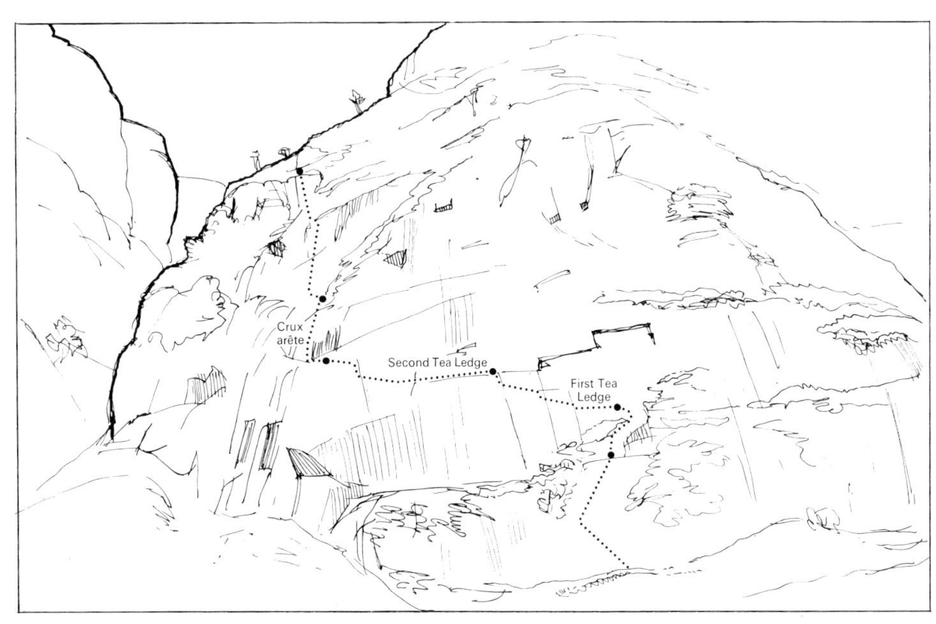

John Sumner

Ken Wilson

Far left: The delicate traverse on the third pitch of Will-o'-the-Wisp. The climber in the background is on the Second Tea Ledge. *Climber: Jill Sumner*

Left: The exhilarating arête pitch that is the crux of Will-o'-the-Wisp. *Climber: Unknown*

Left: The gritstone summit cliffs of Penyghent with their support plinth of limestone outcrops.

Right: Red Pencil Climb (see following chapter). *Climber: Ken Jones*

Chris Hall

44 Red Pencil Direct

by Anthony Greenbank

Route Red Pencil Climb, Severe, 90ft.
Cliff The West Face of Penyghent, near Settle, Yorkshire.
First Ascent A. Greenbank and party, 1956, though it may have been led earlier by A. R. Dolphin.
Map Reference O.S. 1–50,000 Sheet 98 (ref. 836732).
Guidebook Y.M.C. *Yorkshire Gritstone* by M. Bebbington.
Nearest Road A track near the minor road from Stainforth to Halton Gill. It is possible to park (ask permission) by old farm buildings at Dale Head (ref. 841716).
Distance and time from cliff 1½ miles/700ft. Allow 30 minutes. Take the Pennine Way track from Dale Head Farm to Penyghent and traverse round the hillside to the west just below the summit escarpment. There is a slightly longer approach direct from Horton (1 hour).
Good Conditions Allow two days for the crag to dry after heavy rain, except in the summer months. The cliff is very exposed to bad weather and strong winds.
Campsites and Bunkhouses Youth Hostel in Stainforth. Inns in Stainforth and Horton. Camping at Horton. Y.R.C. Hut, Lowstern, near Clapham (11 miles). Climber's shop and cafe at Horton.
Bibliography Mountain Craft 46, Winter 1960: *Rock Climbing on Penyghent* by Tony Greenbank (general appraisal of the crag with photographs and cover photo of Red Pencil Climb).

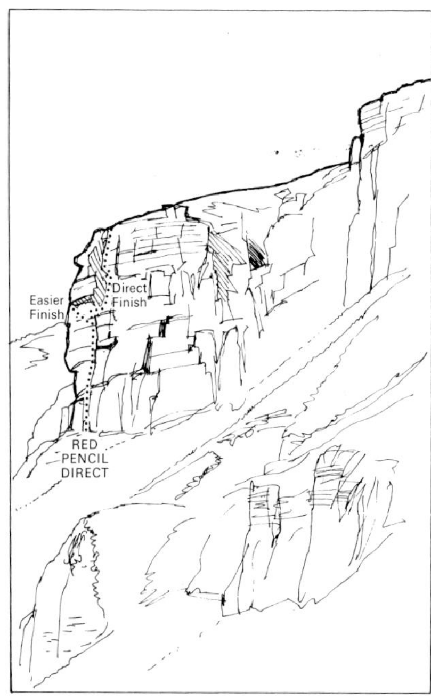

A climb out on a limb, never really in vogue, Red Pencil, which crests the south-west skyline of Penyghent, nevertheless has a striking situation – crowning one of the highest and most remote mountains in the Pennines – and a line so obvious it is easily seen from Horton-in-Ribblesdale, an hour's walk away. It is accompanied by a dozen other worthy climbs on one compact buttress, 90ft. tall, so the visiting climber has a choice ranging from Diff. to HVS, which, combined with attractive walking on the most popular section of the Pennine Way, makes for the complete mountain day.

There are steep crack and face routes pioneered by Ian Clough (Gladiator, Girdle and Agnostic's Arête), and later by Allan Austin (Bilberry Wall and Pitchfork Crack). But it was Red Pencil (recorded by this writer in the October 1956 issue of *The Dalesman* – although it had been visited previously, and presumably climbed, by Arthur Dolphin) which first drew climbing attention to the mountain.

Although Red Pencil is not a classic, in the sense that it is relatively new, and while there are many other routes on grit that are more popular, this climb has a classic aura reminiscent of a real mountain crag. The climbing is sustained at Very Difficult for 70ft. up the corner of a big gritstone box, and then the route slips past a prominent lid overhanging very steep slopes below. The sense of exposure at this point is heightened by the line of white limestone cliffs arranged across the mountainside far beneath. And then, 'tippling away still below these, the scree continues to the moor. Ingleborough is seen away in the distance. The sky is full of the sound of curlew, meadow pipit and grouse. It is a wild, lonely and beautiful setting.

You can walk from Horton, but the short approach is to drive from Stainforth up the Halton Gill road, then turn off along the track to Churn Milk Hole. Park here and take to the moor which leads to slopes running up the nose of the mountain, and just to the south of the crag. Once past the row of limestone buttresses, skirt the slopes leftwards and scramble up to the narrow terrace beneath the crag.

The climbing on this main buttress, unlike that on some of the higher edges, is clean. It lacks the immaculate pavements of a Stanage on top, but up to here the face is sound and rough, and only becomes less reliable on the neighbouring turrets which flank it on both sides.

Red Pencil is 'bigger' and harder than either Flying Buttress on Stanage or 'A' Climb on the Cow at Ilkley – routes with which it is sometimes compared. Its crux is a thin bottomless crack at 25ft., which guards the best of the corner above. Down here the topmost overhangs cast a presence which makes the climbing up to them all the more intimidating. But beneath the roof there is a good crack for a nut runner, and an exciting stride is made across left to a chimney. This cleft looks equally hard from below, as it also overhangs, but there are good holds inside. It was at the base of this chimney that a red pencil was jammed for several years, giving the climb its name.

The climb has a Severe direct finish which crosses the right wall from the nut runner beneath the overhangs. Bridging and jamming lead the climber to a small ledge on the face. A natural staircase then breaks through more overhangs which look desperate from below. There is little to choose for quality, however, between this and the ordinary finish, as both have equally good moments.

Whatever your standard, you won't waste your time here. Red Pencil is an ideal solo warm-up before the rest of the Severes and VSs are attended to, if that is the aim. It is also a route capable of taking any reasonable mountaineer to his limit, for in wind and sleet it becomes an excursion to remember long after others are forgotten. The crag, after all, is one which most people will visit only once; it just happens to have this climb of character near a summit 2,373ft. above sea-level, and good climbing and sensational position make it well worth the trip.

45 Parsons' Chimney

by Angela Faller

Almscliff is Wharfedale's castle of the winds. From its battlements, 600ft. above sea level, you can see the Cleveland Hills, Ilkla' Moor, and Emley mast in South Yorkshire. Leeds, only ten miles away, hides in a hollow until dark, then creates an eerie glow in the sky. Call the crag 'Arms Cliff' if you like, and form a love-hate relationship with it. Certainly, to climb even the easier routes you need strength or technique, and for the harder ones it helps to have both. But what a place to learn! There are numerous boulder problems and more than sixty climbs from easy to utterly desperate, all on perfect rock. The most useful techniques are hand-jamming and conserving your energy in unlikely positions. Even on overhanging rock your feet can be useful.

At 50ft., Parsons' Chimney is one of the longest 'straight up' routes at Almscliff. Traditionally it is climbed as two pitches, of which the lower has two distinct alternatives and the upper at least three, so there are several possible combinations. The more popular start involves laybacking up an obvious crack in the wall to the left of the chimney proper. This crack must be gained by a couple of moves up and left, holding yourself into the rock with your right hand, and stretching for the crack with your other. The edge of the crack is good, fortunately, since the ground has fallen away and you are already in a position where hand-holds are essential. Now you must commit yourself to layback moves and get your feet high up the wall. The left toe can be placed in the crack, and good fluted hand-holds appear on the right. Pull into the cave of the chimney, but beware of birds and their droppings, for the woodpigeons that nest here can give you an unpleasant surprise. Before belaying to a thread in the back of the cave, notice the direct continuation of the crack you came up – Overhanging Groove, steep and reachy, a typical Almscliff VS.

To get here you could also have climbed the first chimney pitch. A few moves are made using small holds on its slabby, green right wall; it is then possible to turn round, bridge on to the impending left wall, and gain the cave. This is about the same standard as the other way, but quite different. The famous North West Girdle (HVS) crosses Parsons' Chimney at this level, entering the cave from the left and leaving it with difficulty round its bulging right wall.

It is usual to start the second pitch in the back of the cave, facing right and chimneying between polished walls. For a few moves the situation is not exposed. But don't go too high before moving out, especially with a helmet on, or your head will be the main obstruction. In the spring, Mrs Woodpigeon will stay on her nest deep in the fissure, temporarily abandoned by her mate. Slender or compressible climbers may struggle up the very narrow innards of the chimney. A point is reached where the shoulders are wedged and the feet hang free. This may be the only Almscliff problem that Allan Austin can't do! It is bolder, but not unduly difficult, to leave the cave by wide bridging near its mouth. Again, the object is to establish a chimneying position facing left (north).

You should now be in a comfortable but exposed position, seated on a sloping ledge with your feet on a smaller one opposite. There is a chockstone above, firmly jammed in the top of the chimney. You have to stand up and go round the outside of it. Good hand-holds make standing up easy. Now the chimney is a convenient width. With your back against the wall transfer a foot to a polished scrape on the edge of all things, push up, reach a jam behind the chockstone or fluted jugs and make a move as exhilarating as you like on to the top of the crag. There's a little hole near the edge or more solid belays further back. Bring up your second quickly, so that Mr Woodpigeon can go home. If you found Parsons' Chimney good value for Severe, well done. If it seemed easy, well, it's the hardest of the Severes, so you must get stuck into the Almscliff VSs. And the best of luck!

Left: Two views of Parsons' Chimney – the strenuous direct start (inset) and the dramatic moves to quit the chimney to complete the route (large photo). The layback crack that forms the alternative start is on the left, its continuation the testing VS problem Overhanging Groove. *Climber: Al Manson*

Route Parsons' Chimney, Hard Severe; 50ft.
Cliff Almscliff Crag, Wharfedale, Yorkshire.
First Ascent W. Parsons and (possibly) F. Botterill, 1900.
Map Reference O.S. 1–50,000 Sheet 104 (ref. 268490).
Guidebook Y.M.C. *Yorkshire Gritstone* by M. Bebbington.
Nearest Road A minor road from Huby to Rigton, two villages close to the A658 Harrogate/Bradford road, about 5 miles south-west of Harrogate. Park on the north-west side of the cliff.
Good Conditions The crag is very exposed to bad weather but dries quickly.
Campsites and Bunkhouses There are no huts or campsites nearby, but there are bivouac boulders below the crag.
Bibliography *Some Gritstone Climbs* by J. Laycock (published privately, 1913); C.C. Journal March 1906: *Almes Cliff Crags* by C. E. Benson.

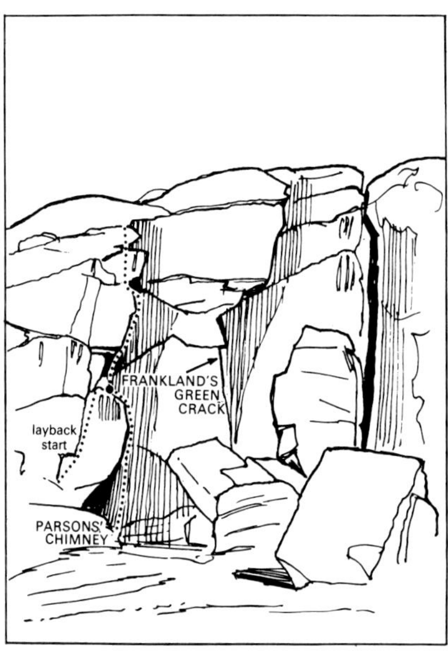

46 Sail Buttress, Topsail and Powder Monkey Parade

by Charles Clark

Routes Sail Buttress, Hard Very Difficult, 45ft.; Topsail, Severe, 40ft.; Powder Monkey Parade, Hard Very Difficult, 55ft.
Cliff Birchens Edge near Baslow, Derbyshire.
First Ascents Sail Buttress – B. Smith and B. Connelly, *c.* 1933; Topsail – D. Penlington and E. Marshall, 1951; Powder Monkey Parade – D. Penlington and E. Byne, 1951.
Map Reference O.S. Peak District Tourist Map, 1–50,000 Sheet, (ref. 278728).
Guidebooks C.C. and B.M.C. *The Chatsworth Gritstone Area* by Eric Byne; *Rock Climbing in the Peak District* by Paul Nunn.
Nearest Road The junction of the B6050 and the A619 at the Robin Hood Inn (ref. 279722).
Distance and time from cliff ½ mile. Allow 10 minutes. Follow a well-marked track that contours the hillside to the north.
Good Conditions The rock is clean and can be climbed in wet or dry conditions with only a marginal increase in standard when wet. The Edge dries rapidly after rain.
Campsites and Bunkhouses New 'official' campsite below the Edge. Oread Hut near Chatsworth Edge (1 mile). Youth Hostel at Bakewell.
Bibliography Climber and Rambler, August 1975: *Birchens* by John Woodhouse.

Note: The grades given above were those in the 1970 guidebook. The climbs were upgraded – to S, MVS and Severe – in 1981, and were pushed up again to HS (4b), VS (4b) and S (4a) in 1985. The 1996 guidebook took them to a heady VS (4b), VS (4c) and S (4b)! This position appears unsustainable if the climbs are compared to Stanage or Froggatt 'yardstick' classics. S, HS/MVS, and HVD are, perhaps, the maximum that the trio should merit if the established grading norms are to be preserved (see also comments on page 253).

Right: The crux traverse on Sail Buttress where a step onto a slabby nose must be made using horizontal jams. The hand traverse fault that leads to this position (left of the runner in this picture) accepts 'Friends'. *Climber: Keith Tomlinson*

'No, I've never been there; it's a bit on the small side to bother about, isn't it?'

'A lot of people who haven't been to Birchen's think the climbing can't be any good because there's nothing over 55ft. But you ought to go there and see for yourself some time.'

I was eating my lunch on a rock at Stanage and caught this snatch of conversation from two climbers who were sitting nearby eating theirs. I'd intended to visit the edge myself, but always seemed to end up at the familiar places, such as Stanage. Birchen, or 'Birchen's', was for beginners; friends rarely went there; Stanage was easier to get to. Conservatism: there are always plenty of reasons for not trying somewhere new. I listened with interest as one of the Birchen routes was described. From about the age of three I had grown to associate grey beards with men of wisdom; therefore, it did not require an oracle to predict that two or three weeks later I would be at Birchen Edge, starting up the classic Sail Buttress.

It was mid-morning. Few people were on the moor as yet; the sun was already on the rocks but the heat of the day was still to come. Ahead, the towers and walls jutted from the heather boldly, while beyond, the expansive flowing curves of the horizon were complemented by the mantle of greenery in the valleys near at hand. I liked the feel of the place – the way the slabs leaned back and invited me to climb them. I tugged out the guidebook.

'One of the most exposed leads for its standard'. The guidebook phrase jingled persistently in my consciousness. I'd been climbing once a month for a year and had led a few V.Diffs., but this was *Hard* V.Diff: could I get up it? Gaining the step on the prominent arête didn't look easy. Allan held the rope as I set off, an inch-thick wad of folded newspaper sprouting from each heel of my oversized Kletts. A large block brought me under the overhanging nose of the buttress, where I leaned right and draped my chest and forearms across a sloping shelf. I flung my right toe on to an awkward, polished hold, pressed up hopefully with one arm and lurched untidily on to the ledge. It seemed I would now need a telescopic leg to reach the crux foothold on the nose, an intimidating distance away: the ground sloped steeply from beneath the overhang, emphasizing the exposure of the swing across. I groped ineffectually with one toe a couple of times; then began to whistle tunelessly.

'What's up?' shouted Allan.

I didn't answer. Then another voice announced loudly: 'That's the first climb I fell off.'

I decided that whoever it was must be talking about that solo climber round the corner. A fly took off from a weathered quartz pebble and zoomed across my field of vision . . .

I finally let go with my right hand and swung into the unknown. My famous Joe Brown hand-jam at once slipped out and I swiftly stabbed my right hand safely back in the horizontal crack, grateful for the rough, crystalline texture of the recess. My left foot hit rock: I was there. Beautiful! I stood up, trembling slightly, but back in balance. The rope dropped away from me and out of sight. The angle was now easier and nervousness slipped away. I stopped my thoughts from rushing headlong and enjoyed the moment. I breathed freely, as exposed rounded ledges took me delicately to the top. As Walter Unsworth said of the whole crag: 'Not big, but significant.'

A few yards to the left of Nelson's Monument is a conspicuous weakness in a stubby overhang. This is Topsail, which continues the Birchen tradition of names with a nautical tang. A straightforward crack soon opens into a shallow recess immediately be-

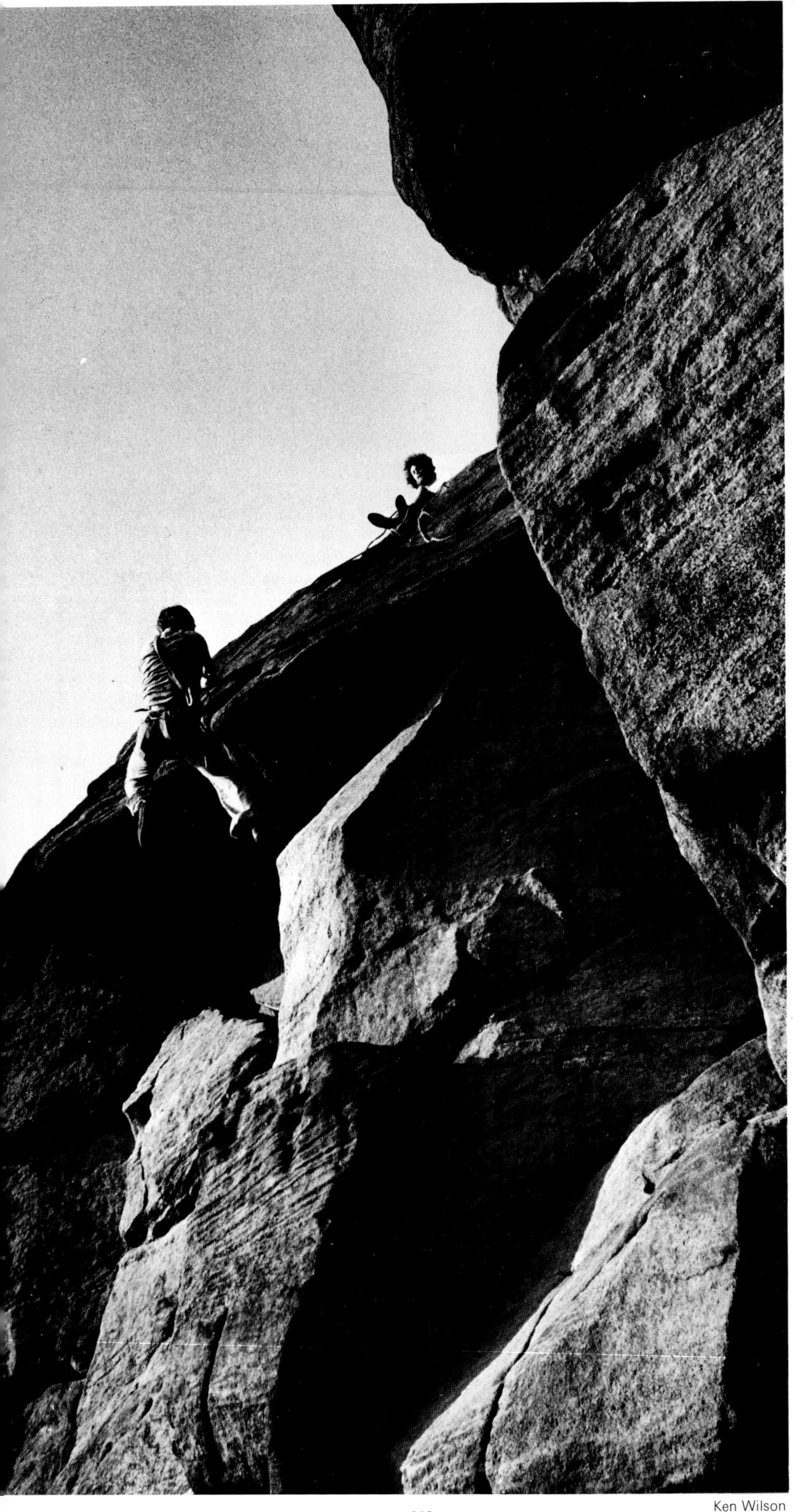

Ken Wilson

neath the overhang. There is a very good hold above the overhang, but you have to be tall to reach it easily.

'Watch it!' The rope above me went tight as I bridged up awkwardly. I knew it could hold an elephant and trainer without parting, but I wasn't yet sure whether it could hold me. I popped my head round the lip of the overhang, right hand spread over a high rounded hold, left foot on a thin toe-crease; a narrow crack twisted above me up the inside of a small bulge. Fingers out of sight, I stretched, and eventually found it. My legs kicked free for a moment as I pulled up strenuously – and the big effort was over. I perched on the lip of the overhang in relative security, relieved that the projecting boot soles above me no longer seemed a hundred miles away. The remainder of the climb, balancing moves up the face, formed a satisfying finish and an agreeable contrast to the preceding struggle.

Some regard Birchen Edge as a practice-ground for so-called better things, but Powder Monkey Parade, like the other two routes, is worth doing for its own sake. The climb starts at the left of Admiral Buttress, a leaning tower which overhangs about half-way up. The sandy bed of Holly Bush Gully is gained over a jammed block, with the help of a slippery crack on the left. The ridge on the right soon leads to the overhang and the start of the fine hand-traverse. The finger crack is a good one, the moves across exhilarating – exposure without anxiety – and a resting place in the centre of the face is quickly reached. A single runner on the route (after the traverse), and a rounded finish ensure that interest is well maintained and that the last 20ft. are no anticlimax. Certainly, I didn't feel that after leaving Birchen Edge.

Left: The bold swing over the overhang on Topsail – a well-protected but demanding move. *Climbers: Unknown*

47 Flying Buttress, April Crack and Black Slab

by Jim Perrin

I began climbing, as is the custom in those bleak, intimate, backstreet cities of the north, at an early age. Prompted by no course, or school, the gaunt outcrops breasting the wind became the haunt of my youth. Such as I was, you see today in odd places: the young boys, awkward and painful often, unconsciously loving a place. As Jefferies to Dorset, Wordsworth to his Derwent, or Hudson to the Pampas, so was I faithful to the Peakland edges, learning beauty from them. Stanage was my favourite, in its mile upon mile, its turns and changes, and then colourful populace. Rags and bags and a sling or two, much skill to develop or watch displayed; these were the gritstone days *par excellence*. Gritstone is so good for youth, for its first principle is movement: the coiled spring to bound one beyond fatigue, or the arched bow on a bald slab, strung with mind's tension to flight the body upwards. All this and the beauty of the place were a powerful spell, and the climbs themselves became most intimate friends. Almost to the degree that one built a relationship with them. As in a playground, there were those with whom one always fought, so with such as the Dangler or Centaur; Agony Crack was a delightful, impudent child; Christmas Crack so big and comforting; Heaven Crack was my first love, for when she grew up she became the Right Unconquerable.

Mostly, during my early days, I climbed in the Black Hawk, Robin Hood's Cave, and Mississippi Buttress areas, not as crowded then as now, and nearer for the Sunday evening dash down to Hathersage, Ma Thomas's cafe, and the Manchester train. I suppose it's rather *passé* now, footworn and teeming. And yet, small part of Stanage though it might be, and contemptible to those who despise popularity, still it contains some of the very best routes on the cliff, particularly among the easier grades. Three of these routes I remember especially from my earliest climbing. Flying Buttress is the first, and here I suppose the visual impression of this tremendous neb is paramount, manifest in the weight of that overhang above its tiny, delicate slab. The climbing on Flying Buttress, in all honesty, doesn't amount to a great deal, but it's not a route where quality of climbing matters. The journey, in its bends and uncertainties, is more than the movement it entails. It starts with a little worn slab, which would be hard were it not so close to the ground. A belay above enhances the character, for always a climb is more complete when both you and your partner are involved. Next to the belay, an awkward little corner leads you into smooth high places above the great overhang, to bring you up short against a roof of your own. Right up there on top of the crag you heave over on knobbly holds to put route and roof behind you. It has, as you might say, its moments.

The other two routes in this trinity are quite different in kind, both from Flying Buttress and each other. They are much of a standard, though one is infinitely more serious a lead than the other; the one is a crack, the other a slab.

Separated from Christmas Crack by a frightening route for tall maestros called Easter Rib, is April Crack. It was, and I remember it vividly to this day, my initiation into the Eleusinian rites of gritstone cracks. In fact, it's not typical of that inimical breed, for much of it can be bridged, and not a little laybacked, elegantly, unlike that ascent of mine fifteen years ago. But nonetheless, if straightness of line and honesty of effort are allowed to be characteristic, then this is a climb of real pedigree. It taxes arms and technique, and one sees it led less often than other, harder climbs hereabouts. The latter characteristic, always a sure sign of a climb of strong character, is shared by the last of

Routes Black Slab (Hargreaves' Original Route), Hard Severe, 60ft.; April Crack, Hard Severe, 55ft.; Flying Buttress, Very Difficult, 65ft.
Cliff Stanage Edge, Hathersage, Derbyshire.
First Ascents Black Slab – A. T. Hargreaves, 1928; April Crack – H. Hartley, 1928; Flying Buttress – F. Graham, 1922.
Map Reference O.S. Peak District Tourist Map, 1–50,000 Sheet (ref. 245834).
Guidebooks B.M.C. *Stanage Area* by Brian Griffiths and Alan Wright; *Rock Climbing in the Peak District* by Paul Nunn.
Nearest Road A minor road below the cliff at the road junction at ref. 245849.
Distance and time from cliff $\frac{1}{3}$ mile. Allow 10 minutes.
Good Conditions The Edge is very exposed to bad weather and can be very windy. The rock on all three routes is clean and they dry quickly.
Campsites and Bunkhouses Campsite at North Lees Hall (ref. 234832). C.C.'s Bob Downes Hut at Froggatt and L.U.M.C. Hut at Grindleford.
Bibliography *High Peak* by Eric Byne and Geoffrey Sutton (Secker and Warburg, 1966) has a general description of the early development of Stanage Edge; Rucksack Club Journal, 1929: *Some New Gritstone Climbs* by A. E. Chisman.

Note: Hargreaves' Original Route on Black Slab is now graded VS (4c) but with patience and subtle route-finding this overstates the climb's difficulty. After the initial 4b (protected) moves to gain the slab a rising traverse to the left (which would surely have been taken by Hargreaves) gains a small nut crack and a point where 4a/b slab moves lead up to the right. The breaks thus reached accept 'Friends' after which a direct line up the final slabby wall is straightforward, exhilarating and well-protected.

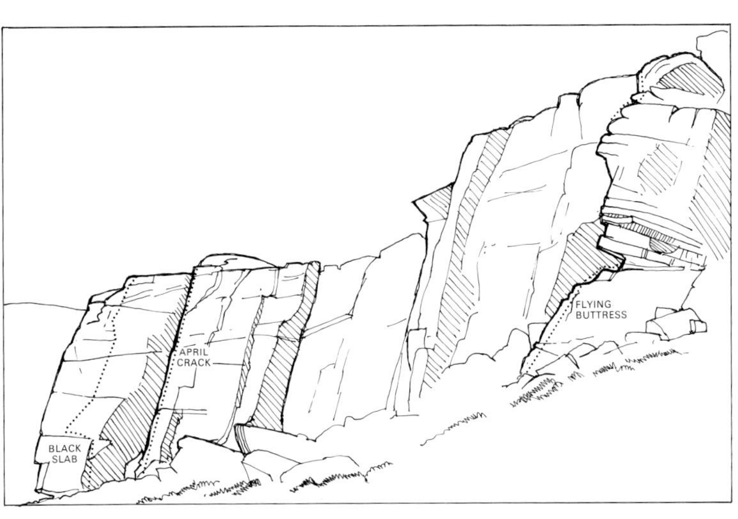

Left: With the hard moves completed the climber can enjoy the splendidly exposed climbing of the upper part of Black Slab. *Climber: Ron Fawcett*

Right: The upper moves on Flying Buttress. *Climber: Andy Walters*

our trinity. I always came to this climb with respect and, more than that, something like fear, the recognition of authority. Just as there are people with whom one is never easy, against whose fine intelligence, straight-seeing and exacting gaze, one can allow oneself no laxity or indulgence, thus it was with Black Slab by Hargreaves' Original Route.

Alan T. Hargreaves, who pioneered many new routes in the Lake District, was one of an outstanding Manchester University group active in the late 'twenties. His route on Black Slab, which he climbed in 1928, is to my mind the finest medium-grade route on gritstone. It isn't, as so many good climbs in the easier grades can be, a promiscuous collection of sweet delights, each short-lived but various. It's rather so many things which one strives personally to attain: direct, open, bold, delicate, serious, tenuous, committing, authoritative.

60ft. of gritstone can mean so much. Let me warn you that here is a climb not to be toyed with, an unforgiving climb. Technically it is no harder than its grade – a goodish Severe – but in every other sense it will test you. Approach it with respect, for in those 60ft. you will find no runner, no easy prop to the mind's balance. You and the rock will be weighed together and you must not be found wanting.

A Black Slab it isn't; sombre it may appear when the clouds lour from the west and a wind scours the edge, but touch it with sunlight and it gleams, silver-grey and furrowed, monolithic and solitary, set forward from the crag. Its first step will shrug off fools; if you falter here, go no farther. A difficult step off a boulder on to small holds around a narrow crack leads off. You realize quickly what lies ahead, for all these furrows are rounded and smoothed by the wind, and the angle is high; nothing here for the fingers to furl around and the arms to secure. You have a friend in friction and an ally in the fine poise of your mind, the tightened bow of movement; throughout those 60ft., these must suffice. Your peril is obvious: you must not miss these moves, one so much like another though each is a taut and pleasurable moment, for the ground would be your landing. There is no placement here for a

John Woodhouse

Ken Wilson

hexentric or a Chouinard 5½, no clear-cut line of chalk-dabs; place only for your courage and confidence to move smoothly despite the threat of situation. And if you see it through, eventually it relents a little, as if to compensate for the heightening fall. A hold or two, even a hand-jam, acknowledge you near the top. Of the climbs in this book, none will be more serious than this, though many will be longer. Remember that, when you are tempted to scoff at outcrops, cragrats, and their brief joys. Last long it may not, but there is a seriousness here, an intensity of experience, which demands a balance, a steady judgement, a courage, which it is no mean or paltry feat to attain.

Ken Wilson

Above: The climber on the left is engrossed in the crux section of Black Slab having moved well to the left from the initial corner. The other party is on April Crack. Christmas Crack (another fine classic Severe) and Central Trinity are the obvious crack lines to the right.
Climbers: Chris Astill and others

Left: A popular section of Stanage Edge, from Black Slab to Flying Buttress.

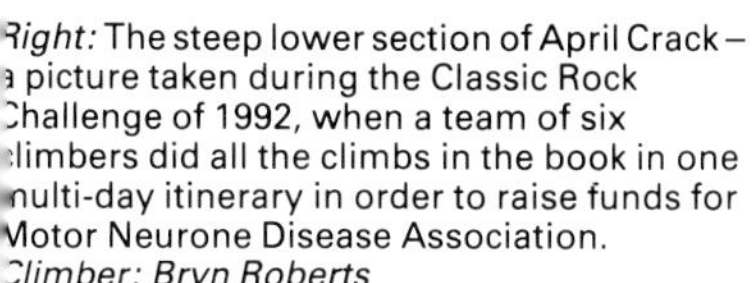

Right: The steep lower section of April Crack – a picture taken during the Classic Rock Challenge of 1992, when a team of six climbers did all the climbs in the book in one multi-day itinerary in order to raise funds for Motor Neurone Disease Association.
Climber: Bryn Roberts

John Stockdale

48 Central Climb

by Paul Nunn

Route Central Route, Severe, 120ft.
Cliff Hen Cloud, near Leek, Staffordshire.
First Ascent J. Laycock (apart from final pitch), 1909.
Map Reference O.S. Peak District Tourist Map, 1–50,000 Sheet (ref. 008616).
Guidebooks B.M.C. *The Staffordshire Gritstone Area* by David Salt; *Rock Climbing in the Peak District* by Paul Nunn.
Nearest Road A minor road below the cliff.
Distance and time from cliff Allow 5 minutes.
Good Conditions The cliff is rather lichenous and remains green and slippery for rather longer than other gritstone edges.
Campsites and Bunkhouses Camping is sometimes allowed at the farms below the cliff.
Bibliography *High Peak* by Eric Byne and Geoffrey Sutton (Secker and Warburg, 1966) has an account of the first ascent; Rucksack Club Journal 1913, Vol. 2: *Climbs on Hen Cloud and the Roaches* by S. F. Jeffcoat; Rucksack Club Journal 1922: *Gritstone Climbing 1921* by Morley Wood.

Note: Upgraded to HS 4a in the 1989 guide and then hiked to VS 4b, 5a in the BMC Selected Guidebook *On Peak Rock.* The former grade is surely correct for though the second pitch is a thrutchy slot that can cause delays, it is only slightly harder than the chimney on Gashed Crag (see page 151) and nothing like as hard as Glyder Fach's Vertical Vice (VD) or Elidir's first Corrugated Crack (S), three similar problems. Climbers should not be misled, Hen Cloud 5a means something rather different.

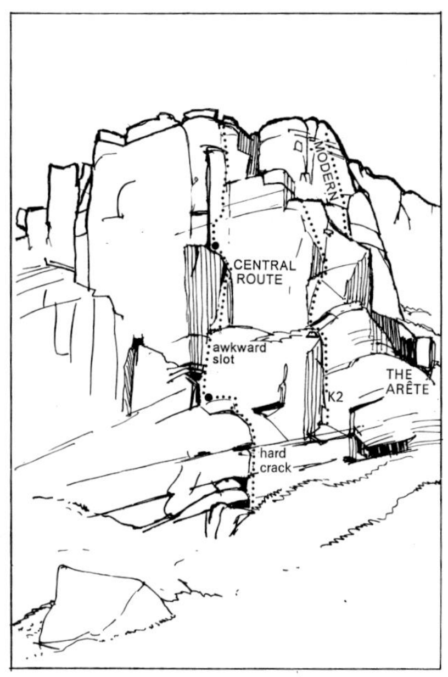

Hen Cloud is the king of all those North Staffordshire Clouds, the sentinel of the south-west Peak, marking the border of the wild country and the wild hill folk of Flash and Goldsitch Moors, sneering down on the lush green pastures of Meersbrook, and across, with even greater disdain, at a miscellany of redundant Leek factory chimneys clustered protectively in the near distance. In the greater distance, a haze of atmospheric grime mercifully conceals an insane menagerie of twisted and 'post office' towers, sky-probing Jodrell Bank saucers and pottery pit heaps.

In the evening sun, Hen Cloud is rosy, a split pyramid, formed almost entirely of rounded, sand-hued, rough gritstone. The pebbled grit holds the lichen, which invades the bloody wounds of jamming scars and colonizes them, delaying recovery to the next weekend or beyond. Unlike the nearby Roches crags, the rock is undisguised by trees and seems exposed, mountain-like. On wet winter days, the wind howls round the upper turrets where the vertical fissures cut through the summit, and thin mists frequently cling to the rocks. There is an air of repulsiveness about the holdless, slimy chimneys and cracks, which is reinforced by closer inspection.

There are great climbs of all standards, though the classics have to follow lines of least resistance amid the formidable rounded walls. Central Route is one of the greatest natural lines, a fault of almost 100ft., which just fails to reach the base of the crag. There is a natural direct start, but it is an inhumanely hard crack, and steep as a way to what is most obviously a more amenable route of ascent. Thus, before the Great War, the pioneers were forced into a steep, wide, 25ft. crack, a little to the right of the groove, and still obviously problematical enough to demand respect. This crack repulsed a good number of pioneers, before being climbed by John Laycock in 1909. Unfortunately his second, A. R. Thomson, was unable to climb it as 'he was handicapped by a congenital disability which made all climbing a matter of heroic endeavour'! Laycock continued, but became benighted below the top of the crag and was rescued after several hours by a sturdy chauffeur. He later confessed: 'Not everyone has been benighted on gritstone

and, though one ought to be ashamed of want of prudence, the episode is delightful to me in retrospect; gritstone has a romance no less than granite.'

The initial crack demands a deep probe into its innards at mid-height, and some knee-jamming technique. Its polished holds smack of the greatest antiquity and many a sweaty palm. Probably it is respectable to fail, but, once underway, a glacis and large ledge are welcome below the main corner. The most difficult section is over.

Ken Wilson

Yet difficulty cannot be equated with interest. The crack above requires a degree of shuffling expertise to reach a ledge on the right, and short grooves end on the great field which can be used for a bivouac, or as an escape route. There remains a fine groove of massively composed gritstone, and a steep section to the summit nick. There is scope for a little individual variation. Beyond is the twisted mass of Ramshaw Rocks and the boggy acres of Goldsitch, stretching away northward towards Axedge and the Peakland core. One can teeter here between the remains of two cultures and in the reality between two climates, as the clouds sweep in from the west laden with the next deluge of rain.

Note: To get the best from Hen Cloud, after Central Climb consider an ascent of K2, a classic climb of some stature on peerless rock. From its final moves a descent of Easy Gully gains the start of Modern, a little-used but characterful Severe. With a slight increase in standard, Hedgehog Crack and Batchelor's Climb (finishing up Great Chimney) could then be added to give a total of 350ft of quality gritstone climbing.

Ken Wilson

Above: The hard initial crack of Central Climb where a precarious arm and foot 'udge' gives access to a finger lock and then a jug at the top of the left-hand crack. This is followed by more struggling to overcome the upper part of the wide crack to gain the first stance.
Climbers: Frank Loftus and Simon Massey

Left: The initial corner pitch of K2 gives Severe (4a) climbing in a surprisingly 'big' situation, with a steep finish over a block. Immediately above this twin cracks in a steep wall provide some well-positioned and entertaining jamming. *Climber: Rob Phillips*

Right: The poorly protected semi-mantelshelf moves that give some anxious moments (particularly in poor conditions) on the exposed finish to Black and Tans Climb (see following chapter). *Climber: Terry Walker*

49 Via Dolorosa, Black and Tans Climb and Technical Slab

by Dave Cook

Routes Via Dolorosa, Severe, 105ft.; Black and Tans Climb, Severe, 100ft.; Technical Slab, Severe, 75ft.
Cliff The Roches, near Leek, Staffordshire.
First Ascents A. S. Pigott and I. M. Wood, 1920.
Map Reference O.S. Peak District Tourist Map, 1–50,000 Sheet, (ref. 005625).
Guidebooks B.M.C. *The Staffordshire Gritstone Area* by David Salt; *Rock Climbing in the Peak District* by Paul Nunn.
Nearest Road A minor road below the cliff.
Distance and time from cliff ¼ mile. Allow 5 minutes.
Good Conditions The routes on the Upper Tier are not unduly affected by wet weather as the rock is quite clean. Via Dolorosa can become rather lichenous however. All routes dry out quickly in sunny weather in all seasons.
Campsites and Bunkhouses Camping is possible at the farms below the cliff.
Bibliography *High Peak* by Eric Byrne and Geoffrey Sutton (Secker and Warburg, 1966). Rucksack Club Journal 1927. *New Scrambles on the Roaches* and Hen Cloud* by Lindley Henshaw.

* Old spelling for the Roches.

Note: Via Dolorosa was regraded to Very Severe in the 1989 guidebook with the final pitch given 4c. This can be avoided by the gully finish and with that finish the climb is still Severe. The direct start to Black and Tans is 5a and the Severe grade only applies if the right-hand (Black Velvet) start is used.

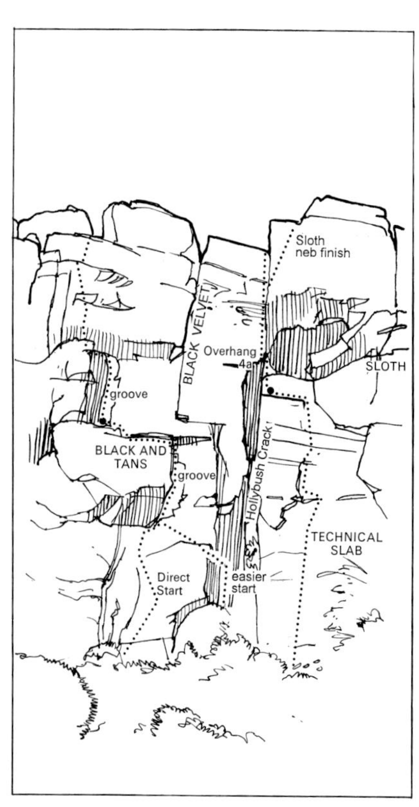

'I don't go much on lower tiers,' Martin Boysen was once heard to remark, a comment which, in relation to the Roches, is so heretical that in the Middle Ages it would have meant banishment from the Pennines for ever. People have been known to get the backs of their hands permanently scarred for less!

Quite a few climbers have never actually penetrated beyond the sombre ramparts of this particular Lower Tier, having either fallen in love with its alluring technicalities, or become so impaled in its spiky cracks that their palsied limbs would carry them no further. Whichever category you fall into (or fall out of), you certainly won't leave these rocks with any feeling of indifference towards them.

This first palisade separates neatly into two, and up the gap a stone stairway leads to the Upper Tier and Skyline Buttresses beyond. To the left are four mouth-watering cracks, climbed variously by Brown and Whillans. On the right stands the great buttress of Raven Rock, looking from some angles like a giant skull, impassively watching the antics on its bones. The climbs which weave across its lips, like Valkyrie, and out of its ears, like Raven Rock Gully, certainly provide plenty of scope for antics, and so too does the splendid Via Dolorosa, which even has the cheek to tickle the head under its enormous chin.

From the carpet of pine needles which skirts the rock, a narrow slab slants rightwards to where a battered holly allows the first belay ledge to be gained. The slab is slippery and hard. If you get up it, a wonderland of magic Severes lies open before you. If you don't, it's back to Stanage for re-sits.

From the belay ledge you can lollop up the steep corner above, and move towards the gully when the jutting roof blocks further progress. Far better, though, is to stride left at once on to a Roches 'Knobble'.

At this point a brief digression must be made for the uninitiated. There is a type of softer, heavily-weathered gritstone which displays all the characteristics of decadence, namely a florid and almost indecent over-abundance (rather like the style in which this chapter is written). For example, cracks are either the ultimate in ecstasy or the grotesque, and sometimes even both at the same time. So it is with holds, too; not so much a rugosity, more a work of art, so to speak. Well, anyway, something like that.

The sculpted projection on to which our initiated reader now strides is one such knob, although I suppose to a boot-clad toe it feels much like any bog standard foot-hold. (The Roches 'Knobble' should not be confused with the Roches 'Wobble', which is another expression of decadence, this time in climbing style.)

Large pulls and hand-jams haul one round on to the gully wall, and then across beneath a chockstone as big as an ice-cream van. It's possible to crawl through a cave to finish up Raven Rock Gully, but, if gluttonous for more, one should layback round the block to climb airily up the forehead of the giant skull.

Why on earth Morley Wood and Pigott named the climb Via Dolorosa is hard to understand. It should be called Via Felicita.

The great overhung facets of the Upper Tier are 150 yards beyond, neat parallelograms, in contrast with the free form chaos below. Although the average grades are much easier here, the atmosphere is more akin to a mountain cliff than a gritstone edge. On a hot day you can fry in its south-facing glare.

Dotting the scrubby space between the tiers are some nasty boulders, glistening from the blister of generations of flailing feet. Because golden oldies on the 'Rock and Ice' label are always worth reissuing, at least with a bit of stereo polish, I won't miss this chance to release one which was first recorded in this never-never land between the tiers. Joe Brown was showing round a visiting expert (who shall be nameless for fear of libel) and inevitably a contest began. The challenge was an innocuous crack up which Brown swarmed, to be followed without trouble by his rival. However, the visitor's premature self-satisfaction changed to disbelief as the game became to climb the crack using successively fewer limbs. The gullibility of the audience, rather than historical accuracy, usually decides with which part of his body the visitor eventually failed to make the ascent.

Ken Wilson

Above: The main part of the Upper Tier at the Roches, with climbers on both Black and Tans Climb and Technical Slab. Sloth's roof crack is above and slightly to the right of the right-hand climbers. *Climbers: Dave Cook and unknown (on Technical Slab)*

Like all classic climbing grounds the Roches has a fascinating history and folklore which, according to the guidebook writers, encompasses all manner of bizarre creatures, ranging from 'the ghost of the singing woman' to climbing marsupials like the wallaby and the whillans. We are also given the intriguing information that the Black and Tans climb was 'named by Pigott in memory of members of a private corps enlisted mainly from the Stockport Lacrosse Club to fill some empty beds on an overbooked Easter meet'. Make what you can of that one!

Left: Moving past the 'knobble' on the second pitch of Via Dolorosa. The climb continues to the left of the huge overhang above. *Climbers: John Cheesmond and Dave Cook*

Right: The first pitch of Black and Tans Climb, if taken direct follows the sunny wall to reach this groove. A stance is taken below the next groove on the left. This gives access to the rib, after which wall climbing leads to the top. *Climber: Terry Walker*

Quite a few people find it hard to make anything of the smooth wall up which Black and Tans begins. This is one of the places where the Roches Knob is not to be found, but delightful balancy moves on ample friction and tiny ledges make up for the deficiency. A few feet to the right is a more difficult and direct way, on which a few action replays are sometimes necessary, to gain the ledge which is the objective of both starts. A steep corner crack connects this to a higher break, rather ominously capped by a sizeable overhang up which one hopes the route does not go.

Sure enough the second pitch sidesteps left, but all is not yet over. A series of bulges have to be crossed; funny mantelshelf moves a long way from home.

In the space of 100ft. of metamorphosis, Black and Tans showcases three definitive types of gritstone climbing for the price of one.

A few feet to the right, just beyond another excellent Severe, Hollybush Crack, is the smooth and stylish Technical Slab. So dominant are the layers of overhang that press down on this central area of the Great Slab that the climbing on it has to be of unusually high quality to stand out in its own right. On Technical Slab it is.

For 40ft. the line goes straight up the steep slab. Little finger rails, good but far apart, lead into a delicate angle, where the slickered sheen of worn gritstone gives the balance just a hint of precariousness. The line of overhang breaks the spell by forcing the climb leftwards into Hollybush Crack.

Over a bulge, the farthest outrider of the monster roof, and then it is all over. A gentle clatter up the corner and you are sniffing the moors that stretch away to the north, studded with islands of gritstone, on which it would be idyllic to be cast away.

If you've read the guidebook you half expect to be assaulted by a keeper or a big-game hunter at this point. In fact, all that greets you is the satisfaction of having climbed the best gritstone crag in the world.

Note: After climbing the bulge, the upper part of Technical Slab can be enhanced by tacking on the final section of Hollybush Crack – an exposed traverse right on ledges and sculpted holds (4a/b), across the side wall of the huge Sloth neb.

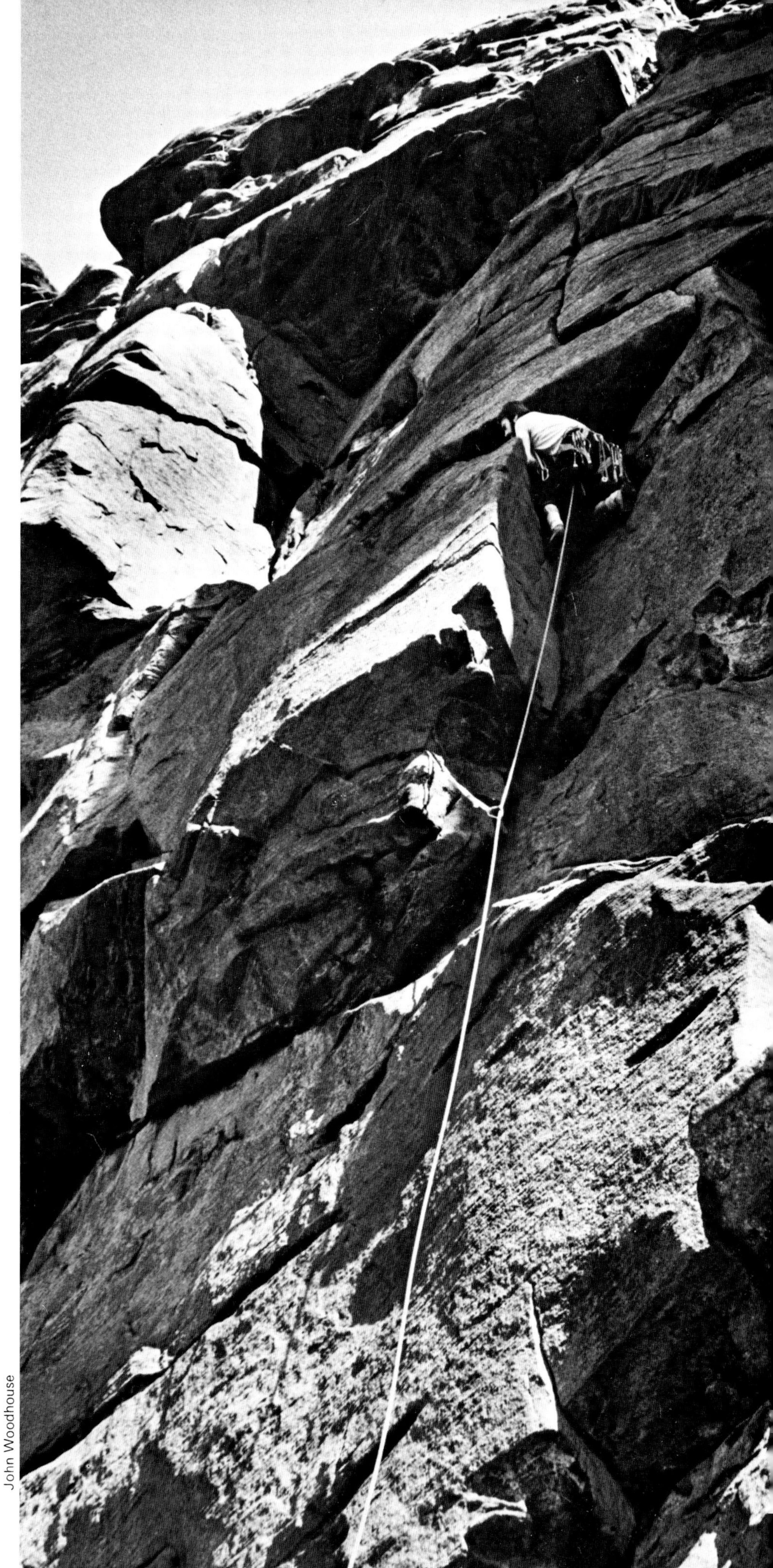
John Woodhouse

50 Piton Route

by Mike Thompson

Limestone climbing, we all know, started in earnest in the 1950s when laconic gritstoners turned to pegging their way up these despised geological formations – an entertaining form of convalescence while their jamming-scarred hands regenerated skin and fingernails. It subsequently came of age in the 1960s, when the next, more voluble generation pulled out the pioneers' pitons and free-climbed up the holes they left. Actually, it wasn't like that at all: the great advantage of myth is that it enables one to avoid even becoming aware of facts that might disrupt such a cosy ordering of history. In fact free climbing on limestone was well developed in the south-west by the 1950s, its origins dating back to the dream-time of the 1930s.*

F. G. Balcombe was one of those meteoric figures who occasionally appear in the mountaineering firmament, illuminate it with discomforting brilliance, and, just as suddenly (thank goodness), disappear. In June 1934 he produced the astonishing Buttonhook on Kern Knotts, the Unfinished Arête and Engineer's Slabs on Gable Crag, Hell Gate Pillar and Lucifer Ridge on The Napes, and a Direct Finish to Central Buttress on Scafell. Two years later he helped to entertain the visiting German climbers who were responsible for Münich Climb on Tryfan. In return for his hospitality they left him a bunch, not of flowers, but of pitons ('Danaos timens ut donas ferrentes'). By this time he had more or less abandoned climbing for caving, and he hit on the ingenious idea of getting rid of this embarrassing ironware on the Avon cliffs, which he regularly passed on his way to the Mendip potholes. But even there, his efforts to rid himself secretly of his pitons were bedevilled by an over-attentive press and public and by his own free-climbing ability. Eventually, he managed to deposit a few around what is now Desperation and the remainder somewhere in the centre of Main Wall, but, before that, he added the almost free Piton Route (originally called Route 2) to his impressive bag of first ascents.

Balcombe is alive and well and lives near Potters Bar where he was recently cornered by the 'Amazing Wilson'. The veteran's welcoming remark, 'You're far too young to be the editor of a magazine', put the precocious pup firmly in his place and thereafter he sat meekly attentive as the pre-war story of pegging, publicity and intrigue unfolded.

Piton Route takes a natural and, as it turns out, a fairly easy line up the sweep of rock now known as the Central Buttress Area. The name, which was given to the climb by later generations, derives from the huge iron spikes left by the nineteenth-century quarrymen, and Balcombe led it free apart from one peg for aid on the first traverse and a protection peg in the initial groove; an awesome achievement when one thinks of the vegetation and loose rock that must have been encountered, and the traditional terror with which limestone was at that time beheld.

The vegetation has long since disappeared, along with the loose limestone and its terrible reputation. Real pitons have sprouted to protect the difficult sections and this classic climb has become a popular Severe. Paradoxically, this very popularity is now reversing the trend. Not content with removing the loose rock, bionic leaders have torn off some of the vital holds, and at the same time shuffled their soft shoes and caressed the rock with their jean-clad limbs until it has acquired the polish of a newly waxed Allegro on a Sunday morning. Despite the activities of that prevalent contemporary pest, the Rock-Pecker, it looks as though Piton Route will soon have to be upgraded.

Suitably primed, the Editor and I presented ourselves at the foot of the climb. But this ascent, something like my fiftieth, was different. This time it was for immortality (if not money) and, what's more, it was to be my first climb following my fortieth birthday. Would my hair turn white and my teeth drop out, or would even worse things, such as even Alvarez could only hint at, cut me down? Thankfully, nothing so dramatic happened. Up the groove that used to have little ash trees growing in it, protected by one of Wilson's wired nuts cunningly threaded, and then a puzzling rising traverse left and up to a gnarled piton, forged and

* Limestone explorations actually began in Derbyshire and Yorkshire at the turn of the century, and there were sporadic discoveries over the years on several of the Pennine and Peak outcrops. (*Editor.*)

Route Piton Route, Hard Severe, 220ft. (The guidebook gives a grade of Very Severe but this is thought to be incorrect.)
Cliff Central Buttress Area, Avon Gorge, Bristol.
First Ascent F. G. Balcombe and J. C. Sheppard, 1936.
Map Reference O.S. 1–50,000 Sheet 172 (ref. 563743).
Guidebook *Avon Gorge* by Ed. Drummond (published privately).
Nearest Road A car park below the cliff, just off the A4 (Portway) through the Gorge.
Good Conditions The cliff is a suntrap and dries rapidly after rain. When wet, the climbs become quite hard. The cliff is recommended for all seasons except on really hot summer afternoons.
Campsites and Bunkhouses There is a good camping spot behind the railings at the west end of the cliff.
Bibliography Mountain 20, *City Crag* by Brian Wyvill gives a general appraisal of the cliff; Northern Cavern and Fell Club Journal 1936–7: *Tyrolean Tactics* by F. G. Balcombe, gives a detailed first-ascent account.

Note: Upgraded to Very Severe in the 1980 guidebook because of its very polished first pitch (4c). Pitch one of Central Rib (4b) avoids this and maintains the overall grade of the climb as a demanding Hard Severe.

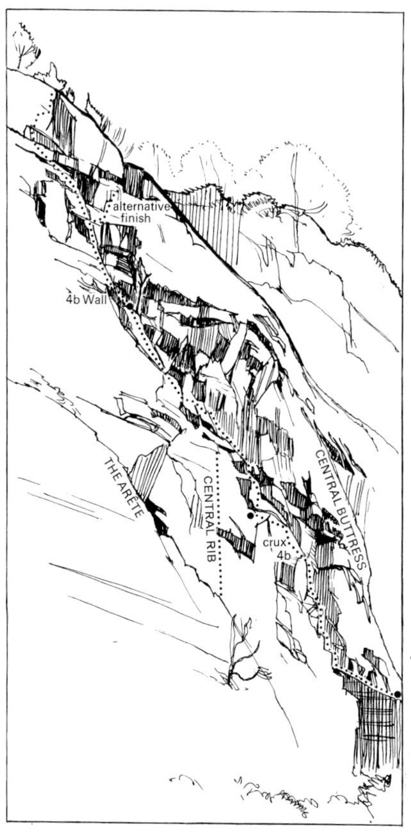

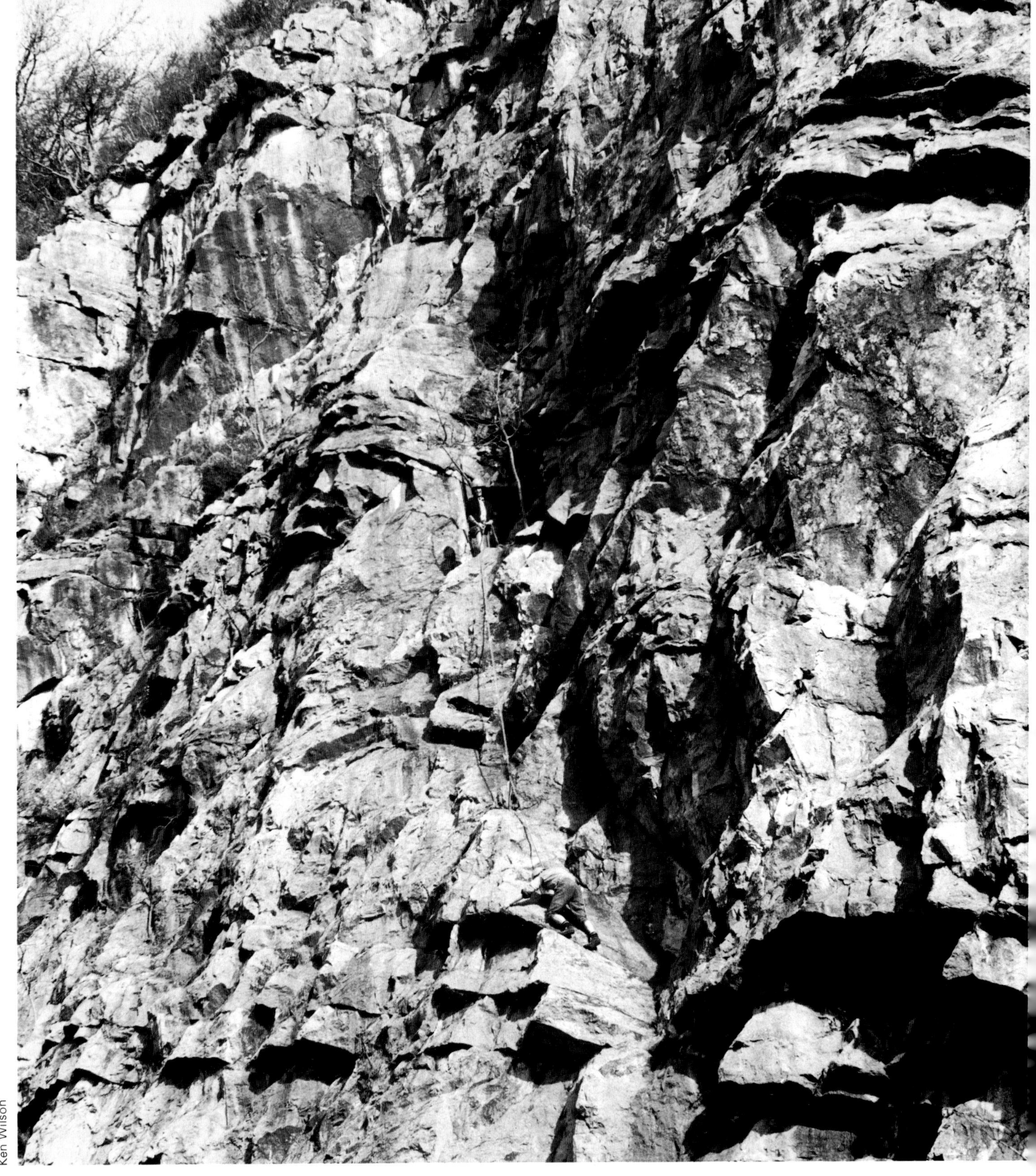

Ken Wilson

Above: Pitch 2 of Piton Route. The steep bastion to the right of the climber is taken by Great Central Route. *Climbers: Brian Shuttleworth and John Peck*

driven decades before the B.M.C. Equipment Committee was even a twinkle in Dennis Gray's eye. The overhangs threaded by Great Central Route crowd in above so one continues leftwards on polished holds to the cave stance; a pleasant spot to shelter from falling leaders and watch the ships, trains, lorries and sewage go by. The next pitch goes through the overhang in that surprisingly unstrenuous manner so typical of Avon climbing and then leads to a smooth and airy slab. This is traversed by the famous Obstetrician's Move – not a fist jam, but a forefinger squashed into a borehole filled with stagnant water. Whether one believes that the stink is inherent or caused by the

Right: Emerging from 4b wall, the second crux of Piton Route. The tree below is scarred with abseil grooves – evidence of the parties that have been forced to retreat having failed to overcome this awkward pitch. *Climbers: John Peck and Brian Shuttleworth*

Ken Wilson

accumulated filth from innumerable prying digits depends on one's position along the continuum that runs all the way from the Women's Lib Workshop to the Male Chauvinist Pigsty.

Rather indefinite slabs lead to a muddy ledge and an over-pruned tree, its trunk almost severed by the action of abseil ropes. The reason for this is soon apparent for directly behind the tree is 4b Wall. Here, even with immoral assistance from the springy stump, the mantelshelf on to a polished projection is not easily achieved. It is possible to avoid this by taking an intricate line on the right, but, though perhaps more aesthetically satisfying, this is probably no easier.

Thereafter, the route tails away leftwards up muddy ledges, but the pleasure can be prolonged a little longer, and on unpolished rock at that, by taking the alternative finish rightwards to gain the front of the buttress. A short steep wall (not unlike 4b Wall) gives access to a rough slab which leads to a skyline notch complete with quarryman's iron spike. Forty feet of delightfully rough easy slabs lead to the top.

The present-day climber will not even draw a passing glance from a public sated with vicarious spectacle but, ironically, Balcombe's and Sheppard's attempt to experiment secretly with the mountaineering moral equivalent of shooting a fox attracted a crowd the like of which would make Bonington or Drummond green with envy:

> . . . pedestrians, cyclists and motorists were packed so densely that such traffic that did wish to pass by, did so only with great difficulty, and much hooting. We seriously feared complications with the police. The cliffs above were lined with hundreds of spectators craning their necks over the top, the railings groaning under the unaccustomed load; the passing pleasure steamers on the Avon hooted at us while their passengers waved and pointed . . . the police were turned out in force to rescue us. They were extremely decent about it all, they took particulars, but promised not to divulge them to the press, and all was well. We slid down to the roadway and sucked ices under a friendly copse until the crowd dispersed, then crept away.
>
> Next time we repeated the route . . . we had to face the mob properly and a reporter rushed up wanting particulars. That had torn it, we thought, but luckily we got away without identities becoming known . . . those newspaper sleuths got very hot on the trail and very nearly tabbed us; friends of ours received offers to spill the beans, but they held fast . . .

Some things stay the same, others change. The modern Avon climber will still lick his ice-cream, but hide from the Press? – they must have been mad.

51 The Devil's Slide

by John Cleare

Route The Devil's Slide, Severe, 390ft.
Cliff West coast of Lundy.
First Ascent K. Lawder and J. Logan, June 1961.
Map Reference O.S. 1–50,000 Sheet 180 (ref. 132469).
Guidebook *Lundy Rock Climbs* by Robert Moulton (Royal Navy and Royal Marines M.C.).
Nearest Road At Ilfracombe: take a boat or ferry (summer only) to Lundy.
Distance and time from cliff 2½ miles/400ft. Allow 1 hour from landing beach.
Good Conditions Dries rapidly after rain.
Campsites and Bunkhouses In order to stay on the island, it is necessary to book in advance (details in guidebook). Bunkhouse accommodation at The Old Light; camping on the east coast; holiday cottages and hotel accommodation are also available.
Bibliography C.C. Journal 1962: *A Reconnaissance of Lundy* by K. M. Lawder and E. C. Pyatt; *Sea Cliff Climbing in Britain* by Robin Collomb and John Cleare (Constable, 1973); Mountain 37: *Lundy Commentary* by Robert Moulton and Pat Littlejohn.

Note: Upgraded to Hard Severe in the 1985 guidebook.

The low, blue shape floating on that line where sea meets sky grew gradually larger and larger. With every churn of the old steamer's paddles, the prospect of spending Whitsun exploring Lundy seemed more and more exciting. Admiral Lawder had assured us that it was indeed a climber's 'Treasure Island', and now at last we were almost there.

According to the Admiral, the finest feature on the three-mile long island was the Devil's Slide, and next morning we were quick to locate it. We scrambled down to the grassy neck linking the rocky pyramid of St James' Stone to the island plateau, and there it was, rising up the other side of a shallow cove. We lay on the yielding turf among the sea-pinks and gazed at it. A sheet of flawless, pink granite, its foot lapped by the swirl of the western ocean, it swept lazily upwards for nearly 400ft., before rearing into a steep headwall below the rocky tor of its summit. The Admiral had been right: it was a truly impressive piece of rock, anomalous on this jagged, be-zawned west coast of Lundy. It was no doubt the greatest slab south of Etive, and we decided that further exploration of the island could wait until we had climbed it.

On its northern side, the Devil's Slide is overhung by a smooth and fierce-crested wall, and there is no way down; but on the southern side a grassy gully leads seawards. We descended this, only to discover that it ended in a rocky gulch, and we were forced to rappel. Standing on the wave-washed ledges at the bottom, the sea sucking at the brown weed a few inches from our PA soles, we examined the slab in detail. It seemed very unsteep, but featureless, except for a slight crease on the far right-hand side – an easy and obvious natural line? We determined to dispense with the rope. What could be pleasanter than to pad effortlessly upwards on this immaculate rock, fingers savouring its rough crystalline warmth, with mind, body, land and sea in harmony – at one in this superb situation?

And that's how it was for nearly 200ft: just sheer carefree delight! Then we reached a fault line, hung with tussocks of sea-pink, running right across the slab. Pausing, we watched the gulls hanging in the vaulted sky

John Cleare

Robert Moulton

Above: The third pitch of Devil's Slide, at a point where the difficulties begin to accumulate. *Climber: Jim Tancred*

Right: A view across the upper part of the Devil's Slide with the lower two climbers completing the third pitch. The higher climber appears to have run out a full rope length on the harder climbing left of the traditional route. *Climbers: Pam Painter and Stuart Caswell. The upper climber is unknown.*

and sun-stars dancing the crests of the blue waves already far below. We were lost in euphoria – euphoria as only a sea-cliff climber can know it.

But the going got harder as the Slide steepened imperceptibly. No longer were we just padding upwards; we were actually climbing. The granite was less friendly and the situation demanded care. A small cloud crossed the sun.

The headwall reared above. Although grooved, it was not inviting. Broken ledges on the right avoided the issue and proffered an escape into the upper reaches of a grassy gully. Leftwards, however, the Slide was slightly rumpled, a sequence of creases leading up and across towards a break in the overhangs of the left wall. The break was a sort of wide chimney, and above it ledges appeared to lead to the cliff-top.

Delicately we tiptoed across the top of the Devil's Slide, ever conscious of the exposure and the holdless slab arcing beneath. A small wooden wedge jutted incongruously from a shallow crack. We wondered. And so into the deep recess of the chimney – rougher granite and real hand-jams drawing blood – its security a welcome contrast. We scrambled upwards and there was no more up to go.

The Devil's Slide has become Lundy's classic climb – and justly so. I've climbed it several times since that day, both on that trip in 1963 and on subsequent ones, and usually with a rope. Once I even climbed it on a quick day-trip on the Ilfracombe steamer. But the first time was the magic one, which is only as it should be, I suppose.

Tom Longstaff must have seen the Devil's Slide when he climbed on St James' Stone in the 1890s, and no doubt again in 1903 and 1927. The history of modern Lundy climbing starts, however, in 1960 when Admiral Lawder and Ted Pyatt made a day-trip reconnaissance. The following year they returned, bringing with them a six-man team including three instructors from Dartmoor Outward Bound School. The Devil's Slide was climbed, along with several other of the island's more obvious rock features. The Admiral recalls that before that first ascent he watched wild goats crossing the final traverse and actually leaping a frictiony section where the holds run out! That was '61, so ours was a very early ascent.

In 1962 Peter Biven, whose name is so inexorably linked with sea-cliff development in the south-west, came to Lundy and led his party up the beautiful *dièdre* on the left-hand side of the Devil's Slide – the angle formed between the slab itself and the beetling left wall. It is a superb line in true 'Cloggy' style, rather harder than the Slide itself and still one of the best pitches on the island. He named it Albion for the then Lord of the Manor, Albion Harman.

By 1970, exploration had proceeded apace and South African Paul Fatti made a delicate and sustained line straight up the middle of the Slide. Satan's Slip, as it's called, is hard climbing and has a bolt for protection high on the third pitch.

I suppose, at a high enough standard, one *could* wander anywhere on the Devil's Slide – but that's not the real point. There was now only one more line left, the steep crest of that overhanging left wall, and in 1971 it provided Keith Darbyshire, a young, powerful and prolific Devon climber, with Shark. It was Extreme climbing for 130ft. up the airy and elegant rock fin of the arête. For a while it was the hardest pitch on Lundy. The Devil's Slide had, to coin a phrase beloved of guidebook writers, 'come of age'.

52 Demo Route

by Robert Moulton

The magnificent ocean setting of Sennen compensates for its lack of stature in comparison with the other popular crags on the peninsula – Bosigran and Chair Ladder. It presents a clean edge of rock, never more than 100ft. in height, rising abruptly from a spacious starting platform, and the climbing is accompanied by the sea booming away among the cracks and blow holes that seam the platform.

Perhaps of all the West Penwith cliffs, it is at Sennen that the holiday atmosphere is at its most pervasive: in the right weather, climbing on the solid, sun-baked granite can be interspersed with swimming in the ocean and eating Cornish cream teas. But somehow my visits to Sennen always seem to be on wild, windy days, when the cliff is exposed to the full force of the westerly winds and their attendant Atlantic breakers. One of my most memorable experiences at Sennen was on a cold, grey Christmas Eve, when working on the guidebook. Undeterred by a few splashes from the waves crashing into the rocks below, I ventured too far along the starting platform and was caught by a massive wave that threw me bodily against the cliff face, leaving me breathless, soaked and with a renewed respect for the force of the sea.

The first time we went to climb Demo Route it was blowing a strong gale, and a tentative walk to the top of the cliff confirmed the inevitable. The waves pounding into the rocks below the starting platform were breaking halfway up the climb, and great plumes of spindrift were blowing high over the top of the 80ft. cliff; the sea was giving its demonstration on Demo Route. The only sensible course of action was a retreat to the Old Success. This friendly pub still displays its earlier Cliff Assault Wing patronage, with commando pennants and framed photo-diagrams of the local crags on its walls. The history of climbing at Sennen is inseparably linked with the Royal Marine Commandos, whose Cliff Assault Wing was based in St Ives. The positive, gymnastic climbing on Sennen's steep, sound rock provided the ideal medium for the commandos, with their emphasis on physical fitness and precise technique.

We were back next day. The wind had lessened, but the relentless Atlantic swell was still sending waves crashing on to the starting platform and my first moves up the climb were hastened by memories of that earlier drenching. The rock on the first pitch was greasy, but good flaky holds enabled swift progress to be made away from the danger zone to the foot of the narrow chimney/crack that forms the main difficulty of the first pitch. No doubt in good conditions more elegant progress could be made up the small, rounded holds outside the crack, but I settled for an awkward but relatively secure technique, wedging my right arm and leg in the crack, and allowing my left foot to make what it could of the holds on the edge. The holds soon improved and an ample belay ledge was at hand.

The top pitch provides the demonstration that gives the climb its name; the line goes steeply up to the right-hand side of a prominent overhanging nose, then down beneath the nose to gain a slab on its left. The moves round the nose call for a positive, determined approach: you lean out on undercut holds, change feet on the large sloping footholds and reach out to commit yourself on excellent layback holds on the left side of the nose. A steep move, bringing your feet high up on the left side of the nose, then leads on to the welcoming finishing slab, which is liberally supplied with those large knobbly holds that are such a reassuring feature of easy granite climbing. The holds on the crux are enormous really, but the commitment required is considerably greater than that normally encountered on climbs of the Severe grade.

Sennen can boast good climbs in all but the very hardest grades, but its nature and situation make it a cliff for light-hearted, enjoyable climbing and for this reason its main attraction lies in its Severes. Although only a short climb, Demo Route possesses a combination of position and character that makes it outstanding. In some ways the perfect time to do the climb would be on a balmy summer evening with the setting sun bringing a glow to the warm, rough granite. However, for me, the conditions of our ascent were more in keeping with the Cornwall I know, with its threatening, grey skies and its uncompromising, windswept landscapes.

Route Demo Route, Severe, 80ft.
Cliff Pedn-Mên-Du, Cornwall.
First Ascent J. F. Barry, 1943.
Map Reference O.S. 1–50,000 Sheet 203 (ref. 347263).
Guidebook C.C. *Chair Ladder* by Robert Moulton and Terry Thompson.
Nearest Road A minor road above the village of Sennen Cove. Turn off the Sennen Cove road just as the hill steepens and follow the minor road to a parking area a short distance from the top of the cliff (ref. 352261).
Distance and time from cliff Allow 10 minutes to reach the base of the cliff taking a descent track that starts just to the left (west) of the Coastguard Lookout.
Good Conditions The climb dries rapidly after rain.
Campsites and Bunkhouses Camping at Sennen. Accommodation at Sennen Cove. C.C. Hut, The Count House, at Bosigran.
Bibliography C.C. Journal 1960 contains an aerial photo of the cliff.

Note: Upgraded to Hard Severe in the 1984 guidebook.

Left: The sensational overhang move on Demo Route, climbed on jams and underclings to the background thunder of the Atlantic breakers pounding remorselessly on the rocks below. *Climbers: John Smith, Ian Esplin and another*

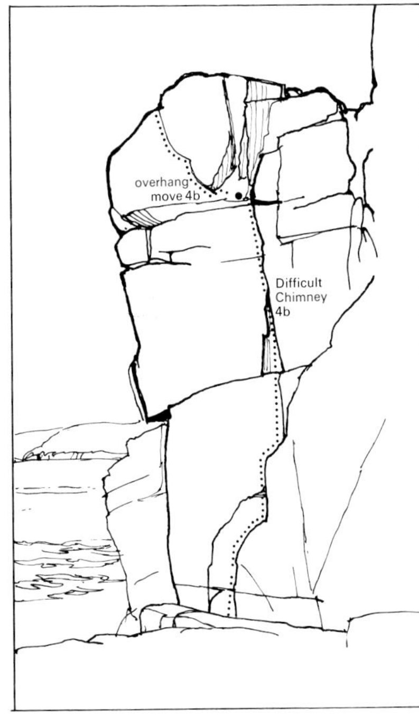

Left: A view down the second pitch of Terrier's Tooth (see following chapter). The initial groove is below the ledge on the left, and below, the Atlantic breakers, on the ebb in this photo, still periodically smash across the climb's plinth of ledges and boulders.
Climbers: Chris Pugsley and Dave Morgan

Below: A view up Terrier's Tooth. The climber is on the easier and more logical groove and corner start. The conventional start takes the quartz seam to the left of the climber. This is quite technical and demands care. The easier start, quickly gained from the descent route, allows height to be gained rapidly if the tide is threatening.
Climber: Dave Morgan

53 Terrier's Tooth and Pendulum Chimney

by Dave Cook

The sea hammered into Cornwall like a rock-a-billy back beat, as Wilson began to boulder-bop along the base of the cliff.

He had it all that day. None of us had been to the Chair Ladder cliffs before, and hence no one could counter the waves of bullshit that cascaded from his lips. 'Yes, that was where the body finally surfaced after three months.' He pointed into a gurgling crevice. 'The Moacs wedged it down.'

Like Moses guiding his people across the Red Sea, he marshalled us along the great platforms of granite, timing each foray to coincide with an onrush of foaming brine. Weaker spirits in our party fell, or rather sank, by the wayside, until at last the prophet gestured upwards.

'Terrier's Tooth,' came the dramatic cry. 'Best conditions for it.' Being somewhat unfamiliar with the mouths of terriers, I wasn't quite ready for the oozing saliva of spindrift and rain that drenched the rock.

Chair Ladder faces the Atlantic like a turreted fortress. Greasy, cavernous gullies separate its great buttresses, throwing their clean steepness into sharp relief. Terrier's Tooth spirals up the right terminal pillar like a helter-skelter.

We set off in a sodden crocodile. Having all been submerged together, I suppose it was only logical to climb so that together we would fall.

The eruptions of spray dropped below us and we shook ourselves dry like dogs.

The first part of the climb mounted a large knobbly slab, and then a steep wall festooned with bizarre jug-handles, more chunky than marmalade. And the rock was so hard. Our numbed hands, grown soft on kinder northern stone, flinched from its bruising coldness. The marmalade turned into jams and our climbing slipped into automatic.

Above the ledge a few feet of chimney; boots crunching on hands below. As if in protest, two cavers in our party disappeared down a hole into Cornwall, making a strange tunnelling variation along a vein of decay and reappearing higher up the route. The climbers, making sure they kept Cornwall tightly in their hands, swung exhilaratingly across a bulge, and then clattered up the triangular slab above.

We all balanced crazily together on the summit *aiguille*, charged beyond measure by the octane of that incomparable coast and the pounding sea.

The lure of cream teas proved too great for some, but Ken and I tobogganed back down to the waves. This time it was neither water nor bullshit that washed over me, but accurate information: 'Some people will say that Pegasus and Flannel Avenue are better climbs on cleaner rock, but Pendulum Chimney is the route of the crag – a bold line of weakness up the front of the highest and most continuous part of the cliff.' Occasionally, as readers of his magazine will know, he is right about such things.

I led off up a steep wedging crack with helpful holds on its left wall. Ken, who had recently been to Yosemite, 'off-widthed' behind me.

Ahead was a delectable right-angled groove, hung on a symmetrical wall like a picture. Obscene commands instructed me to perform some 'flared stemming', but fortunately such defilement was unnecessary. Wholesome back and footing moves, of which Mary Whitehouse would have been proud, levered me to the foot of the towering chimney.

The next pitch was long, hard and magic. A steep crack, appropriately spick-and-span next door to Detergent Wall, led into a gloomy, greasy cleft, which bulged and narrowed like strings of sausages used to be before supermarkets were invented. We bulged and narrowed our way up it, disconcerted by the sparse protection, but astounded by its majestic line.

Wisps of spray still danced in the wind below the gendarmed summit. The history books are wrong: it wasn't bowling that made Francis Drake late for the Armada, but climbing on Chair Ladder.

Routes Terrier's Tooth, Very Difficult, 130ft.; Pendulum Chimney, Severe, 165ft.
Cliff **Chair Ladder, Cornwall.**
First Ascents Terrier's Tooth – J. Mallory, M. A. Roster, A. M. Greenwood and B. Donkin, March 1940; Pendulum Chimney – J. E. Littlewood and party, *c.* 1930 by the final pitch. Direct Start – J. Cortland-Simpson and party, *c.* 1947.
Map Reference O.S. 1–50,000 Sheet 203 (ref. 365216).
Guidebook C.C. *Chair Ladder* by Robert Moulton and Terry Thompson.
Nearest Road A car park behind the village of Porthgwarra (ref. 369219). Continue by a road and track to the Coastguard Lookout above the cliff.
Distance and time from cliff ½ mile. Allow 10 minutes.
Good Conditions The cliff dries fairly quickly but the bottom can remain greasy with sea rime and the top lichenous, unless the weather is hot and windy. Avoid high spring tides.
Campsites and Bunkhouses Camping at Sennen. Huts in Sennen Cove and at Bosigran.
Bibliography C.C. Journal 1957 contains a detailed explanation of the confused first-ascent details surrounding Pendulum Chimney; Mountain 15: *Cornwall* by Frank Cannings gives a general historical picture of Cornish climbing; *Sea Cliff Climbing in Britain* by John Cleare and Robin Collomb (Constable, 1973).

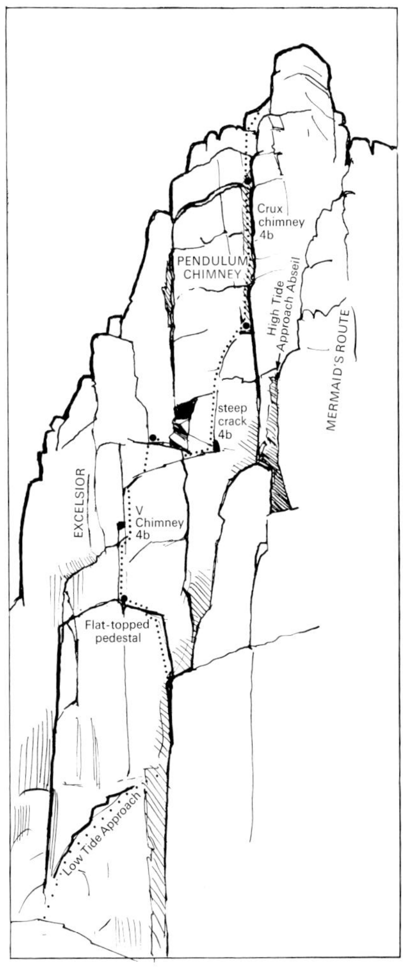

Right: The cracked slab that forms the finale of Terrier's Tooth. *Climbers: Unknown*

Left: The steep crack that leads up into Pendulum Chimney. *Climber: Jim Worthington*

Ken Wilson

54 Doorpost

by Mike Banks

Route Doorpost, Hard Severe, 220ft.
Cliff Main Cliff, Bosigran, Cornwall.
First Ascent B. M. Biven, H. T. H. Peck and P. H. Biven, August 1955.
Map Reference O.S. 1–50,000 Sheet 203 (ref. 413368).
Guidebook C.C. *Cornwall*, Vol. 1, by P. H. Biven and M. B. McDermott.
Nearest Road The B3306 St Ives to St Just road at the Bosigran Count House (ref. 422365). A path leads across the moor to the cliff.
Distance and time from cliff $\frac{1}{2}$ mile. Allow 10 minutes.
Good Conditions Apart from a weep of moisture that stays on the first pitch for some time, the climb dries quickly after rain. The rock is clean and the holds incut so it can be climbed in poor conditions.
Campsites and Bunkhouses C.C. Hut, The Count House. Camping at Rosemergy Farm and Bosigran Farm.
Bibliography *Sea Cliff Climbing in Britain* by John Cleare and Robin Collomb (Constable, 1973); Mountain 15; *Cornwall* by Frank Cannings deals with the general history of Cornish climbing.

Right: The first pitch of Doorpost – a beautiful rising traverse across steep slabs at the foot of Bow Wall. *Climber: Jim Worthington*

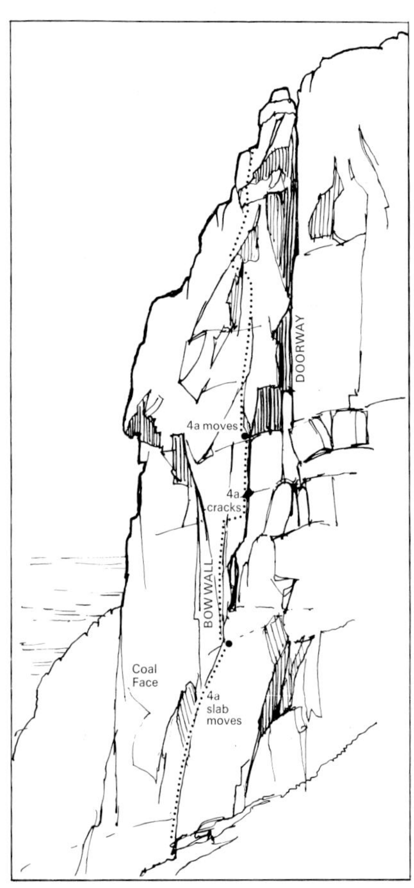

That superb wall of granite, the main face of Bosigran, is arguably the most renowned of all the Cornish cliffs. Yet it is also one of the most atypical. Not only does it run at right angles to the sea, but it is virtually an inland crag. No sea birds nest there and the climber can ignore the state of the tide or the mood of the sea, which normally form part of the charm and challenge of cliff climbing. However, these shortcomings are quickly forgiven in the compensating riches the cliff has to offer: climbing routes galore on steep and irreproachable granite to suit every taste.

Bosigran has atmosphere and, for me, nostalgia. I was taught to climb there, as a Commando, soon after the end of World War Two. In those days you would sometimes see, and have a friendly word with, an old man striding the cliff tops, his white hair streaming in the wind. This was A. W. Andrews, the founding father of Cornish climbing. Andrews made the first route on Bosigran, the Ledge Climb, in 1905, although he had climbed Commando Ridge, on the other side of the cove, as early as 1902.

To a Commando climber, Bosigran brings back memories of night climbs (marginally assisted by the four flashes from Pendeen lighthouse) and sometimes, when an up-country general paid a visit, demonstrations of cliff-raiding techniques, when rockets and mortars hurled ropes and rope ladders over the cliff, until the whole face seemed to be festooned with military spaghetti.

Then, in the mid-1950s, by which time I was in charge of the Commando climbers, activity on the cliff fairly exploded, generating much friendly rivalry between civilians and military. The civilian spearhead was composed of the Biven brothers, Peter and Barrie (tall and straight they were), and the remarkable Trevor Peck. Trevor was an industrialist who, through the accident of giving one young Biven a lift, reconciled the then disparate brothers, cemented the climbing team and, starting at the age of forty-five, put up a long series of fierce routes as well as setting up a manufacturing plant for climbing hardware. In competition were the best of the Commando instructors, including some talented mountaineers undergoing their National Service in the Marines. Names that come to mind include Deacon, Holdroyd, Goodier, Blackshaw and Grey. These were the good days.

One of the most attractive, but by no means the hardest, of the Biven–Peck routes is Doorpost, a sweeping line that curves in an elegant traversing arc and then worries its way up the steep upper face. It takes in some of the finest rock architecture of Bosigran, passes close to several formidably hard routes, yet never goes above Hard Severe itself. It is a gem of a route.

A scramble of 35ft., barely worthy of a rope, lands the climber on a pedestal rock under the towering cliffs of the main face. It is from here that the traverse starts. The granite is clean, and holds small but sharp. The fingers dig into the crisp, undercut holds, the toes find small, fine rugosities on a steep slab. The pitch curves gently upwards and an occasional chock may be slipped into the same crack that provides the finger-holds. After rain, Bosigran often weeps, but the granite is so clean on this route that these damp patches hardly matter. The pitch seems to flow rhythmically until suddenly – full stop. The easy sequence of holds runs out and one of those delicate traversing puzzles has to be solved. Each finger- and toe-hold has to be selected in advance; a pleasant cerebral exercise. The thin moves are made and the traverse leads up to the belay.

The wall above is now much steeper, but split by twin cracks. It is fairly straightforward work to gain the left-hand crack. Now comes the time for arm power. A move is made across to the right-hand crack, then some heavy pulls are made up the crack with the body-weight dragging outwards. This is the hardest part of the climb. I remember once, just as I was making it, a nut hanging from my waist jammed in the crack, anchoring me very effectively on the crux for some agonizingly long seconds until I could free it. Above is the ample ledge under the huge, high roof.

The long top pitch, of about 85ft., starts with some good thin moves, but soon the holds come in generous profusión, often in the form of smooth, black rock adhering firmly (so far!) to the granite. I suppose the upper 50ft. are really too easy, but the situation is wonderfully airy, so that you can

Ken Wilson

Left: The Bosigran cliffs and Porthmoina Island from Commando Ridge.

Right: Looking steeply up the cracks of Doorpost with climbers on the second pitch.
Climbers: Unknown

Ken Wilson

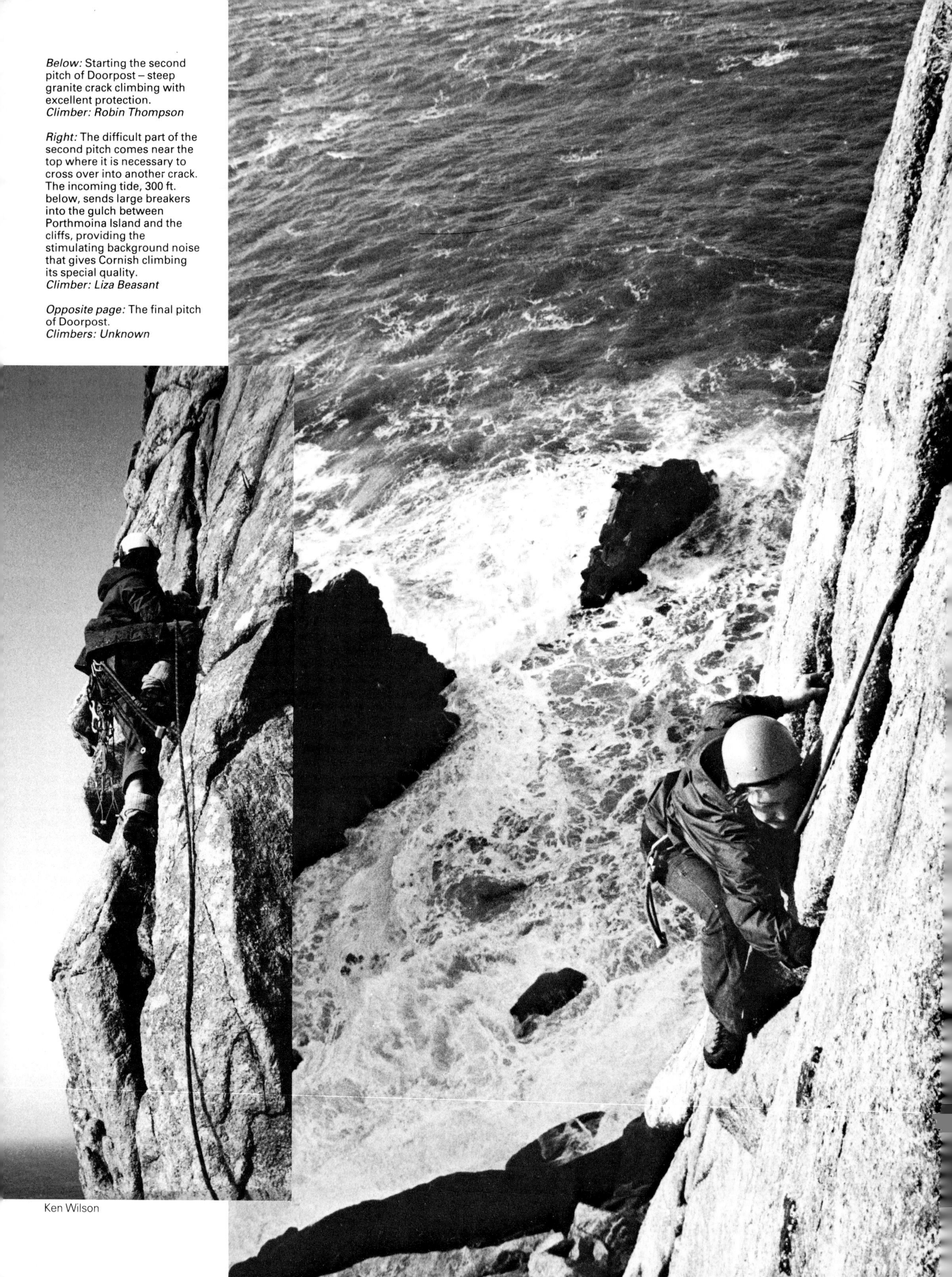

Below: Starting the second pitch of Doorpost – steep granite crack climbing with excellent protection.
Climber: Robin Thompson

Right: The difficult part of the second pitch comes near the top where it is necessary to cross over into another crack. The incoming tide, 300 ft. below, sends large breakers into the gulch between Porthmoina Island and the cliffs, providing the stimulating background noise that gives Cornish climbing its special quality.
Climber: Liza Beasant

Opposite page: The final pitch of Doorpost.
Climbers: Unknown

Ken Wilson

55 Climbers' Club Ordinary

by Mike Banks

Dartmoor is often at its scenic best where the rivers come tumbling off the moor to cascade through steep-sided valleys clothed with mature hardwood forests. The Plym is a fine example of such a river. Partway along its course one side of its containing valley is almost blocked by a mass of granite which thrusts out from the wooded hillside to stop only a few yards short of the river itself. This is the Dewerstone.

The prow of this granite dam terminates in a sheer wall, nearly 200ft. high – the Devil's Rock. It is the largest exposure of granite on Dartmoor and offers the finest climbs. The rock itself is tough, dependable granite, although the surrounding vegetation makes it rather more greasy during humid spells than the cleaner, sea-washed granite of the Cornish or Lundy cliffs.

The Dewerstone nestles somewhat secretively in its valley, and trees mask its true stature. It is not, in other words, a crag that flaunts itself to public view. Perhaps for this reason it seems to have been neglected by the pioneer rock-climbers, although there is a vague reference to the legendary Haskett Smith climbing in Devon.

The story proper opened with a fine flourish on 2 September 1935, when A. D. M. Cox and R. M. Bere climbed Climbers' Club Original. The bold line they took has been tidied up a little and is now known as the Climbers' Club Ordinary. It is graded Mild VS.

The approach to the rock through half a mile of oak woodlands, overlooking the merrily flowing Plym, is a delight in itself. Soon the outline of the Dewerstone resolves itself from among the trees. The scale and steepness of the crag often come as a surprise. Our route follows the only obvious line of weakness up the otherwise unrelenting main face of Devil's Rock.

The climb starts with a traverse up and left across a steep wall. As on any good traverse, the moves have to be studied intelligently and worked out in advance. If you select a line too high or too low, or if your feet end up on the wrong set of holds, then the difficulties suddenly magnify themselves. As the main line of weakness is neared, a sling may be dropped, usually with some relief, behind a flake. A leftwards slither lands the climber in a large sloping niche, where there is a piton and, higher up, a place for a nut belay.

An overhanging roof now seems to block further progress and solving this problem is rather the *bonne bouche* of the route. It was also the scene of one of the rare fatal accidents in Devon: a second man, trying to take the much more difficult left fork above the niche, came off and pulled off his leader, who fell to his death.

It is almost a pity to give the game away, but the move entails launching yourself to the right round the corner of the overhang, hoping something will turn up – or else! Of course, the jug-handle for the fluttering right hand is there, but it might not have been. Soon all becomes sweet reason again and there is a fine belay higher up, round a reassuringly huge bollard.

Next comes a smooth and steep V-groove capped by another overhang. It is not an easy pitch to assess at first sight. The smooth rock offers little for the feet and you will only find out how good the holds in the crack are when you dig your fingers into them. So it is anything from a grunting thrutch to a controlled, if tense, finger-and-toe exercise, according to your mood or technique. A piton under the overhang gives protection for a final heave to the right when, at last, the weight comes off the arms and back on to good foot-holds where it properly belongs. The line goes up and left a little, still demanding, until the wide horizontal ledge of the high girdle traverse is reached.

There is now a choice of routes, but it is a nice thing to finish on a high note and so sustain both the quality and the difficulty of the lower pitches. My preferred finish leads up to a corner, with a narrow crack on the left for the fingers, and small bulges on the slabby wall on the right for the feet. It looks a long way down to the River Plym, so a small chock in the crack can be soothing.

To begin with, the crack goes nicely in a layback. There are then a few distinctly thinner moves as the left wall is used for bridging until a step right gives the comfort of a narrow crack and, quite soon, the summit platform. Then, while your number two climbs, you can gaze lazily at the soft foliage of the oaks, the busy jackdaws or, perhaps, a wheel-

Route Climbers' Club Ordinary, Mild Very Severe, 175ft.
Cliff The Dewerstone, Dartmoor, Devon.
First Ascent A. D. M. Cox and R. M. Bere, 1935.
Map Reference O.S. 1–50,000 Sheet 201 (ref. 538638).
Guidebook R.N.M.C. *Rock Climbing in Devonshire* by R. D. Moulton.
Nearest Road A minor road at Shaugh Bridge near Shaugh Prior. This is 8 miles north of Plymouth, to the east of the A386 Plymouth to Tavistock road.
Distance and time from cliff ½ mile. Allow 10 minutes. Follow the north bank of the stream to the foot of the crag.
Good Conditions The cliff is very sheltered and dries quickly after rain though the first pitch of climbers' Club Ordinary can remain greasy for a little longer.
Campsites and Bunkhouses Camping is sometimes allowed at the farm near Shaugh Bridge but otherwise camping in the area is strictly controlled (restricted).
Bibliography Oxford Mountaineering 1935: *Climbing on Dartmoor* by A. D. M. Cox; C.C. Journal 1937 contains brief references to the climb.

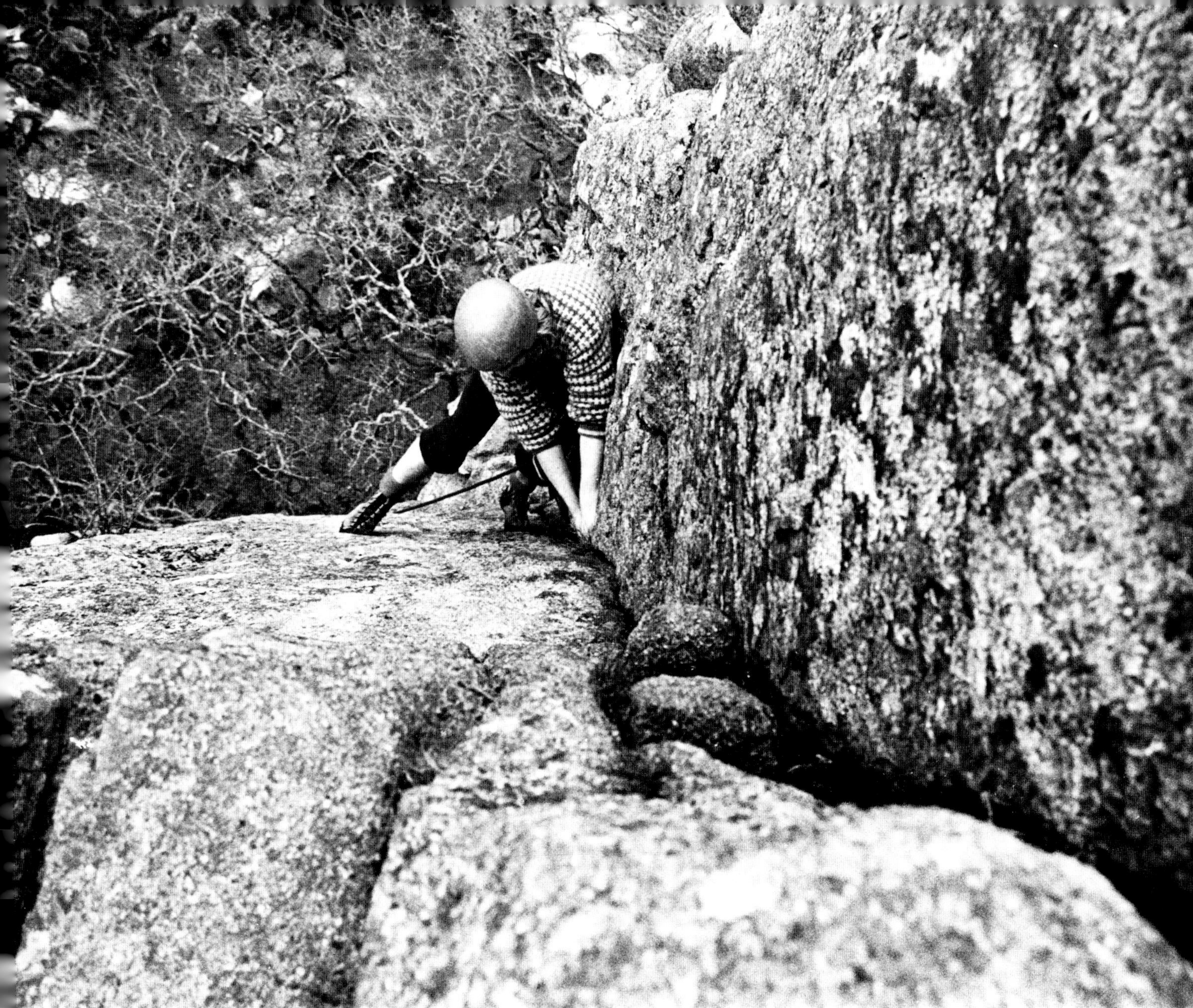

ing buzzard quartering the valley. Even with the motorway to the West Country completed as far as Plymouth, it is still a long day's drive to or from the cliffs of West Cornwall. The Dewerstone can therefore make a delightful break in the journey, particularly on the homeward leg.

Left: The initial wall pitch of Climber's Club Ordinary. The climber has to traverse across the wall on greasy holds, to gain a groove above the knarled tree stump. *Climber: Charles Yonge*

Above: The final pitch of the climb traverses a very steep wall to gain the foot of this layback crack, which provides a satisfying finale. *Climber: Charles Yonge.*

Grading Comparisons

British grading is so beset with complexities and anomalies that it is difficult to give precise grading advice in a book such as this. Though all areas employ the well-tried adjectival system, it has come to represent different degrees of difficulty in different areas, so that unwary climbers may find themselves committed to routes that are harder than expected. Some may feel that it does no harm to have a certain amount of pre-programmed excitement concealed within the grading, but it is well to remember that this could lead to a nasty accident, particularly where inexperienced climbers are concerned.

There is, of course, always an element of imprecision in grading as there are so many factors to be encompassed – length, exposure, protection (or lack of it), technical difficulty, loose rock, size and position of stances etc. There are also geographical factors: gritstone climbs seem to have a more aggressive bite than their mountain equivalents (some subtle compensation seems to have crept in to allow for the generally unserious situation of the edges); sea cliffs have the added possibility of being drowned on approach or even on the lower parts of the climbs; the generally uninformative Scottish grading system allows neo VS nasties to lurk amidst the jungle of Severes, waiting to ensnare the unwary. Then again, how does one compare Ben Nevis's Long Climb – a serious and committing route that is often wet – with a technically harder one-pitch test-piece like Black Slab at Stanage?

So there are problems in correlating climbs in the easier grades compounded by the fact that few people have the sensitivity needed to sort them out. By the time climbers are in a position to pontificate on gradings to be used in guidebooks, their awareness of the nuances of the easier grades will be greatly reduced and they will be forced to rely on memory and consensus. Moreover, the numerical system, so effective in pinpointing difficulty in the higher grades, seems to be of little value for easier climbs.

With these problems in mind a graded list is employed here to amplify the formal grades. Each area has its routes listed in a general order of difficulty (based on a consensus of opinion among a number of climbers), and each list is matched to its neighbour so that general correlations can be made across areas. For example, there is considered to be a similarity between the demands and technicalities of Agag's Groove, Murray's Route, Crackstone Rib and Parsons' Chimney, despite the fact that the local guidebooks grade the climbs Very Difficult, two at Severe and Hard Severe respectively. It must be emphasised that the technical difficulties of some of the one-pitch outcrop routes are still difficult to compare (grade for grade) with the more comprehensive challenges involved in multi-pitch routes, particularly those on high mountains: there is no move on Agag's Groove as hard as those on Parsons' Chimney but the former is in a more exposed and serious situation. The outcrop list should therefore be treated as a rather separate entity.

A note for the 1997 edition: Some of the aforementioned anomalies between areas have disappeared as these days guidebooks are published more frequently and are usually authored by well-travelled climbers.

The relationship between climbs on the list remains the same with the following exceptions: Nea has risen by four places (having become harder because of rockfall); Napes Needle moves up six places to reflect its grade increase from HVD to HS and the view that both its ascent, and more particularly its descent, are not to be taken lightly. The recent excessive upgradings on Birchen Edge reflect a feeling that these very short climbs are much harder than previously recorded – thus, to bend to some of this view, Topsail and Sail Buttress have been moved a few places up the list though both still correlate with S and VD climbs.

The Birchen climbs are the most extreme manifestations of a national upgrading trend. Since *Classic Rock* first appeared in 1978 thirty of its eighty climbs have been officially upgraded – most of them during the last ten years. Some of these, notably the grades given to the top three Scottish climbs and the outcrop-like crux of Ardgarten Arête, merely corrected outdated guidebook norms, but the bulk are less explicable. There seems to be a broad upgrading trend. This is not as a result of a sudden revelation that the climbs are hard as they have been done by generations of climbers without complaint. It seems to be more the expression of a contemporary reluctance to accept that anything that is remotely tough should remain (as a potential embarrassment?) in the easier grades.

All of this has taken place during a period when protection techniques and footgear have greatly improved. Yet only two *Classic Rock* climbs have had their grades officially reduced – Ash Tree Slabs from HVD to VD and Pinnacle Rib (notwithstanding 4b moves on the Yellow Slab) from HD to D – commendable actions that deserve emulation. If *this* book acts as a bulwark to ensure that such great climbs as Tophet Wall, Main Wall, Doorpost and Ardverikie Wall remain securely ensconsed as proud Severes, and are saved from the curiously demeaning grade of Mild Very Severe, it may help to put a brake on this nonsensical grading 'inflation' and serve some useful function.

Comparative Regional Graded Lists of Routes in Classic Rock

*Skye Ridge – individual pitches only (south to north); 1978 official guidebook grades in brackets and revised grades in bold type

SCOTLAND		LAKE DISTRICT		WALES		OTHER AREAS	
The Chasm (S)	**VS**						
The Long Climb (S)	**VS**						
Clean Sweep (S)	**VS**						
Eagle Ridge Direct (S)							
The Talisman (S)	**HS**	Moss Ghyll Grooves (HS)	**MVS**	Main Wall (HS)			
Cumming/Crofton (S)							
Ardverikie Wall (S)				Glyder Fach Direct (HS)		Black Slab (MVS)	**VS**
Long Crack (S)				Grey Slab (HS)	**VS**	Climbers' Club Ordinary (MVS)	
Cioch Direct (S)		Tophet Wall (S)	**HS**	Nea (S)	**VS**	Piton Route (VS)	
Integrity (S)	**MVS**	Jones's Direct (S)	**HS**	The Cracks (S/VS)	**HS**	Doorpost (HS)	
Ardgarten Arête (S)	**VS**			Creagh Dhu Wall (HS)		Pendulum Chimney (S)	
Punster's Crack (S)		Bracket and Slab (S)				The Devil's Slide (S)	**HS**
Clachaig Gully (VD)	**S**					Demo Route (S)	**HS**
North Face Route (VD)		Rib and Slab (S)	**HS**	Red Wall (HVD)		Topsail (S)	**VS**
Archer Ridge (VD)		Napes Needle (HVD)	**HS**	Lazarus (S)		April Crack (HS)	
Agag's Groove (VD)		Murray's Route (S)		Crackstone Rib (S)		Parson's Chimney (HS)	
Labyrinth (VD)		'C' Route (S)		Will-o'-the-Wisp (HVD)		Red-Pencil Direct (S)	
Crypt Route (VD)		Gillercombe Buttress (MS)		Grooved Arête (HVD)		Sail Buttress (HVD)	**VS**
The Cioch Nose (VD)		Troutdale Pinnacle (MS)		Avalanche (VD)		Technical Slab (S)	**HS**
Squareface (VD)				Great Gully (VD)		Central Climb (S)	
Sou'wester Slabs (VD)				Wrinkle (VD)		Via Dolorosa (S)	**VS**
Savage Slit (VD)				The Arête (VD)		Black and Tans (S)	
The Cuillin Ridge (VD)*		Ash Tree Slabs (HVD)	**VD**	Hope (VD)			
		Bowfell Buttress (HD)	**VD**	First Pinnacle Rib (HD)	**D**	Terrier's Tooth (HVD)	
Recess Route (HD)	**VD**	New West Climb (HD)	**VD**	Gashed Crag (HD)	**VD**	Powder Monkey Parade (HVD)	**S**
		Little Chamonix (VD)		Spiral Stairs (HD)	**VD**		
				Milestone Direct (D)	**VD**	Flying Buttress (Stanage) (VD)	
Tower Ridge (D)				Flying Buttress (HD)	**VD**		

Left: On the summit of Terrier's Tooth at Chair Ladder. *Climbers: Janet Davies and Barry Whybrow*

High on Tennis Shoe Climb, one of the fine classic routes on the Idwal Slabs in North Wales.
Climbers: Unknown

Other Good Routes

The following climbs are recommended as worthwhile alternatives to the main routes in the book (including some easy VSs).

Classic Rock routes	*Guidebooks*	*Possible alternatives*
Cioch Direct/Integrity	1/27	Cioch West/Wallworks Route (S), East Buttress Direct (MS), Crack of Doom (VS).
The Cioch Nose	2/27	
The Long Climb	3/27	Observatory Ridge (D), Rubicon Wall (S), Bayonet Route (VD) or Raeburn's Arête (S) to N.E. Buttress.
Tower Ridge	3/27	Route 1 (VD) – Carn Dearg, Pinnacle Buttress of the Tower (D).
Long Crack/Archer Ridge	4/27	The Wabe – Gearr Aonach (VD), Flake Route (VD), Shadbolt's Chimney (S).
Agag's Groove	4/27	January Jigsaw (S), Route 1 (VD), Grooved Arête (HS).
Ardverikie Wall	3/27	Kubla Khan (HS), Hairline Grooves (S).
Savage Slit	5/27	Aladdin Buttress (S), Ewan Buttress (D).
Clean Sweep	5/27	Hell's Lumps (S), Devil's Delight (HS).
The Talisman	5/27	Original Route Direct (S), Crystal Ridge (D) and Grey Slab (HS) – Coire Sputan Dearg.
Cumming/Crofton	6/27	Mitre Ridge Direct (HS), Quartzvein Route (VD) – Coire na Ciche.
Eagle Ridge	6/27	Causeway Rib (VD), The Stack (S), Lethargy – Eagle's Rock (HS).
Recess Route etc.	7/27	Chimney Arête (S), Spinal Rib (HS).
Sou'wester Slabs	7/27	Caliban's Creep (D), South Ridge Original (HS), Prospero Buttress (HS), Pagoda Ridge (S) – A'Chir.
Little Chamonix	8/28	Brown Crag Wall (S), Ardus (S).
Troutdale Pinnacle	8/28	Phoenix Ridge (VD) – Greatend Crag, Bowderstone Pinnacle (D).
Gillercombe Buttress	8/28	Honister Wall (HS) – Buckstone How, Corvus (D) or Raven Crag Gully (VD) – Raven Crag.
Tophet Wall	12/28	Kern Knotts Crack (MVS), Innominate Crack (MVS), Eagle's Nest Direct (MVS).
Napes Needle/Needle Ridge	12/28	Abbey Buttress (VD), Eagle's Nest Ridge by West Chimney (VD).
New West/Rib and Slab	12/28	Walker's Gully (HS), West Wall Climb (VD), North-West Climb (MVS), North Climb (D).
Jones's Route Direct	11/28	Scafell Pinnacle via Slingsby's Chimney (VD), Moss Ghyll (VD).
Moss Ghyll Grooves	11/28	Great Eastern (MVS), Hopkinson's Gully (MVS).
Ash Tree Slabs/'C' Route	9/28	Asterisk/'D' Route (HS).
Bracket and Slab	9/28	Gimmer Chimney (VD), 'B' Route, Stoats' Crack (HS) – Pavey Ark.
Murray's Route	10/28	Gordon and Craig's Route (HVD), 'C' Ordinary Route (D), Hopkinson's Crack (HS).
Great Gully	13/29	Amphitheatre Buttress (D), Pinnacle Wall (S).
Milestone Direct	13/29	Rowan Route (M), Pulpit Route/Ivy Chimney (D), Soapgut/Chimney Route (HS).
Gashed Crag etc.	13/29	North Buttress (M), Apex Route (D).
Direct Route – Glyder Fach	13/29	Oblique Buttress (S), Hawk's Nest Buttress (S), Chasm Route (VD).
Hope, Lazarus, The Arête	13/29	Tennis Shoe (S), Javelin Gully (S), Groove Above (S).
Grey Slab (Lost Boot Climb)	13/29	Manx Wall (S) – Clogwyn Ddu.
Nea	14/29	Scrambler's Gate (S), Hazel Groove Direct (S), Zig Zag (HS) – Craig Ddu.
Crackstone Rib/Wrinkle	14/29	Skylon (HS), Main Scoop Route (HS).
Flying Buttress/Spiral Stairs	14/29	Dives/Better Things (HS), Parchment Passage (VD), Horseman's Route (HS).
The Cracks	14/29	Slow Ledge Climb (S), Black Cleft (S), Little Benjamin (VD).
Main Wall	14/29	Central Route (S), Great Gully (VD), Gambit Climb (VD) – Clogwyn y Ddysgl.
Avalanche	15/29	The Sword/Route 2 (MVS), Roof Route (VD), Yellow Slab – Purgatory Conn. (HS).
Creagh Dhu Wall	16/29	Borchgrevinck/Poor Man's Peuterey (S), Christmas Curry (S), Valerie's Rib (HS).
Will-o'-the-Wisp	17/29	Obvious (VD), Box Trick (HS), The Gem (HS).
Red Pencil Direct	18/30	Meddler's Crack (D), Pagan's Purgatory (S).
Parsons' Chimney	18/30	Pigott's Stride/Whisky Crack (S), Bird's Nest Crack (S), Central Crack (S).
Black Slab/April Crack	19/31/32	Christmas Crack (S), Inverted V (MVS), Balcony Buttress (S), Martello Buttress (S).
Flying Buttress	19/31/32	Holly Bush Crack (VD), Robin Hood's Right Hand Buttress Direct (HS), Heaven Crack (VD).
Sail Buttress etc.	20/31/32	Sail Chimney (VD), N.M.C. Crack – Gardom's Edge.
Central Climb	21/31/32	K2 (VD), Modern (S), Great Chimney (S).
Via Dolorosa etc.	21/31/32	Kestral Cracks (S), Slab and Arête (S), Pedestal Route (VD), Jeffcoat's Chimney (VD).
Piton Route	22/33	Sinister/Direct Route (HS), The Arête/Original (D), Morpheus (VD).
The Devil's Slide	23/33	Hurricane (S), Integrity (S), Walrus (S).
Climbers' Club Ordinary	26/33	Colonel's Arête (VD), Central Groove (HS).
Terrier's Tooth/Pendulum	25/33	Flannel Avenue (S), Mermaid's Route (VD), Pegasus (HS), The Girdle Traverse (S).
Demo Route	24/33	Double Overhang (HS), Corner Climb (D), Dexter Route (HS), Johnstone's Route (S) – Land's End.
Doorpost	24/33	Doorway (S), Autumn Flakes (S), Ding (VS), Ochre Slab Route 2 (S), Bosigran Ridge Climb (VD).

Definitive Guides in 1997
(those relevant to this book)

1 *Skye/Hebrides* (2 Vols) Vol. 1 MacKenzie/Williams (SMC/T 1996)
2 *Northern Highlands* (2 Vols) Vol. 1 Cohen (SMC/T 1993)
3 *Ben Nevis* Richardson/Walker/Clothier (SMC 1994)
4 *Glen Coe* Crocket/Anderson/Cuthbertson (SMC/T 1992)
5 *The Cairngorms* Vol. 1 Fyffe/Nisbet (SMC/T 1995)
6 *The Cairngroms* Vol. 2 Fyffe/Nisbet (SMC/T 1995)
7 *Arran/Arrochar* Little/Crocket/Prentice (SMC/T 1997*)
8 *Borrowdale* Armstrong/Kenyon (FRCC 1986)
9 *Langdale* Armstrong (FRCC 1989)
10 *Dow/Duddon/Slate* Phizacklea (FRCC 1993)
11 *Scafell/Wasdale/Eskdale* Phizacklea (FRCC 1996)
12 *Gable/Pillar* Armstrong/Loxham (FRCC 1991)
13 *Ogwen/Carneddau* (2 Vols) Jones (CC 1993)
14 *Llanberis Pass* Williams (CC 1994)
15 *Lliwedd* Neal (CC 1997*)
16 *Tremadog/Cwm Silyn* Pretty/Farrant/Milburn (CC 1989)
17 *Mid Wales* Sumner (CC 1997*)
18 *Yorkshire Gritstone* Desroy (YMC 1989)
19 *Stanage* Hoey (BMC 1989)
20 *Chatsworth* Radcliffe (BMC 1996)
21 *Staffordshire Gritstone* Gibson (BMC 1989)
22 *Avon/Cheddar* (2 Vols) Crocker (CC 1992)
23 *Lundy* Gibson/Harrison (CC 1994)
24 *Bosigran* Hannigan (CC 1991)
25 *Chair Ladder* Hannigan (CC 1992)
26 *South Devon/Dartmoor* White (Cordee 1995)

*indicates publication expected in 1997

Other Worthwhile Climbs (including some easy VSs): Central Buttress (S) – Coire Mhic Fhearchair; Wisdom Buttress (VD) – Beinn Lair; Pinnacle Ridge (D) – Sgurr nan Gillean; White Slab (VD) – Coir'a'Ghrunnda; Mallory's Slab and Groove (S) – Sron na Ciche; Great Ridge (D), Route 2 (VD) and Butterknife (S) – Garbh Bheinn; Blank (S) – Goatfell, Arran; Kestral Wall (S) – Grisedale; Centipede (S) and the Original Route (S) – Raven Crag, Langdale; Slabs Route 1 (S) and White Ghyll Chimney (S) – White Ghyll; Oxford and Cambridge Climb Direct (VD), Slabs West (HS) and Sauviter (S) – Grey Crag, Buttermere; Bridge's Route and Bower's Route – Esk Buttress; Broadick's Route (HS), Woodhouse's Route (HVD) and Intermediate Gully (HS) – Dow Crag; Western Wall (HS), Thomas (S) and Trinity Slabs (VD) – Wallowbarrow; The Fang (HS) – Thrang Crag, Swindale; Deception Crack (S), Flake Crack (S) and other routes – Kyloe Crag; Hadrian's Buttress (S) and Main Wall (S) – Craig Lough; Devil's Staircase (S) – Devil's Kitchen Cliffs; Wall Climb (HS), Chimney Route (VD) and other routes – Bochlywd Buttress; Janos (HS) and Corrugated Cracks (S) – Elider Fawr; Eastern Arête (VD) – Y Garn; Overhanging Chimneys (S) – Trwyn y Craig; Great Slab (D) or Outside Edge (VD) – Cwm Silyn; Adam Rib (HS) – Craig Cwm Ddu; Angel Pavement (S) – Craig y Bera; Stross (S), Rib and Slab (HS) and Pencoed Pillar (HVD) – Cadair Idris; Christmas Retreat (VD) – Aran Fawddwy; Dental Slab (S) – Rylstone; Josephine and 'A' Climb/Ferdinand (S) – Ilkley; Majola (HS), Cubic Corner (HS) and Owl Chimney (S) – Brimham; Long Climb (HVD) – Laddow; Atherton Brothers (S) and Via Principia (S) – Shining Clough; Vivien (S), Green Wall (S), the Left Monolith (HS), Answer Crack (HVD), Nasal Buttress (HS), Wilderness East Gully (M), Wimberry Route 1 (HS) – Chew Valley; Himmelswillen (VS) – Wharncliffe; Mutiny Crack (VS) and Amazon Crack (S) – Burbage North; PMC 1 (S) and Owl's Arête – Curbar; The Niche (S) and Pilgrim's Progress (HS) – Castle Naze; Medusa (VD) – Ravensdale; Grooved Slab/Notch (S) – Helsby; Classic (VD), Dulfer (S) and Scavanger (VS) – Gower; Bow Shaped Slab (HS), Myola (HS); The Cracks – Pembroke; Strike (S) – Wyndcliffe; Nexus (S) – Chudleigh; Gates of Eden (HS) – Daddyhole, Torbay; Zo-Zo (VS), Wall Street (S), Zig-Zag (S) and Gimcrack (VS) – Swanage; Scrattling Crack (VD) and Shangri La (S) – Baggy Point; Wreckers' Slab (VS) – Culm Coast; Zeke's Route (S), Longships Ridge (D) and Commando Special (S) – South Coast of West Penwith; Right Angle (HS) – Gurnard's Head.

Selected Guides in 1997
(those covering the main areas of this book)

27 *Rock Climbing in Scotland* Howett (Constable 1990)
28 *Rock Climbing in the Lake District* Birkett/Cram/Eilbeck/Roper (Constable 1990)
29 *Rock Climbing in Snowdonia* Williams (Constable 1990)
30 *Rock Climbing in Northern England* Birkett/White (Constable 1990)
31 *Rock Climbing in the Peak District* Nunn (Constable 1987)
32 *On Peak Rock* Dawson/Milburn (BMC 1993)
33 *South West Climbs* Littlejohn (Diadem 1991)

Index